Praise for *The Five Patterns of Extraordinary Careers*

"What *Good to Great* has done for management, *The Five Patterns of Extraordinary Careers* delivers for careers. Impressive in its scope and depth and groundbreaking in the implication that ambition and drive can lead to extraordinary success. Citrin and Smith are true career experts."

—Jonathan Klein, CEO, Getty Images

"This enormously readable book abandons the usual 'how to succeed in business' nostrums in favor of real-life examples. The authors alert readers to search for qualities all of us possess to maximize our chances for professional success. Even the most experienced readers will benefit from the fascinating stories about everyday people who became corporate winners."

—Arthur Levitt, Jr., former chairman, Securities and Exchange Commission, and author of *Take On the Street*

"*The Five Patterns of Extraordinary Careers* delivers secrets for success that crack the code for career achievement. This book is truly inspiring and demonstrates that if you have vision, ambition, and courage, you can realize extraordinary success."

—Howard Schultz, chairman, Starbucks Coffee Company

"*The Five Patterns of Extraordinary Careers* is a book that logically explains and illustrates the amazing consistencies and patterns that exist in extraordinary careers. The writing is crisp and the examples are many. This book should be read by anyone interested in pursuing a special career."

—Terry Semel, chairman and CEO, Yahoo!

"Citrin and Smith, through extensive interviews and surveys, have created a fascinating book describing what it takes to build a successful career. It is replete with examples and experiences from proven executives, which will help in drawing a road map to achieving success."

—Henry R. Kravis, managing partner, Kohlberg Kravis Roberts & Company

"This book transcends the armchair conjecture about careers where people start with the vanity of endorsing their own alma mater and then retrace their own trajectory for others to follow. This is no hasty 'how to guide' shouting platitudes. Instead, this book profoundly asks important life questions, and the answers come from painstaking research utilizing multiple field methods, including original surveys and extensive interviews. Equally refreshing is that the book doesn't offer simplistic, generic prescriptions but rather provides the tools and perspectives to sculpt a highly individualized career plan that considers both internal self-assessment and external opportunity evaluation. Some of the most daunting yet rarely discussed career obstacles are examined in such an insightful way that readers will almost eagerly look forward to life's challenges as now you will feel ready to navigate them triumphantly."

— Jeffrey Sonnenfeld, associate dean, Yale School of Management

"The days of career ladders are over. In these increasingly challenging and complex times, *The Five Patterns of Extraordinary Careers* provides an illuminating suite of knowledge. This work is an extraordinary collection of insights into professional success—timeless lessons for employees, managers, and CEOs. I can't imagine that a read wouldn't trigger ten new strategies to attack on Monday morning! Perfectly timed, an instant classic."

— Paul S. Pressler, president and CEO, Gap Inc.

"Jim Citrin and Rick Smith offer more than conventional career advice for readers. Principled corporate leadership is an essential part of the authors' equation for achieving professional and organizational excellence. Based on extensive research, *The Five Patterns of Extraordinary Careers* adds significantly to our understanding of how individuals and organizations can perform to their greatest potential."

— Daniel Carp, chairman and CEO, Eastman Kodak Company

"When it comes to careers, we are our own best guide, and *The Five Patterns of Extraordinary Careers* provides us with the essential owner's manual. James Citrin and Richard Smith combine compelling personal accounts with breakthrough career principles to identify the tangible steps we can take to propel ourselves from good performance to great advancement."

—Michael Useem, Wharton School professor, author of *The Leadership Moment* and *Leading Up*, and coauthor of *Upward Bound*

"Finally, a breakthrough approach to thinking about careers based on fact, not opinion. An incredibly important work for professionals and organizational leaders everywhere."

—Stephen B. Burke, president, Comcast Corporation

"This is a must-read book for executives and anyone who wants to have a fulfilling life and career. The practical and concrete insights gleaned by the authors from their experiences in assessing real executives and their careers can be applied by anyone committed to pursuing lifelong learning and an extraordinary career."

—Kate DCamp, senior vice president, human resources, Cisco Systems, Inc.

"The adage 'With experience comes wisdom' is especially true when it comes to career building. Citrin and Smith have distilled the essence of what it takes to maximize professional success. Three hours of reading *The Five Patterns of Extraordinary Careers* can save aspiring executives years of 'learning through experience.' It is the equivalent of having a top-notch and highly involved mentor."

—Daniel Schulman, CEO, Virgin Mobile USA

"Whenever you can help a person gain a sense of control, a first sense of understanding, a new vocabulary for the awkward first experience, a fresh mental map, whether in therapy, friendship, learning, or partnership, you've given them a potent gift. This book 'gifts' readers with patterns, rich with anecdotes and wise with experience, to help them begin to understand the skills, attitudes, aptitudes, and experiences essential to the intentional design and implementation of a process heretofore limited to static and predictable 'rules' and lessons."

—Roger Fransecky, Ph.D., president, The Apogee Group, Inc.

Also by James M. Citrin

*Lessons from the Top: The 50 Most Successful Business
Leaders in America—And What You Can Learn from Them*
(coauthor Thomas J. Neff)

*Zoom!: How 12 Exceptional Companies Are
Navigating the Road to the Next Economy*

You're in Charge—Now What?: The 8 Point Plan
(coauthor Thomas J. Neff)

THE FIVE PATTERNS OF

EXTRAORDINARY

CAREERS

THE GUIDE FOR ACHIEVING SUCCESS AND SATISFACTION

James M. Citrin
& Richard A. Smith

THREE RIVERS PRESS
NEW YORK

Originally published in hardcover in the United States by Crown Business,
a division of Random House, Inc., in 2003.

Library of Congress Cataloging-in-Publication Data
Citrin, James M.
The five patterns of extraordinary careers : the guide for achieving success
and satisfaction / James M. Citrin and Richard A. Smith.—1st ed.
1. Career development.   2. Executive ability.   3. Leadership.
4. Success in business.   I. Smith, Richard A. (Richard Alan), 1967–
II. Title.
HF5381.C657 2003
650.1—dc21   2003004340

ISBN 1-4000-8168-8

Printed in the United States of America

Design by Robert Bull

10 9 8 7 6 5 4 3 2 1

First Paperback Edition

CONTENTS

CONTENTS

THE FIVE PATTERNS OF

EXTRAORDINARY

CAREERS

INTRODUCTION:
THE FIVE PATTERNS OF EXTRAORDINARY CAREERS

*You don't just luck into things as much as you'd like to
think you do. You build step by step, whether it's
friendships or opportunities.*
—BARBARA BUSH

*We must believe in luck. For how else can we
explain the success of those we don't like?*
—JEAN COCTEAU

T*he Five Patterns of Extraordinary Careers* reveals the subtle yet
powerful factors that determine career success: why some
people ascend to the top and prosper, while others who are equally talented never reach their expectations. The latter was a fate Timothy
Reynolds suddenly feared might have fallen upon him.

For many years, Tim Reynolds had every reason to think he was
on the path of an extraordinary career. After all, he seemed to have it
all—three kids, a beautiful wife, a four-bedroom house in a leafy
Chicago suburb, and a good job as vice president of marketing at a
leading consumer-products company, all before the age of forty. But
standing beside his classmates at his fifteenth college reunion on an
unseasonably warm spring day, Tim began to feel a little unsettled.

That's no surprise. Reunions are famous for making ordinary
people feel rather unsure of themselves. Especially disconcerting is

facing the former classmates who have somehow blossomed into the next generation of leaders. But Tim wasn't just one of those people who always see the grass as greener on the other side. He was someone everyone admired and considered successful and put together. Yet over the course of this particular weekend, Tim found himself going into a full-scale reexamination of where he was with his career and life and what he had accomplished.

Early in his career, Tim had been a star in his corporation's management training program, which led to rapid promotions and increasing responsibilities. Throughout the first dozen years of his working life, he was spontaneous, optimistic, energetic, and confident, feeling that continued professional success was almost inevitable. But now that he thought about it, he realized that more recently, he wasn't feeling quite as sure of himself—or of his professional direction. He had survived two rounds of layoffs at the company, but it was always possible that more were to come. The prospect of being forced into the job market in a difficult economy was a grim scenario for Tim to consider.

Even more disquieting, however, was a growing sense that he was on a path that wasn't leading him exactly where he wanted to go. He had never even thought about this consciously before. After all, Tim had been on a well-defined career track and he had progressed steadily, achieving many of the milestones for position and compensation that he had set for himself. But as he reflected, he found that the responsibilities, daily activities, and politics associated with his job were increasingly debilitating. Whatever happened to his starry-eyed dreams of becoming an ambassador, a university professor, or a public servant?

Tim had suppressed these feelings, but now that he'd let them out of the cage, he was beset with a sense of being ensnared in a direction that he could not change. He was actually unsure if he even wanted to be promoted again, fearing that this might move him still further away from the things that mattered most to him—a strong family, making a positive impact on society, being passionate and proud about his work, and continuing to develop a broader set of skills and knowledge.

On that particular spring day at the reunion, all of this pent-up anxiety surfaced as Tim was reunited with old friends and classmates.

The alumni association had organized a panel, "Career Success and Satisfaction," that included some of Tim's most successful peers. The star-studded panel went something like this:

• John recently had been appointed the president of a television group for one of the major broadcast networks after a five-year run developing critically acclaimed and commercially successful television shows. John had begun his career as a lawyer and migrated into the entertainment business by coming to represent actors, directors, and writers in Los Angeles.

• Martha was a professor of law and history at an Ivy League university, specializing in the areas of property, religion, and legal history in the university's law school. Before joining the faculty, Martha had served as a clerk in the United States Court of Appeals, which she joined after having been an associate at a Washington, D.C., law firm.

• Stephen was a senior vice president of the National Association of Securities Dealers, with the responsibility to develop programs, services, and technological innovations to benefit the entire securities industry. He had joined the industry trade association after the emerging technology company that he co-founded in 1999 ran out of capital and was liquidated.

• Todd was the founder of a small specialty restaurant company in Chicago that was generating profit in each of its seven locations. Previously he had co-founded and built a natural foods supermarket company over seven years into a twenty-store chain serving five metropolitan areas, which he sold to a major food company. Before moving into the food business, he had been an account executive with a major Wall Street brokerage firm.

• Lynn was a doctor of audiology and president of the parent-teacher association at her daughters' private school in Manhattan, now working three days a week. She had worked full time in private practice for twelve years after medical school.

As Tim listened to each of their stories, he wondered why these folks had met with such good fortune. Thinking back to school, he realized that none of them were necessarily smarter, more energetic, or more charismatic than he, nor did they seem to have any special connections. This certainly wasn't the group the graduating class would have predicted as most likely to succeed. But they seemed to have it nailed.

While Tim thought that his career seemed to have become more complicated and difficult to manage, this group seemed not only successful, but also fulfilled by their personal and professional lives. Somehow they had apparently gained control over something Tim increasingly believed was uncontrollable—their careers.

As his peers told their stories on the panel, Tim took copious notes. He wanted to find clues into the surprising success of his classmates. Each panel member discussed how, over time, he or she had gained command of the job and became valuable within his or her organization or profession. John, Stephen, and Lynn all pointed out how they had benefited from working with exceptionally talented mentors and co-workers. All the panelists hinted at having found themselves in the right place at the right time and having gained access to the kinds of opportunities that mattered most. Todd and Martha articulated how they never took their job descriptions too literally and had always found ways to expand their responsibilities within their organizations. And slowly it became apparent to Tim that each of these individuals was not only highly skilled in his or her chosen field, but also truly passionate about their work. Together, the enthusiasm for their jobs was undeniable, and seemed to provide each with a sense of purpose, belonging, and power that Tim longed to attain. Each had gained a level of control over his or her career direction that Tim so desperately sought.

Just then Tim had an epiphany. As he listened closely, he came to the blinding insight that the key was not the uniqueness of the panelists' careers, but their surprising similarity. Although their careers were completely different, each of his successful classmates had followed a path that twisted and turned, had setbacks and accomplishments and changes of direction. But somehow, each of them kept getting closer and closer to the mark—employing similar strategies and actions to achieve success.

Intrigued, Tim wondered whether the similarities were just coincidence. Or rather, was what he was observing actually the result of cause and effect? And if so, was there specific knowledge that could be harnessed and actions that could be taken to create similar success in his own career?

Do successful careers possibly follow a *pattern*?

. . .

The idea that there are patterns in extraordinary careers is not the conventional wisdom. Many believe that success is the result of either luck or larceny.

Luck, however, is a convenient excuse for a lack of success. A colleague gets a promotion—how lucky. An acquaintance gets a huge bonus—dumb luck. Everyone assumes that he works just as hard as the next guy. So what else could separate those who are successful from those who are less so? It must be good fortune and impeccable timing. If not luck, then perhaps it is political savvy, or worse, something we may refer to as *"assmosis,"* the process by which some people nab success and advancement by kissing up to the boss rather than earning it. Fueling myths about luck is that many high-performing executives make career success seem relatively easy, reinforcing the idea that they haven't done anything special to hoist themselves up the corporate ladder.

The other commonly held belief is even more disheartening—the feeling that high-flying executives are nearly as successful as they are greedy. With the string of corporate scandals and criminal activities of some executives, many have come to assume the worst about what it takes to ascend to the pinnacle of the business world and that ethics run in inverse proportion to success.

The truth is, a successful career is not the result of one critical lucky break, like an actress waiting tables when a star movie producer walks in. It results from a consistent series of opportunities and performance over time. It cannot be faked. And professionals who lack character and ethics and are still able to rise to and remain at the very top are in fact extremely rare. When they do attain career successes, their grasp on what they've achieved is tenuous and ephemeral.

It turns out that extraordinary careers follow a strikingly consistent trajectory, marked by five distinct patterns that distinguish the very top from the rest of the pack. There are two foundations for this judgment. The first is our observation and distillation of these patterns through the lens of our experience at Spencer Stuart, the preeminent global executive search firm. When, over a decade's time, your firm conducts approximately 60 percent of all Fortune 1000 CEO searches (including the CEOs of IBM, AT&T, Honeywell, Merck, Gillette, Hershey Foods, Albertson's, WorldCom, JCPenney, Tyco International, Reader's Digest, and Yahoo!), you gain a front-row seat to study some of the most successful people of our time.[1] We have also recruited board directors, presidents, and general managers of global companies and CEOs of venture-capital-backed start-ups, as well as conducted searches for CFOs, marketing executives, human resource professionals, and nearly every functional role in companies today. Our work has crossed every major industry, ranging from manufacturing and health care to technology and energy. Thanks to our reach and our intensive process of identifying, interviewing, and placing the elite of the global corporate world, we collectively engage in an estimated four hundred thousand conversations each year with professionals about career-related issues. But we didn't stop there.

THE RESEARCH BEHIND THE FIVE PATTERNS

Building on this experience, we conducted exhaustive research on who exceptional executives really are and how they achieved their success. Our goal was to get beyond anecdotes that describe career events and discover the factors that actually *cause* them. What emerged from our analysis was surprising clarity and commonality from diverse individuals.

Our research followed a three-pronged approach. First, we segmented and analyzed Spencer Stuart's 1.2-million-member proprietary executive database, QuestNT. This state-of-the-art system contains detailed employment histories, qualitative information, references, board and other professional affiliations, and a rich contact history of all interactions that our firm has had with these individuals. The database is coded in such a way to permit sophisticated extracting and manipulation. From QuestNT, we constructed a representative sample of executives to survey. Our survey, which formed the heart of our research, asked each participant eighty separate questions about his beliefs, actions, and career. (The survey is available online, along with an instantaneous analysis of results, at www.5patterns.com.)

Relying on the advice of the statistical experts who counseled us in the survey's creation, we were looking to garner one thousand completed surveys to analyze (actually, they felt that four hundred would be more than enough from which to draw conclusions, but we wanted to be sure and therefore set a goal of obtaining more than double the required amount). Based on projected response rates, we would need to invite sixteen thousand executives to participate. So as not to clog up the e-mail system, we decided to send the survey out in two equal and representative waves, eight thousand each.

But it turned out that the response was beyond anything we could have hoped for (or the statisticians would have believed)—the survey was completed by more than two thousand of the initial eight thousand individuals, a staggering 25 percent response rate. We also received hundreds of cover letters and notes passionately expanding on the topics queried. Clearly we had touched a nerve! It turns out that people—even the most successful—want to think about, learn about, and talk about what makes for career success in these volatile times. The respondents, whose careers represented hundreds of industry sectors and more than a thousand different companies, completed the survey in mid-2002.

The third step in our research was conducting more than three hundred in-person interviews of executives over a two-year period. Through these discussions, we attempted to uncover their thoughts, beliefs, goals and aspirations, motivations, turning points, actions, and behaviors. The goal was to identify and explain those factors that really distinguish the different trajectories of the ordinary from the extraordinary executive.

To analyze the information, we segregated the survey respondents into three groups.

- *Average employees,* professionals who have worked for at least twenty years but have not reached a senior professional or executive level

- *Successful professionals,* those individuals who have attained positions within executive management of their organizations or who were top-level contributors, such as senior partners, at professional services firms

- *Extraordinary executives,* executives hand-selected by us and our research team for their documented, consistent, and exceptional track record of success, stellar reputation, value in the marketplace, and impact on their organizations

These three groups provided a distinctive comparison for our research, and we refer to them throughout the book.

What distinguishes extraordinary executives from the wanna-bes is not advantaged connections, higher levels of intelligence, or social connections (although these rarely hurt), but rather the occurrence of the five specific patterns discussed in this book. Executives such as Larry Bossidy, the highly regarded longtime leader of Honeywell, and Lou Gerstner, the former chairman of IBM, intuitively used the patterns to manage and gain control over their careers. Their results in terms of control and compensation speak for themselves.

The extraordinary executive is not the son or daughter of the boss and is not more likely to have an IQ in the 99th percentile than other professionals. The vast majority of executives in the world today began their careers like most others—with a good education, a lot of ambition, and precious little relevant experience. In a process similar to compound interest, the extraordinary executives achieved success slowly and consistently, with each phase building on the prior one. They did not rely on luck, engage in illegal activity, betray their colleagues, or sleep with their bosses. The occasional executive who did get ahead in these ways is, not surprisingly, juicy prey for the media, and surely makes for great fodder around the office or golf club. But this type is exceedingly rare in the real professional workplace.

THE FIVE PATTERNS
OF EXTRAORDINARY CAREERS

So what are the five patterns of extraordinary careers? As the five chapters that follow will detail, they are to:

1. Understand the value of you. People with extraordinary careers understand how value is created in the workplace, and they translate that knowledge into action, building their personal value over each phase of their careers.

2. Practice benevolent leadership. People with extraordinary careers do not claw their way to the top; *they are carried there.*

3. Overcome the permission paradox. People with extraordinary careers overcome one of the great Catch-22s of business: You can't get the job without experience, and you can't get the experience without the job.

4. Differentiate using the 20/80 principle of performance. People with extraordinary careers do their defined jobs exceptionally well but don't stop there. They storm past predetermined objectives to create breakthrough ideas and deliver unexpected impact.

5. Find the right fit (strengths, passions, and people). People with extraordinary careers make decisions with the long term in mind. They willfully migrate toward positions that fit their natural strengths and passions and where they can work with people they like and respect.

MANAGING COMPLEXITY VIA PATTERNS

The five patterns are not a simplistic formula for distilling the complexities of a career into a set of rules. Many of us desperately yearn for a set of simple rules for dealing with the complexity of our working lives: Do these ten things, avoid these five. If this, then do that. The problem is that in managing a career in real time, where you have to make important decisions without all of the facts, where there are important and sometimes painful trade-offs, cookbook rules are simply not effective.

Careers, like weather systems or financial markets, *contain patterns.* When a cold front collides with a warm front, thunderstorms are likely to appear. When interest rates decline, the stock market tends to rise. In any complex system, there are usually a handful of factors that govern the vast majority of the behavior of that system. So while in situations with great complexity, such as careers, there are no easy, rational answers that will always lead to the most positive outcomes, there *are* patterns that correlate very strongly with success over time.

Careers based on success patterns are quite different from those most people feel they are in. Many believe that success is out of their control. Yet careers guided by success patterns are understandable, predictable, and manageable over the long run. Our goal in this book is to answer two questions that lie at the heart of what you would presumably like to accomplish on your lifelong career journey: How are extraordinary careers really achieved? And what deliberate thoughts and actions can you institute to create extraordinary success and fulfillment in your own career?

WHAT PROFESSIONALS ARE UP AGAINST: CAREER UPHEAVAL

This isn't your parents' career ladder anymore. Gone are the days of *The Organization Man* and *The Man in the Gray Flannel Suit,* which described a world in which you moved steadily up a preset career ladder at the same company until you retired with a gold watch and a pension.[2] While large corporations historically attempted to create career opportunities for their employees, today we are all on our own to navigate an increasingly complex and competitive business environment, as well as a daunting number of career choices and jobs along the way. Four of the most important forces at play:

- Executive turnover is at an all-time high. Fifty-eight percent of large and medium-size companies changed CEOs from 1998 to 2001, according to an international study of 481 corporations by management consulting firm Drake Beam Morin. The median tenure for CEOs is now 2.75 years (down about a year from 1999), and only 12 percent of CEOs have held their position for 10 years or longer.[3] Low-performing companies have nearly twice as much turnover among top-performing employees as high-performing companies, according to the consulting firm Watson Wyatt Worldwide.[4]

"You'll go far in this organization, Taylor, unless I manage to stop you."

• Career choices are much more unclear. There is no single perfect job out there, and in a world of increased specialization, there are many more forks in the road and avenues to take. This means many more career decisions, with each one potentially leading you down a slightly different path. And with an increasing number of choices comes the danger of career drift along with the vagaries of the market. For example, in the mid- and late 1990s Internet and technology companies were hot and drew hundreds of thousands of people. Subsectors such as technology consulting firms or outsourced customer service providers also flourished. When the recession hit, traditional corporations with perceived stability came back in favor, so back many people went—or tried to go there. Other sectors, such as pharmaceuticals and private companies, are coming into vogue and will certainly attract many of the most opportunistic professionals. But keep this Ping-Pong game going and you risk a severe case of career vertigo.

• You are going to move through more jobs in a decade than executives did in a lifetime thirty years ago. The average professional with thirty-five years of experience has worked for just over six different companies during his or her career. Yet those with only ten years of experience have, on average, already worked for four companies. This trend is likely to persist for two major reasons. On one hand, companies are going to continue to be rigorous about their cost management and efficiency drives, making reductions in force a normal part of doing business. On the other hand, individuals are going to feel simultaneously less loyal to their companies in the face of potential layoffs and increasing career alternatives, and liberated by the portability of their IRAs, 401-K plans, and pension plans. Addressing individuals' deeply held desire for stability in an environment of unrelenting uncertainty and change will require new guideposts and principles for successful career management. Specifically, managing the experiences and perceptions associated with working for many employers, including those who are viewed as archcompetitors, is a challenge that today has no simple solution.

- There is no safety net. Until recently, if you or your company stumbled and you lost your job, there was a long list of companies that would be interested in hiring you. Now, with huge waves of corporate downsizing and the fall of once high-flying companies, nothing is guaranteed. The seemingly safe company you join today could possibly turn into tomorrow's downward spiral. As the Internet boom and bust illustrated, one can go from MVP to persona non grata in a matter of months.

Your individual career is becoming more complex, and so is the overall business world. Competition is driving every business to lower costs, wring out inefficiencies, compete globally, and outsource non-core activities. "The rapidity of change has clearly raised the level of anxiety and insecurity in the workforce," said Federal Reserve chairman Alan Greenspan.[5]

Even the factors that are positively impacting the value of individual professionals, such as the increasing competition for top executives, often are accompanied by additional challenges and complexity. With a shrinking pool of people between thirty-five and fifty-five—the future generation of top executives in the years ahead—companies are becoming more sophisticated and creative about attracting talent, and navigating the many forms of incentives, compensation, and opportunities will only become more complex.

The good news is that despite what you may be feeling in these volatile times, your actual value is higher than at almost any other time in modern history. As the complexity and specialization of the business world increases, more value is placed on intellectual property and specialized skills such as financial acumen, direct marketing, and turn-around expertise as well as intangible factors like teamwork and the ability to work across organizational lines. Consequently, companies are investing more time and money to seek out executive talent.

THE ULTIMATE PAYOFF

Career success is not achieved easily. Like all things of value, it requires significant investment—in time, effort, focus, emotional exertion, and personal sacrifice. Yet as Tim Reynolds realized longingly during his college reunion weekend, and as our own research clearly confirmed, those achieving the highest levels of professional success are more satisfied with their jobs, their lifestyle, their compensation, and the balance in their lives.

Understanding the five patterns of extraordinary careers and tailoring them to you—your personality, aspirations, personal situation, and strengths and weaknesses—is well worth it and will help you accomplish the ultimate payoff: career success and satisfaction, under your control, and beyond your grandest expectations.

UNDERSTAND THE VALUE OF YOU

I conceive that the great part of the miseries of mankind
are brought upon them by false estimates they have
made of the value of things.
—BENJAMIN FRANKLIN

Value is not intrinsic; it is not in things. It is within us;
it is the way in which man reacts to the conditions
of his environment.
—LUDWIG VON MISES

THE POWER OF CAREER KNOWLEDGE

Before he was diagnosed with testicular cancer, Lance Armstrong thought he had all that he needed to be a champion cyclist. He had oversized lung capacity, explosive power in his legs, and fiery ambition stoked by a tormented youth. So when he began racing as a professional on the European circuit, he expected to win and quickly emerge as the best rider in the world.

But he soon learned about the *peleton,* a swarm of cyclists that makes up the mass of road racers. To the spectator, it seems like a colorful blur of riders storming by. But inside the pack, there are subtle forces at play and a culture that governs how things really work. One rider helps another one day and gets the favor returned the next. The

deans of the sport, who have worked their way up the hierarchy by paying their dues, demand—and are accorded—respect and recognition.
For one without an understanding of how the game is really played,
the *peleton* could prevent you from winning by blocking you out, slowing you down, even running you off the road. Why? Because in racing,
the *peleton* is often more powerful than the individual.

In his book *It's Not About the Bike,* Armstrong said, "As an American, I was a gate-crasher in a revered and time-honored sport, and I
had little concept of its rules, written and unwritten, or its etiquette."[1]
Since he raced with no deference to the elders and never backed
down, he was making enemies. It wasn't until after his miraculous
recovery and the maturation and self-awareness that went along with
it that Armstrong truly understood all the elements required to win in
cycling. It was not all about bulldozing straight ahead, pushing aside
everyone else. It was not about parading, mouthing off, and shoving
his fists in the air after winning a stage. It was about respect, a continuous give-and-take between competing riders, an appreciation of
the proud history and traditions of the sport. And, of course, it was
also about ferocious competition, explosive speed, and lung-bursting
endurance. When he coupled his talents and his drive with knowledge
and experience, Armstrong went on to win four consecutive Tours de
France and become the unassailable best rider in the world.

What's the moral of the Armstrong story for you? Careers, like
other important activities in life, are governed by subtle yet pervasive
dynamics that significantly influence your value in the marketplace for
professional talent. Once you truly understand them, you are bound
for glory. Remain ignorant of them at your own peril. Many talented
professionals come unmoored from the path they set by failing to
appreciate what really determines their professional value, never achieving the level of success and fulfillment attainable to them. The most
successful professionals have come to understand the underlying factors that determine value in the job market, how to maximize their
market value at different stages of professional life, and why some
careers prosper while others peak and decline.

Does the fact that some professionals have a much better
understanding of how value is created in the workforce really make a

difference? You bet it does. Our survey asked this question: "Do you have a strong understanding of what drives value in the marketplace for professional talent?" When we analyzed the responses, we were stunned by the results. When professionals answered "strongly agree" to this question, they were more likely—by a factor of two to one—to have the degree of success to which the vast majority of people aspire. They are extremely satisfied with their career and compensation, passionate about their job, and optimistic about their future. In addition, those with the greatest self-reported knowledge about the dynamics of careers were 35 percent more likely to be performing at or near peak productivity levels, believe their value within the organization is growing at above average rates, and are much less likely to consider external job opportunities. For both the aspiring professional and the organizations they work for, an understanding of the drivers of professional value turns out to be a most critical asset.

What are the underlying factors that determine value in the job market? How do you maximize your market value at the different stages of your professional life? Why do some careers prosper, while others peak and then decline?

THE VALUE OF YOU

What are you worth? For many, the answer to this question may seem a matter of simple math. Just take your total annual compensation, add benefits, and *voilà*—you've got your answer. Not so fast. Placing a monetary figure on your talents may be correct for a static moment in time. However, the equation for determining your true worth over time is more nuanced than you might first imagine. In addition to the critically important characteristics about you as an individual—intelligence, interpersonal skills, leadership, and ambition—there are key macro factors at play as well. Age matters, influencing where you fit into the demographic trends of the population at large. So too does the demand for professional positions similar to yours at any given point in time. And all that volatility among companies is not necessarily a bad thing—increasing fluctuations in corporate valuations turns out to actually enhance your value in the marketplace as well. Finally, recognize that this is the age of intellectual capital. With technology-enhanced productivity improvements working their way across the economy, the value of specialized knowledge is at a premium.

These factors together constitute the foundation of the job market—or more accurately stated, the human capital market. While most workers don't understand their worth in the broader job market, our research suggests the extraordinary executive is instinctively aware of the forces that drive her value at each and every stage of her career, and single-mindedly focuses her energies and actions on maximizing that value over time. But most have gained their knowledge through trial and error, often over many years.

What we will do in the remainder of this chapter is help you understand what determines value in the marketplace and how you can influence it, thereby avoiding the difficult process of the hit-or-miss approach.

Solving the talent-worth equation is partly a matter of testing the job market waters, in much the same way that you might market-test a product to gauge consumer acceptance. But while this will give you some information, it is not the most complete measure of your true value. To do this, you will need to get beyond short-term compensation data and look at the underlying factors that determine real value in the employment market.

Specifically, you must first understand four key macro factors:

- *Demographics.* You need to assess where you fit in the aggregate supply and demand of professional talent.

- *Market liquidity.* Is your supply in demand? You need to gauge the number of professionals seeking positions versus the number of open positions seeking professionals.

- *Company volatility.* You need to evaluate how fluctuations in corporate valuations enhance or diminish your value in the marketplace.

- *Intellectual capital.* You need to consider how the financial markets value intangible assets, notably intellectual capital, relative to hard assets, or book value.

To help professionals and their companies understand where they stand in the evolving market for talent, we have developed an analytical tool that measures these four factors over time, which we call the Human Capital Market Index (HCMI). Details about the methodology and research behind the HCMI can be found at www.spencer stuart.com. But the bottom line of our research is this: Given the massive structural changes in the economy over the past thirty years, professionals as a collective whole are worth far greater today than in all but a couple of the years of the past three decades. Your individual characteristics are still essential, of course, but at a macro level, your value should be enhanced by the rise of an economy dependent on the service sector, which means that there is a much greater demand for talent and intellectual capital. (Note that the number of jobs in the manufacturing sector has fallen from 40 percent of total employment in 1950 to less than 18 percent today, while service sector employment has grown from less than 14 percent to more than 35 percent over the same time period.)[2] Despite increased economic turmoil, the upward trend in the value of you should continue in the years to come, based on demographics, continued technology-based productivity improvements, and the ever more valuable role of knowledge in the workplace. In short, talented individuals will continue to be able to create more economic value in the years ahead, and this will in turn pull up their own value.

How is this possible at a time when many people feel less valuable than ever before? We cannot ignore that only a few years ago, with the technology bubble swelling to a bursting point, the behavior of both supply and demand became almost irrational—employers going to outrageous lengths to lure talented people, and employees abandoning loyalty and security for potential riches and fame. The most talented professionals became "rock stars," and the employers regressed to screaming teenage fans. But the stark reality of the postbubble employment market is indeed rather different. During the last few years, compensation dropped, layoffs flourished, and the pervasive calls from corporate recruiters disappeared. You weren't dreaming if you felt less valuable during the last recession: You actually *were* less valuable. But as the saying goes, everything is relative.

Now for some good news: Despite the recent sharp downturn, you're likely to be more valuable than you might think in the future. Looking out to the year 2020, we expect the value of executive talent to grow appreciably, even if substantial volatility continues. Many forces have led to a recent downturn in the economy, but the key components of the human capital market remain strong. Today's marketplace for extraordinary talent is as competitive as it's ever been. And the competition for top executives is expected to accelerate well into the twenty-first century.

THE NATURE OF PROFESSIONAL VALUE

When managing your portfolio, tracking the movement of the various financial indices is important, but what really matters most is what is happening to the value of *your* stocks and bonds. The same is true in the talent marketplace. Similar to an individual stock, your value in the marketplace is far from static. In fact, it changes at every stage of your career and in every different position you are in. So there's no single answer to the question "What am I worth?" However, once you understand what affects your value, you will have the insight to increase that value. To find out how, let's now examine the marketplace for professional talent at its most basic level, the individual.

Consider the early career of Allen Chan, who graduated with a bachelor's degree from Texas A&M, and soon after earned an MBA from Stanford University. Although he had a few years of work experience, Allen knew little of practical value in the market, yet several companies offered him excellent employment opportunities with lucrative compensation. Later in his career, after several successful work experiences, recruiters would call Allen constantly, offering him increases in pay and prestige if only he would switch employers to perform the same role. Clearly, Allen knew he was in demand during both of these stages in his career, but for different reasons. When Allen was coming out of business school, he was valued for his potential, the value that he would be able to bring to employers in the years ahead. Later, when he was fielding calls from corporate recruiters, he was being valued for the experience that he had already gained. That in its most simple form explains it. Your value in the talent marketplace is derived from two distinctly separate elements—the value of your potential and the value of your experience.

Over the course of your career, value changes and actually follows a pattern strikingly similar to the properties of energy: potential (energy at rest) and kinetic (energy in motion). A child swaying to and fro on a swing has both forms of energy in action. Careers follow a similar pattern. When you enter the workforce you have a store of potential value—the value you will be able to add over time as you exercise your intellectual and interpersonal energies. Then, as this potential is translated into experience, you gain momentum and become more valuable, just as the child swinging his legs takes him higher and higher. In essence, we begin our careers with a bag full of potential and an empty bag of experience. The trick is to fill the bag of experience before you empty the bag of potential.

Experiential value—not unlike kinetic energy—is the value of your career momentum. It is the perceived value of what you have done. As your career progresses, other departments in your company or other employers may notice your achievements and attempt to bring you into their fold. If you are in marketing, they might be impressed with your successful product launches and want you to do the same for theirs. If you are a CFO, they may want you to take them public given your prior experience leading an IPO. They may want you to apply your brand marketing know-how, sales force management experience, Six Sigma quality control expertise, or turnaround track record to their situation. This was the thinking of General Motors CEO Richard Wagoner, who recruited one of the most successful and experienced auto executives in the world, Robert Lutz, into the company in August 2001 to overhaul all of GM's auto design and product line. With twenty-five years of experience at Ford and Chrysler, and hit designs such as the PT Cruiser and Dodge Viper to his credit, the newly restyled Cadillac line and other hot products have been a direct result of this manifestation of Lutz's experiential value brought to bear for GM.

Experiential value is usually more highly compensated than potential value for the simple reason that it is much easier to measure what you have done than what you can do. This is also true given that specialized expertise can be measured against the specific demand that a company has at a point in time. But this does not mean it's more important. True, the value of your experience is easier to quantify, and often is a key determinant in how you are compensated, but your perceived potential is frequently essential to gaining access to the most value-building opportunities, which, we will learn later on, is critical to extraordinary career success. Similarly, employers who focus on experiential value to the exclusion of potential value are fundamentally quite conservative and understate the true value of professional talent. It is true that today few, if any, companies hire with the expectation of providing lifelong employment. But while an important and logical approach to hiring, looking only at the skills someone has today ignores how that person may develop or what she may become. At its most unimaginative extreme, this limiting approach is what we refer to as seeking to put a square peg in a square hole.

Your true worth in the marketplace is determined by the combination of both potential value and experiential value. At any point in your career, your value can be thought of as a combination of these two elements. Even if you find yourself considering a role similar to one that you have been in, it is important to look for and discuss the growth potential of the new role itself and you in it. And while experiential value and potential value are distinct, they are closely related. For a child to continue to swing, potential energy must be transformed into momentum, which in turn builds up potential energy again. The path of your career is similar—you must turn your potential value into valuable experiences, which together can be converted into renewed potential.

WHY DO SOME CAREERS CONTINUE TO PROSPER WHILE OTHERS DECLINE?

This basic way of thinking about your value has powerful implications for some of the most important questions about your career: How do you maximize your market value? Why do some careers prosper, while others peak and then decline? Before delving deeper into the value of you, let us take a look at one of the most extraordinary business leaders of our time, Lou Gerstner. The former IBM chairman and chief executive officer is a highly visible example of potential and experiential value in action.

Born in Mineola, Long Island, in 1942, Gerstner had an outstanding education as the foundation for his career, graduating from Dartmouth College in 1963 and Harvard Business School in 1965. At the fresh young age of twenty-three, on the basis of his enormous potential represented by his academic performance, his intellect, and his strong communications skills, he was hired by McKinsey and Company. Over the next decade he developed invaluable strategy, business planning, and client management expertise as a consultant. He was a star at McKinsey, one of the youngest people ever to make senior partner. Working with a wide variety of clients around the world, from consumer products to financial services companies, Gerstner gained a broad and valuable perspective. His internal reputation at the firm was unparalleled. But at thirty-six years old, with enormous problem-solving capabilities, intellect, experience across many industries, and a demonstrated talent for project management, he was also perceived as having significant general management potential. His combination of potential and experience made him very attractive in the corporate marketplace. He had general management aspirations and realized that moving over to industry would add even more to his career. So after thirteen years with McKinsey, he accepted a position as an executive vice president at American Express Company. When Gerstner joined American Express, it is said that the secretaries in the New York office of McKinsey bought stock in the company, a move they would repeat when Gerstner joined IBM.

As the head of Amex's flagship Travel Related Services (TRS) division, Gerstner was credited with helping the company start to think and act as a marketing company. He recruited and mentored several marketing professionals who went on to become among the very best direct and consumer marketers in the industry. Gerstner's management approach was notoriously demanding. Over eleven years at American Express, his track record and leadership earned him the role of president of the parent company and chairman and chief executive officer of the TRS division. But he was increasingly in disagreement over the direction of the company with James D. Robinson, the American Express CEO at the time, and he was itching for a CEO job, which was not in the offing, at least in the near term.

By 1989, Gerstner hit the radar screen of the giant buyout firm Kohlberg, Kravis & Roberts, which recruited him to join RJR Nabisco to be CEO of the (then) largest LBO in history. Even at this stage of his career, at age forty-seven, it was Gerstner's combination of experiential and potential value that made him an attractive candidate to take on this management challenge. On the experiential value side, his reservoir included the general management track record of successfully leading a multibillion-dollar consumer services business, demonstrated problem-solving and strategic capabilities, exceptional decision-making and prioritization skills, and the proven ability to develop and lead large teams of people. However, it was also KKR's bet on his potential value, as he had never been the CEO of a major organization, had never led a highly leveraged company, and had never worked in the tobacco and food industry. KKR concluded that the blend of experiential and potential value coupled with his driving ambition was immensely attractive.

When he got to RJR Nabisco, Gerstner thrived in the CEO role. He built a strong management team, developed and implemented a restructuring plan that focused on the most important leverage points of the operations, successfully reduced costs and increased cash flow, and also got the top line of the giant company moving again. But progress was hard won. He confronted a debilitating price war against market leader Philip Morris while trying to dig the company out from a mountain of debt from the LBO. While Gerstner was both enjoying the role and making slow and steady progress against the plan, he was fighting an increasingly uphill battle. Due to the ferocious bidding war, filled with greed and intrigue (well chronicled by Bryan Burroughs and John Helyar in *Barbarians at the Gate*), KKR ended up paying too high a price, $25 billion, for the company in the buyout. This meant that despite all of the operating and financial progress that was being made, it just wasn't possible to achieve the desired return on investment.

As he learned that KKR's exit strategy for RJR Nabisco might be changing, Gerstner started to think about his own plans for the future as well.

As Gerstner wrote in his book, *Who Says Elephants Can't Dance?* this is what left the door open for an approach by the CEO search committee for IBM over the weekend of President's Day in 1993 (the search was co-led by our partner, Spencer Stuart's U.S. chairman, Tom Neff).[3] When Gerstner met with Jim Burke, CEO of Johnson & Johnson and search committee chairman, Burke made an emphatic case that what the company needed was not a technology-industry executive, but rather a change agent and a broad-based business leader. Gerstner was skeptical at first, but this was the consistent message from the board committee during the entire process. As he did his own research and due diligence, he found widespread skepticism about the company's ability to survive, much less thrive, in the Microsoft-dominant era of computing that had dawned. In addition to the shift from mainframe to PC computing, IBM was a hierarchical, change-resistant, insular bureaucracy. And its fortunes had shifted rapidly. IBM swung from its most profitable year ever in 1990 to losing a record-breaking $16 billion in just three short years. But having studied the problem, Gerstner concluded, "The IBM proposition was daunting and almost frightening, but it was also intriguing. I have always been drawn to a challenge."

So at the ripe age of fifty-one, he ended up taking the plunge of his career. Gerstner had run neither a technology company nor a global corporation near the size of IBM when tapped to take over the world's largest computing company. But the board perceived a blend of experience and untapped potential—strategic, marketing, and general management skills, coupled with intelligence, an obsession for the customer, an understanding of technology from the perspective of the corporate clients, and an ability to make tough decisions—that was unique in the marketplace.

The story of Gerstner's turnaround of IBM is now cemented into the business hall of fame for all time. While the details do not need to be retold here, the highlights still delight. When Gerstner started at IBM, in April 1993, pundits and employees generally thought that he would keep in place the current plan of separating the company into autonomous business units with different names and try to maximize value by leading a breakup. The IBM printer division, which became Lexmark International after its spin-off, was the road map for other divisions to follow. Investment banks were all over the company, valuing the different businesses, and accounting firms were building historical financial statements. However, it did not take Gerstner long to put all this on hold. He concluded that one of the company's major strengths was its size and breadth and that it could win by turning itself into the complete set of computing solutions for its corporate customers. With that decision made, he focused on getting the right managers in the right jobs and holding them all accountable. He made sure that they all bought into the mission of a single, integrated IBM dedicated to being a customer-focused provider of computing solutions.

What became "IBM E-Business" and the growth of IBM's Global Services business combined to constitute as bold a new vision for the company as Gerstner or any other executive could have conceived. Before Gerstner's tenure, IBM went from perhaps the mightiest company in the world to the brink of extinction. He and his management team brought it back to a position of market dominance once again. During his tenure, IBM's share price increased by more than 800 percent and its market value increased by over $180 billion. In March 2002, when Gerstner retired as CEO, and in December 2002, when he retired as chairman, he passed the leadership baton to longtime IBM executive Sam Palmisano to take the company into the post-Gerstner era.

True to form, Gerstner has not rested on his laurels, not even for a moment. He turned his vast experience into renewed potential once again, signing up on November 21, 2002, to become chairman of the Carlyle Group. Established in 1987, the Carlyle Group is one of the largest and most influential private investment firms in the world, with over $13 billion under management and a roster of former top world leaders as firm members, including former U.S. president George H. W. Bush, former prime minister of England John Major, and former U.S. secretary of state James Baker, among others. The firm focuses on management buyouts, minority equity investments, private placements, consolidations and buildups, and growth capital financings. Since its inception, Carlyle has invested nearly $7 billion of equity in 252 corporate and real estate transactions with an aggregate acquisition value of over $19 billion. Gerstner has committed to spending about 20 percent of his time at Carlyle, providing strategic guidance on the firm's global business activities, meeting with clients and potential clients, giving management input to Carlyle portfolio companies, and serving on the firm's investment committees.

There are many lessons to be gleaned from Gerstner's extraordinary career. But one of the most important is his ability to consistently build both his potential and experiential value throughout his professional life.

THE POTENTIAL VERSUS EXPERIENTIAL PROMOTION

While the value of both your potential and your experiences can be used to land a new job or get a promotion, the type of new opportunity is actually related to the kind of value used to obtain it. In other words, potential value is leveraged to gain a potential promotion, and experiential value is leveraged to gain an experiential promotion.

A *potential promotion* happens when you are given an opportunity to do a job you have never done before, perhaps because you have demonstrated the skills that make it likely you will succeed. These promotions are not easy to come by but are critical to career advancement. They are a leap of faith by your employer. An example would be an opportunity for a functional specialist to move to a general management role, or a move from a stable management role in a core market to a multicountry assignment overseas. Kirk Siefkas benefited from a potential promotion when he was hired as the chief information officer (CIO) for the John Deere Corporation. Kirk was an exceptionally talented IT professional and had worked as a technology consultant for his entire career. He had successfully written computer programs, led product evaluations, and managed large technology implementations for global companies. But he had always been a consultant, where valuable experience is gained but full-blown credit stingily received. Kirk felt his talents would be effectively utilized as a CIO, yet he had never worked directly in this capacity before. But the CEO of John Deere had seen Kirk in action, leading several projects within his company. Even though the CEO knew Siefkas had never been a CIO, he felt strongly that Kirk had so much potential for this position, it was worth any perceived risk. Kirk was hired for this new role and has performed up to every expectation.

The critical element to potential promotions is trust. Although you haven't done it before, your superiors, who have become comfortable with your capabilities over time, believe you should be given the chance to succeed. When a career is just starting out, employers rely on trust in your educational background, perceiving that a graduate of a certain program has met admission standards and been given a specific level of learning. Either way, throughout your career companies will look to your potential as a measure of your value. As one senior General Electric executive was quoted as saying, "Don't be afraid to promote stars without specific relevant experience, seemingly over their heads."[4]

It should be noted that the potential promotion illustrated by Kirk Siefkas is relatively rare. Because these are promotions of trust earned over time, they seldom occur when changing employers, since senior people in the new organization are usually not yet familiar with you or your capabilities. When we are retained to fulfill an executive search, the most common approach is to identify and attract candidates with successful track records in comparable situations. Rarely are clients open to finding candidates with little relevant experience, of course. However, in our search assignments we typically try to include on our slates candidates who have related but not necessarily direct experience as long as we believe that the patterns of their experience and successes combine to demonstrate the *potential* worth taking a chance on.

Positions in the *experiential promotion* category increasingly fall under the realm of an executive recruiter. These are promotions that usually result in a change in employer or even industry and in higher pay. In effect, companies are investing in the belief that because you have done something successfully before, you are likely to be able to do it again. If you happen to have done something of great value once, such as take a company public if you are a finance executive, transform a sales force from selling products to selling solutions, or reduce costs through business system redesign, others are likely to have a keen interest in you doing it again, for them.

Doug Boothe benefited from an experiential promotion when he was recruited away from Xerox to Pharmacia, a global pharmaceuticals company. For several years, Doug had been the general manager of Xerox.com, the company's online distribution site. There, his team had developed this innovative channel for the company's distribution partners and customers almost from scratch, enabling a new, more profitable, customer-focused means of interaction. Xerox had won several awards for its online operation, and revenues derived from this channel were starting to grow at a rapid pace. Executives at Pharmacia learned of the specific results that Doug had generated, and were interested in recruiting him. The health care industry was undergoing dramatic change, and building a strong presence on the Web represented opportunities to lower costs of distribution, directly communicate with doctors, and even develop one-to-one relationships with end customers—something unprecedented in the industry. Pharmacia recognized that the opportunity was significant, but there was no one in their organization with experience in this area. They needed someone who had already cut his teeth in the space—and they were willing to pay for it. They approached Boothe with an offer that was hard to refuse, and he ultimately joined the company with great enthusiasm.

Drawing from his previous experiences, once at Pharmacia Boothe was able to quickly create an e-business organizational model and an executive steering board for direction setting and support, and focus operational teams to develop solutions and capabilities aligned with the growth-based initiatives of the company. Within a year, Boothe successfully integrated the newly developed online channels into the U.S. Sales and Marketing group, and emerged as a leader for the company's high-priority sales force automation and customer relationship management initiatives.

This pattern of leveraging successful experience in one company or industry for the opportunity to do something similar in another plays itself out in a majority of the four thousand searches that Spencer Stuart conducts annually. The key to building experiential value in your career is straightforward: Gain experiences that really matter. However, as we will see in the next chapter, this is often easier said than done.

Which type of promotion, potential or experiential, is more important in your career? Actually, a successful career is almost always made up of both. Remaining with one company may keep your pay lower on a relative basis, but you are more likely to receive a potential promotion within your current organization than through a move to another company. Being given the chance to move into general management or dramatically increase your scope of responsibility is crucial to continued career advancement. So understanding when it is in your long-term interest to do something in the short run, such as going for a potential promotion within your current organization to position you for an experiential promotion later on, is a key trait of extraordinarily successful executives.

Promotions based on experiential value are also a basic element of a strong career progression. Although it is dangerous to switch companies too often, our research shows that making well-timed transitions between employers is valuable to a strong career. Executives switch employers every 4.6 years on average.[5] The fact is that when companies recruit someone they are confident about, they are generally willing to pay the candidate handsomely for it. Our data suggest that when an individual is recruited to a new employer, the appointment is typically accompanied by an increase in compensation of between 15 percent and 30 percent. In general, potential promotions tend to be accompanied by the more typical 5 percent to 10 percent pay raises.[6]

In addition, when building a portfolio of career experiences, experiential promotions allow you to leverage the currency of your demonstrated skills for a more prestigious opportunity, company, or industry. Finally, if you are ever between jobs, your experiential value will be your most critical asset to land a new opportunity.

RECOGNIZE THE PROS AND CONS OF LOYALTY

Chances are if you ask a CEO between fifty-five and sixty-five years old, he or she will tell you that unwavering loyalty to a company over many years is a foundation for career success. Yet many of today's younger professionals are rather comfortable switching jobs every eighteen months or two years. With such divergent opinions on employee loyalty, is there a right answer? Is success more likely achieved by demonstrating commitment to a company or by taking advantage of opportunities to change employers as they present themselves? Of course the answer is some of both. Employers want their star employees to be loyal to the company but also to have gained broad experience in the marketplace. Many prospective employers actually shy away from individuals who have experience in only one company. We've had numerous conversations with clients who eliminate a potential candidate out of hand, saying, "It's too risky hiring a one-company guy," or "It's always better to hire an executive from GE, Time Inc., or P&G *after* they've left and had another experience where they've had to prove themselves without all that support." But they are equally nervous about job hoppers who show no continuity, loyalty, or time to allow results to be derived from actions. Achieving the right balance is difficult, but extraordinary success requires it.

THE THREE PHASES OF YOUR CAREER

Where are you in the arc of your career swing? Is your value more potential or more experiential?

Before you jump to an answer, recognize the fact that your value changes throughout your career, shifting from potential to experiential to potential again. As we'll see, one of the patterns of successful careers is to build and harness both potential and experiential value to maximize your value whatever the stage of your career.

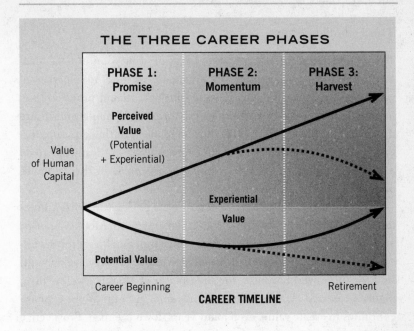

THE THREE CAREER PHASES

Everyone thinks her career is unique. The reasoning goes that a career in manufacturing bears little resemblance to a career on Wall Street or in high technology. The experiences must be different for each and every sector of the economy. Job titles must vary widely in scope and responsibility. And career paths must differ greatly depending on where you live.

However, there are many similarities. The solid line in the chart shows the steady, upwardly sloping career arc that describes career success. The path of successful professionals often visibly diverges from that of the less successful in the middle of a career. Of course it's not quite as simple as that. The path of careers varies greatly among professionals, and minor differences in trajectory early on can lead to big differences in career success over time. But the fact is that over the course of your career, no matter what your rate of ascent, you will likely experience three distinct phases, regardless of your specific occupation, industry, or geography: the promise phase, the momentum phase, and the harvest phase.

The Promise Phase

The *promise phase* unfolds from the years following your formal education until generally sometime in your early thirties. Your perceived
value is significantly weighted toward your potential or promise. During this period, you can have a dramatic impact in shaping your future
direction by affiliating with blue-chip companies, getting exposure to a
wide variety of experiences, and figuring out what you really like to do
and are good at. Our advice to young professionals in their promise
phase: Go blue chip early.

Great companies such as General Electric, PepsiCo, Pfizer, Procter & Gamble, Starbucks, IBM, Booz Allen Hamilton, Morgan Stanley,
and Microsoft have long built their staffing strategies on recruiting talent during this early phase in a person's professional development.
And for those who have left, the imprimatur of having a well-known,
highly respected company on your resume in your promise phase
continues to create value, even many years down the road. Prospective
employers, recruiters, and even boards of directors will look to your
employer immediately after graduation as an early indication of the
trajectory of your career.

The importance of this stage is often underestimated. Compensation is relatively low, and the differences in work experiences among
peers are often almost indiscernible. Yet this phase is critical. There is
no better time to steer the direction of your career. In our survey, those
executives who ultimately achieved extraordinary success were more
than twice as likely as average employees to consider their first five
years as a professional as very successful. Akin to investing for the long
term, seemingly small differences in career momentum early on can
pay large dividends down the road.

Contrary to the well-intentioned advice of many parents to their
children getting ready to enter the workforce, there is no single best
path for the promise phase. One path to always be considered is the
traditional large corporation with training program, but there are
many different alternatives. The military, public service, Peace Corps,
and teaching can all provide valuable experience and reveal a great
deal about your interests and skills early in a career. In whichever

direction a career begins, our advice to new college graduates is to choose wisely and start something that will begin the process of building experiential value. As innocent as it may seem, you should think carefully about the true cost of taking a year or two off to travel or waiting tables at a resort. Going blue chip early offers the opportunity for young people to "find themselves" just as effectively, and the early professional experience will provide feedback and input into what you enjoy and are good at. And it will certainly create the most freedom and alternatives later on.

Whatever your choices early in your career, make sure that the experiences you gain provide you with a better understanding of your talents and interests. This is one of the key objectives you should have for yourself for the promise phase. If you remain out of the marketplace during the years when your potential is most valued, your swing still continues to descend. And this is not just the case in the promise phase. After attempting to reengage in a career after a long sabbatical, professionals later realize that much of their potential value has been diminished, making it difficult at that point to rebuild career momentum. The bottom line is this: If you choose not to use your potential, you will have still spent it.

Working in the promise phase is in fact one of the best times to identify your strengths and passions, and by combining this increasing self-awareness with greater and greater experiences, you will form the foundation for future opportunities and accomplishments. An individual's ability to convert potential into valuable experience is one of the most important elements to achieving long-term success, and the greater the perceived potential you can build early on, the more fuel you have to gain worthy experience. The promise phase is also the time to develop your human capital assets—skills and credentials such as an MBA or other advanced degree. Although achievement in this phase is important, successful career management at this point looks much more like broad exploration and testing of opportunities than single-minded devotion to a chosen field.

To summarize, there is a twofold goal for the end of the promise phase: to have achieved the endorsement of having worked for at least one recognizable company or institution while having learned enough about yourself to become directed toward a situation that plays to your strengths and interests in the years ahead. This combination, which we will revisit in more depth in the chapter "Find the Right Fit," will enable you to perform consistently and in an environment that you enjoy over a sustained period of time.

Michael Reene: The Value of Potential

Michael Reene excelled in the promise phase of his career and benefited from his early success for decades thereafter. He grew up in a suburb of Chicago, attended the University of Illinois, and received a degree in engineering. "Just before graduation," he told us, "it was clear to me that I was never going to compete successfully with my fellow engineers on the basis of either skill or enthusiasm." Lacking interest in the typical engineering jobs, Reene applied directly to the University of Chicago for its MBA program and was accepted. After graduation, he explored many different opportunities but chose a position with the Information Consulting division of Arthur Andersen (now Accenture).

"I wasn't sure what I wanted to do with my career, but I knew that with Andersen, I could leverage both my engineering and business education and would be exposed to many different companies and industries," Reene reasoned. "My strategy seemed to pay off early, as there were very few engineering MBAs within the company." Andersen did not pay Reene a premium for the incremental potential value that his MBA represented, but having it increased his value within the firm subtly yet meaningfully. The engineering and business training made him a natural to be chosen for certain of the most prestigious assignments that he otherwise would not have had access to, for example. He reflected, "That minor bit of differentiation seemed to separate me from the pack quickly, getting me onto key engagements with the most successful partners."

During his early years with Andersen, like many of his peers, Reene worked very hard on his assignments. But he also made it a point to try to get involved in other activities beyond his day-to-day responsibilities. "I helped out in recruiting, on office management, even small things like the annual party. These extracurricular activities not only taught me how to get things done in a professional services environment, but they gave me a lot of visibility with the partners that I otherwise could not have gotten from pure assignment work." Reene offered to lead all recruiting activities with his alma mater, the University of Chicago, and developed close relationships with entering students and alumni within Andersen. He proactively offered any available time to the most senior partners for basic tasks such as editing presentations, and he gained both exposure and knowledge from these interactions. Reene reflects, "Although I never failed to complete my primary tasks, I also never missed an opportunity to connect or to learn."

In the early 1980s, Reene took a calculated risk and moved from Chicago, Andersen's corporate headquarters, to Atlanta, a fledgling office with strong growth prospects. "The move to Atlanta was clearly a risk," Reene said. "But by then I had developed a strong support base among the senior partner group, and I felt that the upside of trying to make a large impact on a small office made it a risk worth taking." Indeed it was, as both the Atlanta office and Reene performed exceptionally. "Looking back, I am convinced that not taking a risk at that point in my career would have been an even riskier strategy, because I would have been just another associate." Based on his assignment success, visibility among the partnership, and track record building the Atlanta office, Reene went on to become one of the youngest partners ever named at Andersen.

With demonstrated success, Reene was poised for a major experiential promotion. A few years later he was recruited to IBM into the Global Services division, and he eventually found himself managing its multibillion-dollar global telecommunications consulting practice.

In the initial phase of his career, Reene was able to create significant perceived potential by achieving a top education, early consulting experience, and exposure to a broad group of executives within his firm. He was then able to steadily translate this potential into career momentum through greater and greater impact on clients and the firm at large. And all the while, testing various industry areas through multiple engagements, different office environments from headquarters to an outpost, and experiences from line consulting to office management, he was able to zero in on a career track that was best suited to him. Reflecting on his early years, Reene commented, "It's amazing how seemingly minor differences in momentum and perspective that you establish very early on in your career can lead to such major differentiation later in life. Investing your energy as best as you can early on really pays off down the line."

The Momentum Phase

As you migrate through a series of positions and most likely companies in the first five or seven years of your career, you begin to build up experience and therefore value based on the skills you've acquired and the different situations you've encountered. Your potential value is steadily converted into experiential value as you master functional skills, develop a track record, take on broader responsibilities, manage other professionals, and cultivate a network of business relationships. This is the period, often in your mid-thirties, when you shift into the *momentum phase* of your career. This phase corresponds to the downward fall of the swing, or the point of greatest acceleration. The momentum phase is when many professionals approach their maximum experiential value.

Your potential value hasn't gone away—after all, you still have many years of energy, vitality, and interests ahead of you. But at this point, you are experienced enough to start breaking through to the top levels of an organization or to attract the attention of outside employers. It is at this stage when experiential promotions most frequently occur, based on what you've actually done. Because your track record is now demonstrable, you are in a position to have skills and experience relevant to a broader marketplace. Executives at this stage are frequently targets of an executive search firm, and the number of employers interested in recruiting them typically peaks. Not coincidentally, in our research, the number of recruiting contacts peaked for the average professional between thirty-eight and forty years of age.

For prospective employers, hiring professionals in their momentum phase is about filling organizational holes or deepening the management bench while simultaneously mitigating risk. They want someone who has a track record of success over a sustained period of time and who can replicate that success for them. In most cases, your experience at this stage, represented by roles such as vice president of marketing, logistics director, assistant treasurer, regional sales manager, strategic planning director, and the like, is still sufficiently generic that it is often applicable to multiple companies. On a highly simplified basis, the thinking goes something like this: If you manage a hundred-person sales region with $50 million in revenue, then you will be a sound potential candidate to take over as a national sales manager with two hundred salespeople and $150 million in revenue. If you are a business unit manager at a company such as General Electric, Honeywell, or Emerson Electric, overseeing a $100 million P&L, and your results have been on budget, you will generally be well positioned to be considered for the role of division head or chief operating officer of a $200 million to $500 million business across multiple industries. If you are the top human resources executive for a $3 billion company, you will be a logical potential candidate for the same top HR role at a $5 billion to $10 billion company, or if you are number two at a $5 billion company, then you would be a logical possibility for the number one slot at a $1 billion company. These are the kinds of discussions hiring managers tend to have about professionals in their momentum phase.

If you are on the right track by this middle stage of your career, then you are in a position to take maximum control over your career's direction. The promise phase was still about testing different waters, becoming aware of those things you do well and enjoy, and getting yourself positioned in a role of increased responsibility, leverage, and impact. The most successful executives in the momentum phase achieve positive impact at an accelerating rate. You are the IT professional whose design and implementation skills attract the most important assignments and greatest demand. You are the business development professional who is creating the best reputation in the market and thereby attracting the most interesting deals to the company. You are the editor whose feel for the audience allows you to commission the right articles and therefore attract the best writers.

If you have managed this phase well, you will typically have multiple options within your current organization. Your visibility among other employers is also increasing, especially if you meet with customers, clients, and suppliers and have the occasion to speak at industry conferences. Unfortunately, those who haven't managed this phase are at serious risk of seeing their career stall. If you have been unable to migrate your career toward roles that play to your strengths and passions, enabling the kind of impact to attract the most important opportunities, then you may have lost your greatest opportunity for momentum. This is the place where you and many of your peers begin to fan out along different career trajectories.

Even if you have managed this phase well, you are now in a position that requires you to make difficult decisions: navigating between numerous opportunities, striving to continue gaining new experiences while still playing to your strengths, and strategically cashing in your experiential value in exchange for new career opportunities.

Dan Rosensweig, Yahoo!:
Turning Potential into Momentum

Let's take a look at someone who has done an exceptional job accelerating into the momentum phase of his career: Dan Rosensweig, chief operating officer of Yahoo!, Inc. At forty-two years old, Rosensweig runs all the day-to-day operations of the venerable Internet company. While most everybody knows Yahoo! today, not everyone knows how successful it has become transforming itself from an advertising-supported Internet portal to a diversified online search, access, information, commerce, and marketing business. A major catalyst in this transformation has been the operational leadership of Rosensweig.

Yahoo! is the number one Internet brand globally and is the most trafficked destination worldwide, reaching well over two hundred million individuals each month (in thirteen languages) and 70 percent of U.S. workplaces during the daytime. The company today offers a broad array of communications, commerce, search, and content services in over one hundred distinct properties, including Yahoo! Mail, Messenger, Calendar, Chat, Greetings, Photos, and Shopping. And through partnerships with hundreds of content providers, Yahoo! offers content and media programming in popular areas of interest, including sports, music, movies, news, finance, and games. The company also offers a range of services for businesses and enterprises and has more than twenty thousand merchants on the Yahoo! Store platform.

Yahoo!'s relationships with leading advertisers, as well as with the agencies who serve them, have deepened, and Fortune 500 customers represent a growing share of Yahoo!'s advertising revenues. At the same time, Yahoo! has launched a number of strategic new businesses that generate subscription and fee revenues, including a major initiative to serve corporate customers and a variety of new services targeting consumers. The purchase of recruiting company HotJobs and the development of Yahoo! Personals have helped to increase the revenues from subscribers and fees as well as additional premium services in mail, access, and messaging. And the company recently launched its ambitious subscription video service that features news, sports, and entertainment.

How did Rosensweig win the operational helm of this complex and exciting business? He was recruited to Yahoo! in April 2002 by chairman and chief executive Terry Semel, co-founder and "chief Yahoo" Jerry Yang, and a committee of the board of directors. His selection from a highly competitive field of candidates illustrates career momentum at work from a combination of experience and potential. There were numerous executives with an even greater number of years of professional experience who were just as intelligent and knowledgeable about technology and media as Rosensweig. But in the end, he was the unanimous choice for the Yahoo! job based on how his experiential value had accelerated over the previous eighteen years and on the strength of the fit with the culture and the people.

After graduating from Hobart College in upstate New York in 1982, Rosensweig joined Ziff Davis, publisher of leading technology trade magazines, as an advertising sales representative. He dove into his new role with a passion, learning from some of the most seasoned sales leaders in the company. He also solicited and got mentoring from legendary publishing leader William Ziff, the company's CEO. Rosensweig applied the lessons learned along with his natural ability to listen to and relate well with people to become a top sales professional. This performance earned him management roles early on in his career, where he often had to manage individuals many years his senior. In one telling case, he was asked to take on an important new management assignment as a publisher, to the chagrin of one of the more experienced sales executives. Rosensweig met with the older gentleman in an effort to win him over and after an icy conversation concluded that the only way to earn his respect would be to lead by example. He committed to signing on $1 million of new business for the magazine, which the salesman thought was mere bravado. But deliver he did, and Rosensweig earned the credibility upon which he built a high-performing team.

By the mid-1990s, the Internet was gaining momentum, and Ziff Davis was well positioned to respond because of its leading role as a publisher in the middle of the technology industry. With his track record in sales and strong people skills (experiential value) and high energy level and ability to grasp key technology developments (potential value), Rosensweig was assigned the responsibility to build a new online company, ZDNet. This is a clear-cut example of a potential promotion, as Rosensweig had never built an online company before (few had at that stage). But Rosensweig was not at all deterred. Drawing on the tech positioning of the company, the company's editorial content and technology expertise, and established advertising relationships, he had all that he needed to build a successful enterprise. ZDNet was an immediate success. Rosensweig became increasingly visible in the online community, and the company was becoming more and more valuable to the parent corporation. So valuable was ZDNet that the company was able to execute a successful initial public offering with Rosensweig as CEO. Now he had secured the additional experiential value of leading an IPO and being CEO of a public company.

As it grew, ZDNet found itself fighting it out in the market for advertising dollars, technology news, and product reviews with arch-rival CNET Networks, a San Francisco-based Internet company that had a similar product offering, audience base, and advertising clientele. After going at it head to head, the larger company, CNET, agreed to acquire ZDNet and merge the companies and operations. But defying the conventional wisdom and normal practice whereby the management teams of acquired companies end up taking severance packages and leaving the company, Rosensweig became president of the new, much larger CNET. The company's board quickly determined that he was the linchpin in making the merger work. It turned out to be a fortunate move, as the majority of management positions in the new company ultimately went to former ZDNet executives. Rosensweig's experiential value was again expanded, this time from executing a public company sale, leading a merger integration, and making all the tough resource allocation and people decisions.

At this stage of his career, Rosensweig's career momentum was accelerating. Only forty years old, he still had many years of his career in front of him, but he also had an almost unique degree of relevant experience in the market. He was now president of one of the leading advertising-supported Internet companies, and the leader in the technology vertical. The quality of the CNET advertising sales effort won renown from the company's much larger rivals, Yahoo!, MSN, and AOL, based on its ability to bring the disciplines and Madison Avenue relationship building of traditional media to the online world.

So when it came time to search for a chief operating officer at Yahoo!, Rosensweig was clearly among the top on the list. In fact, it was co-founder Jerry Yang who first suggested Rosensweig due to his reputation and track record and was heavily involved in bringing him into the company. Rosensweig's relevant general management experience in an advertising-based online business, his traditional media experience, his depth of technology understanding and industry relationships, and his leadership qualities combined to make him the top choice, even though Yahoo! was nearly four times the size of CNET. Along the way, another important factor came into play as well—the diversity of Rosensweig's experiences across numerous roles (sales rep, sales manager, publisher, president, CEO) and across three different companies (Ziff Davis, ZDNet, and CNET Networks) coupled with the stability and loyalty that he demonstrated to his organizations (he never left any company; one was a spin-off and then it merged). This is an interesting consideration to keep in mind as you think about achieving maximum value in the momentum phase of your career.

Given all of his relevant experience and personal qualities, Rosensweig was able to dive into his COO role at Yahoo! with abandon and add value immediately. Both CEO Terry Semel and human resources chief Libby Sartain commented to us that Rosensweig has been a hand-in-glove fit for the company and that he has been a fabulous addition to the top management team. Why? Specifically, Rosensweig's background and personality have complemented those of the company's other top executives, especially in finance, strategy, and development. Not only has Yahoo! benefited from him personally, but also the whole exceeds the sum of the parts. Rosensweig's people and leadership skills have also energized the team very quickly, which has been critical considering the tough competitive environment and where the company is in its lifespan.

With Yahoo!, Rosensweig is in a top leadership position at a visible, dynamic company with a significant brand and global platform on which to continue to perform at a critical moment in time. His case provides great clarity as to what *your* goal should be toward the end of the momentum phase: to have reached a point of significant responsibilities in your area of expertise that stretch you to the max, to have performed strongly in these responsibilities on a sustained basis, and to have achieved the appropriate level of visibility in your organization or industry. All of these achievements combined will result in the ultimate objective at this point—to generate many different career options. This, as our research and experience have confirmed, is the mark of the extraordinary executives as they move into the most mature stage of their career, the harvest phase.

The Harvest Phase

Most people experience the *harvest phase* when they have been in their careers about twenty-five or thirty years, or beginning in their mid-forties to early fifties. Career trajectories do start to diverge in the middle of the momentum phase. The most successful executives are the ones to whom the most important roles and responsibilities are flowing. Talented managers with fewer years of experience start managing those with more years. And it is clear that some careers are continuing to progress while others have reached their highest level. However, on a relative basis, executives still progress reasonably predictably through the momentum phase. After all, the vast majority of professionals are still gainfully employed at this stage.

The most visible differentiation in career success occurs in the harvest phase. At this stage, extraordinary executives have an increasing array of career options from which to choose: other companies to run, boards to join, investment firms with which to affiliate, consulting engagements to pursue, articles or books to write, television appearances or speaking engagements to make, not-for-profit projects to lead, and so on. These fortunate executives find a way to continue advancing their careers, while others inevitably plateau or even decline. It is not surprising to see average employees, even successful professionals, retire early in today's economy, exiting the traditional career track. And this, of course, is the clearest way to distinguish where on the trajectory someone is.

How does one maintain the upward trajectory moving into the harvest phase? The explanation for this is quite simple conceptually but rather more challenging to act upon. The formula for continued career success in the harvest phase is all about transforming the varied components of your now much deeper experiential value into renewed potential. There was no single perfect fit for the role of CEO of IBM, but Lou Gerstner had assembled such a powerful portfolio of experiences in his career that he emerged as the choice with the greatest potential. When Yahoo! sought to land a COO, there was no one in the emerging industry that had the exact set of experiences directly applicable to the position, but it was the *combination* of experiences that the search committee recognized as potential in Dan Rosensweig. Maintaining or even accelerating career value is possible well into the harvest phase if you are able to link your experiences in a way that represents renewed potential. Often this requires personally assessing the potential that your aggregate experiences may embody. A good executive recruiter or human resource professional should quickly be able to connect the dots in your experience and see the value that the combination represents, but you never want to leave this interpretation to chance. Review your career history and identify the competencies gained, the various skills demonstrated, the exposure to various industries and business models. Then become skilled at articulating how your unique career path represents an opportunity for continued promotion or other new and exciting professional challenges.

And with the ability to articulate this renewed potential, find an organization, group of people, or audience for whom it is both relevant and valuable. Not everyone can host a talk show, go on the lecture circuit, take on a new CEO role, or join a corporate board (although they are all sound things to which to aspire). Other, more down-to-earth approaches are to join a not-for-profit board or your industry association, help raise funds for an academic institution, mentor small-company business executives, teach in an after-school program such as Junior Achievement, or volunteer to work on a political campaign. And herein bears mentioning an important point: that the vertical axis of our career value chart, which reads "Perceived Value," is not necessarily the same thing as financial value or compensation. Any of these aforementioned activities will be valuable to your career provided that you enjoy doing them, that they add value to someone, and that they keep your mind sharp and spirit engaged.

A Harvest Phase to Aspire To: Arthur Levitt Jr.

Arthur Levitt Jr., the longest-serving chairman ever of the Securities and Exchange Commission, is a magnificent example of someone who has accelerated all through his career, well into the harvest phase. In the 1960s, he was a founding partner of a small New York brokerage firm, along with three other individuals who would also go on to renown: Sanford Weill, now chairman and CEO of Citigroup; Arthur Carter, now publisher of the *New York Observer*; and Roger Berlind, who became a Broadway producer. By the late 1960s, Levitt's success and that of the firm earned him the role running Shearson Hayden Stone, which later became Shearson Lehman Brothers. In 1977, after leading a search committee for the next head of the American Stock Exchange, he was persuaded by the board to accept the position himself. Levitt had a long and distinguished tenure leading the exchange, and this also helped bring him into public life.

By 1993, when President Clinton appointed Levitt to run the SEC, he had become well connected in both political parties, having served three prior presidents: Jimmy Carter as chairman of the White House Conference on Small Business, Ronald Reagan with the Commission on Private Sector Initiatives, and George H. W. Bush as chairman of the Sanford Commission on Central American Economic Recovery. In 1980, he had also founded and chaired the American Business Conference, an organization to represent the interests of high-growth medium-size companies on Capitol Hill (similar to what the Business Round Table does for the largest companies). At the SEC, Levitt earned his reputation as a tough regulator and activist for the individual investor, taking on the powerful accounting industry with its armies of lobbyists and millions of dollars in political contributions. But it was his consistent calls for aggressive corporate accounting reform that look so prescient now in the aftermath of the multitudinous corporate scandals.

Levitt's success, visibility, and network of important relationships have helped generate more alternatives than are seen even with the most extraordinary executives in their harvest phase. After Levitt's tenure as SEC chairman concluded with President George W. Bush coming into office in January 2001, he was able to construct a portfolio of activities that ensured that he would remain active, vital, engaged, and adding value. He joined a prestigious investment firm, the Carlyle Group, as a partner (the same firm that Lou Gerstner joined more recently). He continued to serve on the board of Bloomberg, the financial news and media company founded by Michael R. Bloomberg, now mayor of New York City, and also began a weekly television and radio show. He had numerous board directorship offers from which to choose. And he devoted two years to writing his book, *Take on the Street,* which became a blockbuster best-seller with its call for aggressive corporate reform and populist message of investor responsibility, which he has brought to a broader audience than ever before.[7] In addition to all of this, he maintains an energetic and positive private life, enjoying a beautiful family and keeping in great shape. Levitt is truly an inspiring role model for what the harvest phase can ultimately look like!

THE VALUE OF YOU:
PUTTING IT ALL TOGETHER

The marketplace for talent has seen significant ups and downs over the last several years, and there are so many factors at work that it's easy to get lost in the confusion. However, we hope that by reading about this first pattern of extraordinary careers, you will find the dynamics at work and changes at hand understandable. The talent market, although complex, really does operate based on the same fundamental principles of every other market, supply and demand, and despite increased volatility and uncertainty, the trends are still at hand for driving up the value of executive talent for years to come.

Now that you better understand the market you're participating in, you are well positioned to take control and proactively steer your career in directions that will maximize your success and satisfaction.

Understanding value is important, but even more important is how you behave in leadership positions, how you treat people, and how other people respond to you in return. To do that, let's turn to the next pattern of extraordinary careers: practice benevolent leadership.

PRACTICE BENEVOLENT LEADERSHIP

A leader is best when people barely know that he exists.
He is the teacher who succeeds without taking credit.
And, because credit is not taken, credit is received.
—LAO TZU, 6TH CENTURY B.C.

SUCCESS THROUGH OTHERS

Sometimes you just need to let go. That's the lesson Mark Kaiser learned back in 1987. Kaiser was hurtling up the corporate ladder in the communications industry when he realized that he had a problem: With each success came broader and more difficult assignments, until his responsibilities had outstripped anything that he could accomplish alone.

It seems like a simple enough problem. At some point many exceptional workers move into management and need to hand off responsibilities to the next generation of up-and-comers. Easier said than done. Kaiser's journey demonstrates just how tough it can be and provides clues about how you can learn to let others come into their own without clamoring for all the credit.

The son of a utility executive, Kaiser graduated from Furman University in South Carolina. He joined IBM in 1979 with the ambition of becoming CEO of the company, but "quickly realized there were quite a few of the three hundred thousand or so other employees that had a similar aspiration." A bit disenchanted with the rigid structure of such a large organization, he left IBM and a few years later took a job as the head of a small marketing department for a newly formed company, TelecomUSA. The company was just starting, and although it was expected to grow quickly, Kaiser was confident that his capabilities would be able to keep up. But the growth quickly accelerated to a frenetic pace—$100 million, $200 million, $300 million, new markets, new offerings. Not only were there not enough hours in the day, but Kaiser's responsibilities had expanded beyond his experience and areas of competence. He was overworked, stressed out, and becoming unsure of his abilities.

Kaiser became visibly exhausted. One weekend while at the CEO's home for a gathering, his boss said to him: "Mark, who ever told you that you had to do this all by yourself? You know, the curse of the highly talented person is that everyone wants him to do everything." Kaiser realized it was time for a major change. Rather than go it alone, he would become fanatical about wooing, hiring, and retaining the most talented people in his business. Ultimately, he developed a plan to create an environment that would be the most attractive to the very best people—one of open communication and deep trust, in which his subordinates' success would be more important than even his own.

It wasn't long before Kaiser's strategy began to pay off. He began retaining top performers on his team and attracting highly sought-after prospects. And there were additional benefits as well. Other professionals, some of the most talented he ever met, sought him out. In a virtuous cycle, word spread like a brushfire about his leadership and mentorship abilities, and professionals began to come to him, longing to work closely with him and join his team. With so many talented professionals wanting to join up, Kaiser had the luxury of selecting only the very best. And it allowed him to upgrade his team over time, raising the bar of performance with every new hire. Even more inspiring, he observed that many of his existing employees began to thrive in this new environment of trust and delegation, far surpassing any expectations he had had for their performance. With such a distinct advantage in the attraction and development of resources, Kaiser's teams consistently performed beyond expectations, and his own career took off.

Kaiser built a world-class marketing organization that he was still leading when TelecomUSA surpassed $1 billion in revenue. Confident and far more secure of his position in corporate America, Mark went on to become CEO of a company called Caredata, which he grew from a start-up through its successful public offering in 1997, largely by following the same leadership principles.

Today, as the CEO of Cendian, a logistics outsourcing company, he has turned his knack for harboring talent into an art form. During a particularly poignant corporate ceremony not too long ago, Kaiser stood with his top lieutenants before Cendian's entire management team and lifted up a silver baton. "This small team of professionals has contributed greatly to the growth of this company, and indeed we have come a long way together," said Kaiser. "But today we stand before you, willing and ready to pass the baton to the next level of management that will take Cendian to even greater heights. As we continue to grow, success cannot be achieved alone." Kaiser and his team then handed out these symbolic batons to each member of the management team, and with this gesture, the message of trust and delegation was clearly communicated. With a strong, motivated, and loyal team in place, Cendian has grown steadily, and it finished 2002 with a run rate of more than $500 million in revenue, grown from a standing start in less than three years.

Kaiser had no choice but to build a strong team or be crushed under the weight of too much direct responsibility. He had been in a role where he had limited experience and capacity while his responsibilities were expanding exponentially. Ignoring his personal limitations based on a belief that he could do—or learn to do—anything was not a viable option. "Once I understood what was really happening, it was a fairly easy choice," Kaiser said. "Build a strong team around yourself or perish."

But for most people, the choice rarely seems as stark—and the case for plausible denial is great. You make excuses for why in fact no one else can do what you do. And while you take on the world you unknowingly leave your team in the lurch. If you are not careful, you risk drifting along through the majority of your career driven by ego and grasping to perform as many tasks as you can physically manage, all for fear of entrusting them to others. As author Peter Block succinctly stated, "We are reluctant to let go of the belief that if I am to care for something, I must control it." So many people progress in their careers hoping to ensure short-term success by tight oversight, while long-term success slips away. For the few who do manage to let go and focus on achieving success through others, the rewards of an extraordinary career become highly attainable.

Mark Kaiser practiced benevolent leadership, an approach based on ultimate trust and alignment of individual and organizational goals. His ability to create a positive working environment, inspiring and galvanizing a loyal army of professionals working toward common success, highlights a vital element in managing your career: *Extraordinary success is achieved by making those around you successful.*

Benevolent leaders may have various interpersonal styles—some are humble and self-effacing, others are charismatic, and others still are demanding taskmasters. But regardless of style, they all create an environment of open communication, honesty, and confidence, delegating both minor and critical tasks. Moreover, they demonstrate how the success of the team directly benefits each team member. In today's skeptical business environment, where one crisis after another has come to light, the benevolent leadership approach is more important and appropriate than ever. People long to work in an environment where bold aspirations for success are clearly defined and commonly shared, and team behavior is governed by a strong set of ethics and core values. Perhaps most importantly, when the leader's attention is focused squarely on the success of team members, strong results, organizational performance, and employee loyalty are achieved as a natural end result.

The benevolent leader maximizes performance through facilitation. She eliminates barriers for subordinates and leads with authority, even though at times appearing to be just one of the pack. It's easy to know when a benevolent leader is in charge. The telltale signs? Information and authority flow freely. Honesty abounds. People feel free to question authority without retribution. Creativity reigns. Each member of the team feels just as accountable to the other team members as to the leader. With a benevolent leader, the environment of work is changed for the better.

Witness the powerful turnaround of consumer products juggernaut Procter & Gamble under the benevolent leadership of chief executive A. G. Lafley. Since taking over the top job in 2000, he has refocused P&G on its core brands, such as Tide, Pampers, and Crest. More importantly, he has liberated the tradition-bound company from a stodgy, formal corporate culture through empowering actions that are both symbolic and substantive. He switched out the mahogany paneling and an executive dining room in the executive suite, for example, to put in a training center to bring employees from around the world close to the company's top management. And business planning meetings have been transformed from one-way presentations defending a particular course of action to engaging, interactive discussions about various scenarios. Lafley has led this process by example, having been known to sit for hours in product and business review meetings listening carefully, taking notes, and contributing occasional soft-spoken questions such as "Have you thought about it this way?" The result: P&G is expected to post an 11 percent increase in operating income this fiscal year on a 6 percent rise in sales to $34 billion, and the morale of the company is at its highest in years.

DEPARTURE FROM CONVENTIONAL WISDOM

At first blush, career success seems to hinge upon personal performance and outperforming others around you. That's what many people believe is the route to get promoted. Most see climbing the corporate ladder as a treacherous journey—the higher you climb, the more cutthroat and nasty the environment. Just take a look in the business section of any bookstore and you'll find reinforcing titles such as *Swim with the Sharks Without Being Eaten Alive.*[1] Those who've battled their way to the top, therefore, must be the most aggressive, self-centered type of people, right?

Not necessarily. Happily, the facts show that the most successful individuals populating the top rung of the corporate ladder are more often those who can attract top talent and inspire them to exceptional levels of performance. When we examined the experiences of hundreds of top-performing executives, it was apparent that they were the beneficiaries of the talents and performance of their peers, subordinates, and superiors.

This fact by itself is not unusual. Nearly all of us have worked with exceptional teams at some point in our careers. We may have been rewarded for our association with a truly outstanding boss, or been recognized for the superior performance of our subordinates. What is unusual about the most successful professionals, however, is the consistency of this occurrence. They almost always seem to be surrounded by other top performers.

In our survey we asked people to describe a particularly successful executive they knew. Extraordinarily successful executives, it turns out, were not perceived as overly self-interested. Quite the opposite was true. *Nearly 90 percent* were described as being concerned about the careers of their subordinates as much as or more than their own careers. Further, a mere 4 percent were described as being most concerned with their own careers. The aggressive, take-no-prisoners executive represented less than one in twenty of the top executives we identified. Our research clearly demonstrates that a leadership approach *focused on the success of others* is truly a significant pattern among successful executives.

But the findings beg two critical questions. First, what is it about the benevolent leadership approach that makes it so related to successful careers? And second, how can this pattern be replicated in your own career?

Let's start with the first question. Do customers feel more comfortable when executives don't steal the spotlight? Possibly, although for the better part of the 1990s, high-profile executives garnered a disproportionate share of press and exposure, in effect gaining cheap advertising for their companies. Do investors prefer an executive who is more concerned with the team than himself to be at the helm of the companies they invest in? Perhaps increasingly so, in the post-CEO-scandal environment of 2003. However, there are still ample examples where in-your-face CEOs, such as Barry Diller of USA Interactive, Ed Whitacre of SBC Communications, and Larry Ellison of Oracle, engender more respect and confidence from investors than their more self-effacing peers. Are benevolent-leader CEOs more competent?

There is certainly no evidence to support this. Yet, looking beyond some of the highly visible CEOs to mainstream executive leaders, research clearly indicates that benevolent leadership has a direct, positive impact on success.

Why is this the case?

The answer lies not in the ability of the CEO per se, but rather in the environment that this style of leadership generates within an organization and the resulting effect it has on the performance of team members. It is the creation of this type of organizational environment, we have found, that is consistently linked to superior long-term performance for these executives and their companies. Quite simply, benevolent leaders achieve advantage by creating an environment where the very best performers want and even seek to work, will perform at peak levels, and will remain loyal. In turn, the leader successful in creating this environment is rewarded by the performance of those working with him.

Ed Woolard graduated from North Carolina State University in 1956 with an industrial engineering degree and took a job at DuPont's Kinston, North Carolina, plant the next year. From these humble beginnings, over the next forty years Woolard ascended within the organization, ultimately becoming DuPont's chairman and chief executive officer. When asked to what he attributed his extraordinarily successful career, Woolard replied, "A good B player can surround himself with a lot of A's. My job was really just to nurture them and make them successful." Our caveat to Woolard's self-deprecating comment is that this is what actually made him an A—identifying the opportunity and creating the conditions for attracting the best people and letting them do their best work.

To put this lesson another way: The extraordinary executive does not claw his way to the top—*he is carried there.*

SEEING THE PATTERN

To understand this more clearly, let's examine the characteristics of different working environments. We set out to identify if in fact there were certain types of environments—large company versus small, high growth versus stable, and so on—that increased the likelihood of career success. We looked into what really motivated executives, and sought to identify the places in which they most preferred to work. Further, we wondered if there were environments viewed so positively that executives would proactively seek them out. These questions led us to some important insights. As we had hypothesized, there were indeed environments that were strongly linked with career success. But to our surprise, it was not necessarily the fact that professionals had steered their careers toward these beneficial environments that led to their success. In many cases it was the working environments that they themselves had created that contributed to their success. Success is therefore not entirely dependent on finding the most attractive environment, but can also be attained by creating the most attractive environment for others. As did Kaiser, the extraordinary executive creates an attractive, powerful, and positive environment by practicing benevolent leadership—and in so doing, dramatically advantages her own career.

So what really does motivate the best and the brightest? In our survey we asked how respondents personally defined career success. Two key factors emerged. The first—one of the most often cited—was "freedom in my job to do the things I want." Professionals, particularly high-performing ones, do not like to be micromanaged. In fact, they really don't like to be managed at all. They prefer to be led, being provided with a clear set of goals and objectives and given the creative freedom to accomplish their targets. They want to be trusted with the information and resources necessary to achieve a task, and then to be given the accountability, authority, and flexibility to accomplish their objectives. They feel smothered and undermined by managers who are afraid to truly delegate responsibility or who view information as power, providing it only on a need-to-know basis. They seek empowerment that comes from a leader who trusts them completely. This unusually high degree of trust, then, is the first element of the most desired professional environment.

The second most often cited definition of career success was "to be well regarded in my company or industry." Beyond money, prestige,

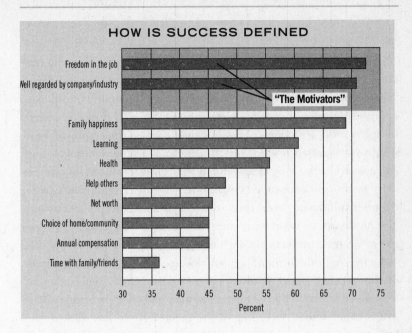

even lifestyle, the successful executive wants to have an impact and to be recognized for it. He wants to get something done. He has specific goals for personal success and is most passionate when there is alignment between his objectives and those of his boss, team, or organization. "How will *this* job, working for *this* boss, help me achieve the level of respect and impact that I desire?" he asks, explicitly or implicitly, about each new opportunity. Most people hold each opportunity up to the lens of self-interest: "What's in it for me?" Highly successful individuals do this, but they also add another question: "If I am successful, will the organization or team be successful?" Alignment, therefore, is the second element of the most desired environment.

Yet not all leaders can create both of these conditions in the workplace. The closer they get to these ideal conditions, the more likely it is that they will attract and retain top talent. As we continued to explore the ability of leaders to create trust and alignment, we concluded that there are four categories of leaders: *pirates, mercenaries, good citizens,* and *benevolent leaders.*

Pirates

A pirate is a successful yet not particularly well-liked leader who may have a winning strategy but who also bands people together by appealing to common wants and greed. Often ruling by fear and internecine competition, pirates create an environment of high turnover, except for a few loyal lieutenants. They are able to retain the employees they want with outsized rewards or stringent employment contracts. Loyalty created by this type of leader can be fleeting, however, for often as soon as the golden handcuffs are lifted (by a declining stock price, contract fulfillment, etc.) there is a corresponding exodus of talent. The pirate can be successful over the long term only if he is far superior in strategic thinking or deal making than the competition and uses seductive rewards to retain key employees. One well-known example of this type of leader is also one of media's most respected—and feared—executives, Barry Diller, chairman and chief executive officer of USA Interactive. According to one executive who has worked with Diller over many years, "not only is this description generally accurate, but I think Barry would be proud to be referred to like this."

Mercenaries

A mercenary focuses on personal success above all else. Self-motivated and not overly concerned about the success of others around them, mercenary leaders are viewed as extremely competitive. Yet these professionals not only fail to motivate others to help them succeed, they often create dog-eat-dog cultures and stimulate co-workers to cheer for each other's failure, and in some cases prompt it. Michael Ovitz, former superagent and chairman of the once all-powerful Creative Artists Agency (CAA) in Hollywood, is said by associates to have followed this approach in building his firm. While Ovitz was successful for a long while in the talent agency business, mercenary leadership did not translate well to corporate America—his tenure as president and chief operating officer of Walt Disney Company lasted only nine months. But consistent with this school of behavior, he shrewdly walked out the door with some $100 million in severance.[2]

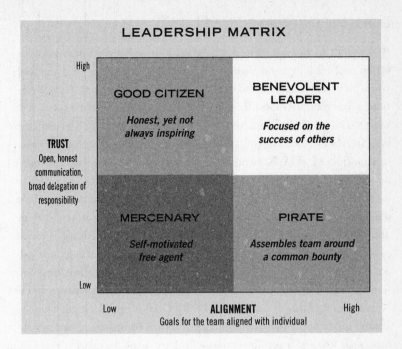

Good Citizens

Good citizens are honest leaders who engender personal trust, though not always inspiration nor organizational alignment. They are perceived as having the best of intentions and the willingness to delegate, but not always able to hold people accountable, make the tough calls, or deliver success. Professionals remain with these leaders often based on personal loyalty or out of pleasant inertia. However, strong performers often become frustrated under good-citizen leaders because their career goals are not being met, and eventually they leave to seek more promising opportunities. Gerald Levin, former chief executive officer of AOL Time Warner, for example, was well known for his soulful personality and his vision and philosophy about the future of media. However, he found it challenging to align the goals and objectives of the powerful and decentralized division chiefs at the company for the common good of the overall enterprise.

Benevolent Leaders

Benevolent leaders are those whose primary agenda is team success. Often self-effacing and egoless in style, but also firm and decisive when necessary, benevolent leaders motivate by setting clear, ambitious goals that are mutually shared and by creating an environment of both trust and goal alignment. They attract the best and brightest, and benefit from incredible loyalty. Tom Freston, chairman and chief executive officer of MTV Networks, the multibillion-dollar cable television powerhouse owned by media conglomerate Viacom, Inc., has proven over the years to be able to build and retain what is arguably the best management team in the industry. By employing a genuinely humble and self-effacing style and truly caring about his subordinates as much as or more than himself, Freston has developed a deep, stable, and talented bench of business leaders running the multiple television, film, publishing, and consumer products businesses that constitute MTV, Nickelodeon, VH1, Showtime, CMT, BET, TNN, and Comedy Central among other networks. The company has thrived by having unambiguous goals for the overall company and for each network chief and allowing them to run their business as they see fit.

In business, benevolent leaders find themselves at a distinct advantage because they create the most attractive professional environment and, as a direct result, consistently have their pick of the most talented people. Similar to collegiate athletics, where competition for star athletes is intense, the schools perceived to have the best programs consistently win the best recruits. Often, the result is that the schools where athletes believe they are most likely to win keep on winning.

Like athletes, professionals understand the importance of joining the best program and actively seek it out. This becomes a virtuous circle—the best people create the best results, which in turn attract the best people. The ability to create the most attractive environment, therefore, pays tremendous dividends. Professionals who create a winning environment, usually end up winners.

WORKING WITH THE FOUR
LEADERSHIP TYPES

When managing your career, it is important to recognize the distinctions between these four types of leaders. Working under a manager who tends toward the mercenary approach has many clear pitfalls, but this type of individual is the easiest to spot and thus is also the easiest to avoid. There are environments, however, such as securities trading or talent agencies, that have lent themselves to this style. Working for a good citizen can be comfortable; however, his or her lack of decisiveness and organizational alignment often results in different parts of a company working at cross purposes or makes an environment susceptible to counterproductive politics. And beware the comfortable atmosphere created by these leaders, for as difficult as they are to leave, long-term success often requires it.

When working under a pirate, the benefit-pitfall distinction may be the least clear. Pirates are not all mean-spirited, ravenous plunderers, as the name may imply. And many, including Barry Diller, have proven over the years that their approach works, uncomfortable as it may be to work for them. There is one specific type of pirate, however, who can be particularly dangerous to your career—the narcissist.

In 1990, the psychologists Robert Hogan, Robert Raskin, and Dan Fazzini conducted research into various forms of flawed managers and identified a particularly dangerous type they referred to as "the narcissist."[3] Narcissists are managers who possess a high degree of energy, self-confidence, and charm, which often allows them to rise very quickly up the corporate ladder. Although their charisma naturally attracts others to them, narcissists are usually poor leaders. They rarely delegate critical tasks, fearing they will appear weak, and they discount suggestions their subordinates may offer. "Narcissists are biased to take more credit for success than is legitimate," Hogan and his fellow psychologists wrote, "and are biased to avoid acknowledging responsibility for their failures and shortcomings for the same reasons that they claim more success than is their due." Despite the frequent absence of substance or insight, narcissists also make decisions with a very high degree of confidence and conviction, so much so that others believe them and follow their lead, blind to the potential hazards of the path.

Narcissists attract people with their beaming confidence—you might think that this person offers an easy ride on their coattails. Don't be fooled. Their apparent success is often an illusion, and ultimately their poor management skills translate to poor performance that even they cannot gloss over. Those professionals who align themselves with narcissists on the way up are at risk of being thrown out with the bathwater on the way down. Their projects rarely have lasting positive impact, and under the tight ego of the narcissist, subordinates are not given room to develop.

The self-consumed manager was particularly popular during the 1990s technology bubble. Analysts touted the expected dramatic growth of market segments. Venture capitalists poured money into every conceivable company with a good story. Investment bankers competed aggressively to take companies public. It was a period of time when merely having the right concept, the right CEO, and the right investors almost guaranteed IPO success. And along the way, the storytellers themselves—the leaders of these companies with exploding values—became stars.

Two factors were characteristic of the boom. One was that truly gifted, charismatic leaders emerged, who through their own strength of personality could paint beautiful pictures of how their company would soon dominate this new frontier. The other was even more dangerous—the premise of these companies was that all the old assumptions were wrong. The market seemed to encourage the CEOs to tout their new, unorthodox strategies and assumptions, even though many of these CEOs lacked critical experiences upon which to draw. These two factors caused the emergence of a particular profile of leadership—a charismatic and dynamic speaker who could hypnotize a room, who also had the arrogance to really believe that he was personally destined to rewrite the rules of business.

One such individual we have observed—we will call him Maxwell Kennedy—was at one point worth more than $200 million on paper, having started a company only a few years earlier. Max had left a top-tier business school after his first year to start a company. Within months, he had secured funding, and within two years, with the help of his investors and Wall Street, he had taken the company public. A truly gifted speaker, he was able to captivate his audience with the story of his company's new technology creating a new market, their first-mover advantage, and the destiny of success. He seldom answered the tough questions head-on, responding in generalities, avoiding specific facts, and openly disparaging anyone who challenged his assumptions, either internally or externally. With a high-flying stock and market analysts cheering on his company, few seemed to have the credibility to challenge him.

In December 1998, after a strong year of sales for his company, he decided to withhold all bonuses. His company had the cash, and there was no dispute as to whether the bonuses had been earned, but January 1 came and went, and none of the expected payroll checks appeared, to the great surprise of employees who had been counting on the money. Max had simply decided that his employees might be getting too cocky, and he wanted to let everyone know that he still controlled the company. On March 1, the bonuses were paid, two months late. The point had been made.

Later in 1999, Max flew all of his company's salespeople to Palm Springs for their annual meeting, to recognize strong performers and kick off the coming year. When each person arrived, he received an itinerary, but unknown to the attendees, there were two separate itineraries separating the sales team into two groups. The next morning, they were directed to separate rooms. Max entered the first room, welcomed everyone, and then bluntly informed them that they had all been fired for poor performance. He then proceeded to the next room, where he informed the group of what he had just done, and threatened to do the same to them if performance did not improve. He turned and walked to the helicopter waiting for him, leaving the remaining employees sitting in stunned silence.

Max was an extreme case of the narcissist—arrogant, charismatic, and very dangerous. As Max's company's stock had continued to rise, employees became locked in with golden handcuffs. Many desperately wanted out of the company but were unwilling to give up the stock options that on paper were worth small fortunes. Some actually believed that Max's style of management, albeit unorthodox, was what was driving the company's success. But with the market crash that started in mid-2000, Max's company's stock price plummeted. The very best employees abandoned the company as soon as they were able. With the organization in tatters and Max now commanding virtually no respect from his employees, he was removed in disgrace from the company he founded. But those who really lost were the employees, having clung to paper wealth in a mismanaged and unsophisticated company. In the end, they were left with worthless options, a resume highlighting a tarnished employer, and precious little relevant work experience.

Learning to spot and avoid narcissist leaders is essential to long-term success. Aligning yourself with benevolent leaders is also important. But practicing this style of leadership yourself, creating an environment that will pull the best resources toward you is most critical.

NAVIGATING PROMOTIONS

Another aspect of the pattern of benevolent leadership plays out in companies' promotion decisions. In addition to attracting the best talent to work with you and achieving excellent results through others, there is another reason why practicing benevolent leadership can increase the likelihood that you will be promoted—it helps you to avoid the limiting consequences of becoming "indispensable" in your current role.

We recently sat with the CEO of a Fortune 100 company who wanted to recruit a new general manager for one of his largest and most profitable divisions. He felt that although there were two executives in leadership positions within the company who could take on this broader role, he was hesitant to promote them from their current jobs. "They are just too valuable where they are," he confided to us. Little did they know it, but those two otherwise qualified executives had not done what was needed to develop a chain of talented up-and-comers.

And that brings us back to Mark Kaiser, because that was precisely the skill that he honed. He developed his team, delegating responsibility to them wherever it made sense, and made others aware of their success. As promotional opportunities arose in his own career, there were usually one or two people on his team who could readily step in and fill his role—thus making him all the more promotable.

When it comes to you and your own promotions, it is not always as easy as it sounds to develop great people to make yourself expendable so you can be promoted. Some are able to get around this challenge, such as fast-track employees at large companies who have the opportunity to move rapidly through a series of jobs as their experience is broadened. But if you are not on a rotational management development program, there is a natural inclination to cling to the belief that the job couldn't get done without you. If you do not balance this belief with the additional reality that helping develop your own bench strength is a key to your success, your superiors may use this as an excuse when passing you over for a promotion or reassignment.

THE SUCCESSFUL BENEVOLENT LEADER

One business leader who is famous for building a company based on the benevolent leadership approach in business is Herb Kelleher, co-founder and longtime CEO of Southwest Airlines.

For Kelleher, the pattern of benevolent leadership has long been a key part of the DNA of Southwest Airlines' corporate culture, which is frequently atop lists of the most admired companies in America. Many other organizations have sent teams of managers to visit the company in the hopes of establishing a culture similar to that of Southwest. But as Kelleher told us in our interview, it cannot be forced. "When we tell visitors that all we've done is just treat people right, it's too simplistic for them. They want something far more complex. They want a program. We always felt that making it 'a program' murders it."

Kelleher co-founded Southwest Airlines in 1967, battling rival airlines all the way to a Supreme Court victory that allowed them to start flying in 1971, within Texas only. He became president, chairman, and CEO of Southwest in1982, retired from the president and

CEO positions in 2001, and still serves as chairman. Over the course of his career, the fun-loving leader built Southwest into the fourth largest airline in the United States. But with its customer-obsessed, labor-friendly, and efficient point-to-point airline service, it is the most valuable airline in the country by far in terms of market capitalization.

Contrary to his self-effacing comment about the lack of a program, there are in fact disciplined management processes that the company has put in place to give teeth to Kelleher's philosophy of benevolent leadership. Over the years, the company formed and empowered something called the Southwest Culture Committee. Each year this committee brings forth a cross section of company employees to brainstorm issues to address, blockages to break down, and opportunities to improve the culture of Southwest. The daylong session typically generates scores of ideas, which are then grouped and prioritized. Then teams are set loose to work across the company, focusing on the top priorities. Kelleher and his successors, James F. Parker, CEO, and Colleen C. Barrett, president, take a personal interest in making sure these teams have the access, resources, and mandate they need to succeed. Management is updated. Progress is made. And this feeds back into the next annual meeting of the overall Culture Committee, when the process starts once again.

Although his leadership philosophy is deeply rooted in doing right by people, Kelleher also provided us the economic rationale. "In a business where everyone has similar planes, the same gates, and basically the same fares, the only thing that differentiates one airline from another is the people who work there." He elaborated on his management philosophy by posing a rhetorical question: "Do you think people work better and are more productive if they enjoy what they're doing?" He then answered his own question. "I've always felt that you shouldn't have to change your personality when you come to work. So we decided that we were going to hire good people and let them be themselves. We were going to create an environment where we pay a great deal of attention to them, their personal lives as well as their business lives. We wanted to show them that we don't regard them as automatons. We wanted to create an environment where people can really enjoy what they're doing."

Many corporate managers talk like this, but as the Culture Committee example demonstrates, Kelleher is quick to stress that you cannot just provide lip service to these concepts. "People know whether you're treating them this way for some kind of purely economic reason or whether you're doing it because you genuinely like and value people." He also confirmed something that we strongly believe: that the best people are looking for deeper meaning in their work these days, especially in a post-9/11 world. "There has been a real change in American society in the attitude that people have toward their work and what they are looking for out of their working lives," Kelleher said. "So you have to change in order to accommodate that. We believe it's important for everybody to realize that we're in an enterprise that has a worthwhile meaning. We're like the bricklayer. If he understands what the ultimate goal is, building a home for a family, he will probably do a better job."

Kelleher has indeed achieved success by making others in Southwest successful. This is clearly visible to customers, who enjoy the genuine spirit of service provided by gate agents, flight attendants, and pilots. But at the executive level as well, Kelleher has focused on making his top lieutenants supported, empowered, and accountable—it has been Parker and Barrett who have run the day-to-day operations of the company for years. While the rest of the airline industry slumped into the depths of the 2002 global economic slowdown, the Southwest veterans kept the airline thriving by consistently implementing the employee- and customer-obsessed, low-fare and cost-conscious strategy. As a whole, the industry lost nearly $10 billion in 2002 and laid off thousands of workers, but Parker and Barrett were able to protect jobs, turn a profit, and remain true to the benevolent leadership approach instilled by Kelleher.

ATTRACTING THE BEST, UNLOCKING THEIR POTENTIAL

To understand just how a truly benevolent leader is able to change the workplace for the better—and benefit in the process—let's explore some of the specific attributes of this style in more detail, particularly, the self-effacing nature that focuses attention on the leader's subordinates and team, rather than herself.

In *Good to Great*, Jim Collins identified eleven companies that had undergone a transformation from lackluster performance to market leaders.[4] The companies were not the usual suspects—in fact, a dowdier crew might not have been assembled, including Walgreen's and Kimberly-Clark. But more was surprising than just the companies identified. Collins also discovered that the leaders of these firms were not the typical, larger-than-life superstars that are often written about in the business press. Instead, they were level-headed, self-effacing leaders who were often longtime corporate insiders.

Our own research findings are similar. For one particular track of research about professional performance, we thought it would be interesting to focus on entrepreneurial companies, since their success or failure (sometimes their very survival) hinges on the performance of the top executive team. Also, without the "noise" of the organizational politics found in many larger organizations, executive performance can be isolated and examined more easily.[5]

The conventional wisdom is that brash entrepreneurs lead companies against all odds to amass personal fortunes, and arrogance and ego almost seem a price of entry. Surprisingly, our research shows that although arrogance and ego were clearly present within the chief executives of some of these companies, this trait did not win the day. In fact, our research indicates the best-performing entrepreneurial CEOs, like Collins' "good to great" Fortune 1000 CEOs, are relatively self-effacing and humble. "It's the team, not me," these talented leaders consistently stress when talking about their success, even in this most unlikely of worlds.

But neither these findings nor Collins' could explain this relationship between a self-effacing style of leadership and the success of professionals and their organizations; all they could say was that the correlation was strong. It was not until we delved deeper into the issue of career success that we fully understood why this correlation existed. What we discovered was that this modest style of leadership has two major advantages—it results in an environment that attracts and retains the very best, and it allows employees to develop to their ultimate potential.

While the concept of benevolence is simple, it may be one of the most difficult forms of leadership to actually practice because it can run counter to some ingrained human emotions. In any leadership role, there is a natural tendency to want to be perceived as the boss. When professionals work hard at something, they yearn for recognition. The prestige associated with being the point person is actually a form of compensation. It's natural for managers to want to keep their hand in mission-critical activities—ultimately it's their career on the line. Unfortunately, the more limelight they take and the more control over the team they wield, the less credit and responsibility are left over for the team, all of whom also share the desire to succeed in their careers.

The benevolent leader is not a micromanager, "protecting" a subordinate from succeeding or failing on his own. Nor does this leader simply hand off responsibilities to employees without providing guidance and continued involvement. The benevolent leader spends a great deal of time defining the resources that are available, and the expectations and objectives for success, but then observes from a safe distance as subordinates define and execute the process for meeting the objectives. In this way, growth of subordinates is accelerated, performance of the team is maximized, and costly employee churn is greatly reduced.

Now that you have seen the linkage between benevolent leadership and career success, let's take a look at how you can create this pattern in your own career. The benevolent leader knows that he must lead, follow, and get out of the way.

LEAD, FOLLOW, AND GET OUT OF THE WAY!

Lee Iacocca, the former chairman of Chrysler, famously said: "You either lead, follow, or get out of the way." But while focusing singularly on the first of these three options may have been sufficient for an auto company in Iacocca's time, leaders today must do all three.

Lead

Beyond getting results, there are three things for which a leader is absolutely accountable: (1) creating a strong values system, founded upon living with integrity and leading by example; (2) setting the vision and developing a winning strategy; and (3) building a strong management team. Nothing is more important in today's scandal-ridden era than the establishment of a strong values system based on integrity. This is the necessary foundation on which a strong organization can be built. By setting the right example—"walking the talk"—the leader forms the norms and expectations of behavior for all employees, and also establishes a foundation of trust. Equally important is setting and communicating a lofty, aspirational, yet realistic goal to provide direction to the team, create context for each team member's function, and help people visualize how the team's success is consistent with their own. Then, in order to generate the positive results that are, in fact, the natural end result of effective leadership, all that aspiration must be turned into perspiration. And the means to do this is by developing the right strategy for the company to fit the times—getting the right people in the right jobs doing the right things.

Follow

Once the right values system, vision, strategy, and management team have been put in place, the benevolent leader must now *follow* people. Contrary to notorious commanders and controllers, the best leaders know what they don't know and have the self-confidence to truly listen to and empower the very best players within each functional area of the enterprise. A key part of leadership is followership as well.

Get out of the Way

Delegation is as critical to leadership as it is to career progression. Being a micromanager is *not* the best path to achieving your professional aspirations. Success requires giving your people the creative freedom to accomplish their tasks as they see fit. In a telling finding from our research, extraordinary executives were only slightly more comfortable delegating their *basic tasks* to their subordinates than were the average employees—simple delegation comes naturally to many. However, extraordinary executives were 58 percent more comfortable delegating their *most critical tasks* than their less successful peers. The latter of the two findings is most important, as it is these extremely critical tasks that subordinates most want to own. And it is this aspect of benevolent leadership that creates the most attractive environment for the most talented people. We must stress, however, that delegation is not the same thing as abdication. Effective delegation also requires keen observation to ensure things are on track, holding people accountable for results, and taking corrective action when commitments are not met.

Bill Burke, the president of one of the most well-known and valuable sets of media assets, the Weather Channel Companies, puts the benevolent leadership approach to work every day. Just walk through the employee cafeteria, the broadcast studios, and the technical center with Burke and you can see that he is one of the pack. Employees feel completely comfortable in his presence, readily switching between talk about the weather (small talk in other settings) and business-building ideas.

Burke had early and effective training on this leadership approach from a young age. The son of one of the most well regarded media executives of all time, Daniel Burke, former president of Cap Cities/ABC, Bill was instilled with values of integrity, humility, hard work, and a philosophy of doing right by people. After graduating from Amherst College with a major in history in 1988, Burke worked at National Geographic as a programming intern and at Mattel Toys in product management. Coming out of Harvard Business School in 1992, he joined Turner Broadcasting in Atlanta, Georgia, where he led business development for the entertainment group. Burke played a key role in the formation of new networks, such as Cartoon Network, Latin America, and Turner Classic Movies, when he was given one of the most attractive but riskiest jobs in the company: president of TBS, founder and chairman Ted Turner's personally favorite network.

At TBS, Bill put his benevolent leadership approach to work with full force. All of the approximately two hundred employees watched him closely as he found the delicate balance between listening carefully to Turner's continued wishes for the network and developing a new strategy that he thought made sense for the future. His actions showed that it was in bounds to question sacred cows but also that it was necessary to take careful stock of the lessons of the past. In the end, he and his emboldened programming team changed the on-air mix to eliminate poorly performing documentaries and develop original movies and series. Burke and his team also led the controversial move to convert TBS from a "superstation," generating advertising revenues, only to a fee-paid cable service, adding subscription fees to the revenue base. This translated to adding more than $100 million to the network's bottom line (with the additional subscriber revenue more than offsetting the lost advertising revenue). And he made some decisive people calls as well, replacing the heads of marketing and on-air promotion and recommitting to other long-standing managers on the other, which showed that he could make the tough decisions and get the right people on board. In the end, once he had his team in place, they were set free to act, and act they did. From 1995 to 2000, a time of increased fragmentation, the TBS audience grew and earnings increased dramatically (the company does not break out financial results at that level of detail).

Burke took this same benevolent leadership approach to Portland, Maine, where from 2000 to early 2002 he led Resort Sports Network, a company dedicated to bringing extreme sports programming to demographically attractive viewers in vacation spots ranging from Vail, Colorado, and Stratton, Vermont, to Park City, Utah, and Lake Tahoe, California. Although the market for niche cable and Internet programming became extremely difficult during his tenure, Burke still managed to keep the company on a solid footing. He developed a more conservative strategy to reflect the reality of the times, cutting costs and people, but did so with compassion. He also "followed" by letting his sales leadership and the company's charismatic founder persuade him to redirect the company's efforts on traditional advertising sales while moving away from e-commerce and selling the company's travel division.

Burke's greatest leadership opportunity came in early 2002, when

Landmark Communications, the private company that owns the Weather Channel Companies, recruited him to become president. He found a situation where the company was well funded but not organized optimally. Now with two general management experiences under his belt, he was able to quickly get off to a strong start, employing the benevolent leadership principles of lead, follow, and get out of the way. He set the right tone by establishing himself as an approachable but decisive leader and setting a new vision for the enterprise. He made a series of critical structural decisions designed to liberate the energies of the organization, including combining the television and dot-com sales forces, resulting in the departure of some senior sales and marketing managers. He also made the decision to close the company's Latin American operations, a very tough people and cultural call that prioritizes the company's energies on its core U.S. businesses—the Weather Channel and Weather.com. Today, the company is hitting on all cylinders, taking the subject of weather to new heights.

The most talented individuals are attracted to an environment where leaders do lead, follow, and get out of the way. In a sense, it allows them to fly with a safety net. They feel empowered to manage their areas, they feel ownership over their accomplishments, and they get the sense that calculated risks are not only tolerated but encouraged. This is the environment created by the benevolent leader, and talented professionals don't just like these leaders, they brag about them. Listening to employees and alumni rave about Herb Kelleher, Tom Freston, A. G. Lafley, Mark Kaiser, Bill Burke, and other benevolent leaders is enough to make their families blush. Over time, great benevolent leaders develop a tremendous following, creating an army of the best and brightest professionals competing to be part of their team. Once you have created a team or a company working to make you successful, there is almost no way not to have an extraordinarily successful career.

THE SUCCESS OF OTHERS

The notion of benevolent leadership could not be more timely. There has been a notable diminution in the most basic level of trust between employee and organization: "Is my employer being honest to me, the market, and our investors? Whose interests really come first?" The recent environment compelled Intel chairman Andy Grove to declare that in all his working years (he co-founded Intel in 1968), he had never felt more embarrassed to be in business. We have all watched with horror the recent parade of executive misconduct, greed, theft, and fraud that has lined the pockets of CEOs with cash while their unassuming employees were wiped out, left only with the baggage of their previous employer's tarnished image. Employees have trusted their business leaders with the health of their companies and the strength of their investments. Sadly, in many cases, this basic level of trust has been betrayed.

But the benevolent leader creates a truly different environment altogether. No, you might not be Herb Kelleher or Andy Grove or even Mark Kaiser or Bill Burke. But that doesn't mean you can't focus on the success of those around you, communicate openly and honestly, and create an atmosphere in which the triumph of the team is viewed by all as the best path to any individual's success. This will create an organization that communicates clearly, critiques and congratulates with candor, and relies on each other to win. Trust is established, and everyone benefits from the success of the team.

In the end, it is the ability to create an environment in which subordinates, peers, and even your superiors want to work—a place where they feel they can maximize their own personal success—that maximizes an individual executive's chances of greatest personal career success. To position yourself for success, create success for others. To advance your career, seek to advance the careers of others. Take the most blame, give the most credit, set ambitious objectives, and let your people strive to realize them, holding people accountable. Excel in giving direct feedback and hands-on mentoring and you will reap the rewards of consistently better teams and consistently higher performance levels from team members. Over time you will create a virtual army of professionals willing to fight in your corner. Follow this pattern of benevolent leadership and you'll be well on your way to creating success and satisfaction, for yourself and others.

PATTERN 3
OVERCOME THE PERMISSION PARADOX

Ability is of little account without opportunity.
—NAPOLEON BONAPARTE

Big jobs usually go to the men who prove
their ability to outgrow small ones.
—RALPH WALDO EMERSON

THE CAREER CATCH-22

The permission paradox is one of the great Catch-22s in business: You can't get the job without experience, and you can't get the experience without the job. Many people are confident in their abilities if given the chance to perform. But the hard part is getting permission to demonstrate these skills and to gain new experiences. This is the permission paradox. You may want to become a CEO, move into a general management role, or make a bigger impact within your company, but unless you have permission to take on a broader role, you won't reach your goals. How do you go about getting permission to make the big impact?

The permission paradox can be a paralyzing obstacle to overcome, and it is often a self-fulfilling prophecy. Successful executives, unlike a large number of their peers, rarely have trouble gaining access to the most critical opportunities in their careers. They know that the secret is finding some way to get the experiences they need to get ahead.

Sometimes these are the once-in-a-decade, career-defining experiences, but other times they are the incremental but concrete incidents that move your career to the next level. All the same, extraordinary careers are set apart from mediocre ones by the ability to gain access to critical experiences.

CAREER LAHARS

Life-altering moments occur in careers in much the same way as in nature. The primary forces shaping the Grand Canyon were not centuries of steady erosion (contrary to what many people assume), but earth-shaking mud flows, known as lahars.[1] These geologic events occur infrequently, as massive flash flooding sends tons of boulders cascading down. A single lahar can reshape the landscape more dramatically than hundreds of years of steady erosion. The constant flow of water over the countryside does shape the path of rivers and form valleys, but "grand" canyons are usually the result of grand events.

Careers are similar. Like a river flowing continually over time, steady access to new experiences met with strong performance is required to keep your career on an upward trajectory. But there will likely be a limited number of lahar opportunities in your working life— events that, if taken full advantage of, will positively and dramatically change your career's direction. Successful executives learn to identify and gain access to these intermittent events and use them to their advantage. They employ numerous creative strategies and all the resources at their disposal to gain the experiences required for an extraordinary career.

BIG PROBLEM? BIG OPPORTUNITY

Part of solving the permission paradox involves identifying valuable opportunities that others may not see. It is natural and comfortable to be drawn toward the places in an organization that are successful and running smoothly. But this may not be the best strategy for success in the workplace.

The most significant opportunities may be found in the most distressed parts of an organization. Often the best you can do in an already successful situation is to maintain the status quo. In a distressed or untested unit or company, however, the expectations can be much lower but the potential to generate a positive impact can be much greater. The parts of the organization that cause the most pain are also often the most highly visible. Fix them, and management will stand up and take notice.

Take, as one example, Dennis Lacey, a former partner at audit giant Coopers & Lybrand. In 1989 he was offered an opportunity to join a major client, Capital Associates, a $2 billion Denver-based leasing company, as vice president of operations with the understanding that he would become chief financial officer shortly. But as he learned rather quickly, the company was in deep trouble and heading toward bankruptcy. Capital Associates was in desperate need of a successful turnaround. Rather than crack under the pressure or limit his actions only to the financial function, Lacey dove deeply into the operations of the business. First he took over the administrative roles for the company, and for his tenacity at attacking the underlying problems he was named chief operating officer. He kept his eye on his core financial responsibility by recapitalizing the company and arranging new bank financing, but the board of directors rewarded Lacey for stepping up to the company's problems by installing him as CEO. Once he gained access to this position, he delivered. He led a restructuring of the company, which included a downsizing, and implemented new management, information, and rewards systems to instill business discipline. He built a new management team, developed a new vision and strategy, and executed it soundly. Lacey therefore played the key role in moving the stock price from 13¢ to $5 a share during his seven-year tenure as CEO. Once he completed the business turnaround, the company achieved twenty-one consecutive quarters of profits, and Lacey led a successful sale of the company, positioning himself for further success down the road.

THE TWO FORMS OF PERMISSION

Clarifying and expanding the scope of what you have permission to do is a skill you must master for extraordinary success. And when you do, you will be in a position to extend this opportunity to others by creating a culture that welcomes permission seeking and attracts the best talent through innovation and risk taking (see "The Patterns of Extraordinary Organizations" for more on how to apply the success patterns at the company level).

Before formulating your strategy to get the permission you need to advance your career, you first need to understand the two primary forms of permission: direct and implied. Direct permission says, "You can do it because somebody says you can," whereas implied permission states, "You can do it because no one said you *can't*." As you will see, the distinction between the two is critical.

Direct Permission

Direct permission is the most common and readily identifiable source of authority within an organization. For many people, however, it can also be very limiting. Through scores of conversations with executives on this topic, we've concluded that the more you rely on being *allowed* to do something—because your job description says so, because your predecessor did it before you, or because your boss asked you to do it—the more likely it is that you *won't be allowed* to do something else by co-workers and other people when your direct permission to act is not as clear. Similar to the boy who cried wolf, people who rely on the granting of permission by someone else are often stuck when formal permission is absent.

Implied Permission

Implied permission is a more subtle but potentially much more powerful form of permission. The reason is that direct permission is usually handed out cautiously and conservatively, because once given, it is awkward and difficult to take back. Implied permission, on the other hand, is not given but *taken*. It ultimately affords people who use it much more latitude. It occurs when you are able to create the presumption that permission is yours: by having the right degrees from a prestigious institution or if you are mentored by a powerful figure, associated with a leading company or brand, a rainmaker, or a great creative talent.

Similar to direct permission, implied permission can appear in various forms, but all share a common premise—you are perceived to have permission if no one has visibly denied it.

THE ABSENCE OF PERMISSION

To illustrate just how important permission is, it is useful to look at the often severe consequences that occur when permission is absent. Even if you perform exceptionally well at your task, your efforts can explode in your face if you are not perceived by the right constituencies to have appropriate direct or implied permission. You may be labeled as a ruthless self-promoter who is putting your own interests ahead of those of the organization. Worse, you can be accused of trying to win at the expense of other people. And despite the positive associations and track record of being proactive, the combination of too much initiative with too little permission can be deadly.

A well-known Fortune 500 company was developing a comprehensive plan to spin off an important part of its business into a high-profile joint venture. The spin-off would impact every part of the company, since the function was a shared service for all the divisions. The investment bankers were coming in to review the plans early the following week so that they could help develop the financing and strategic marketing process for the deal. With the meetings bearing down on the management team, Ellen T., one of the company's senior executives, took the initiative to write a draft of the strategic plan for the whole company and how the spin-off fit into the strategy.

The CEO told us that it was the single most spectacular piece of work he had ever seen in thirty years of business. He added that the fact that Ellen took the initiative and pulled it off in a single weekend was incredible. However, rather than getting the plaudits of the other members of the top management team, Ellen's initiative ended up causing a different kind of fireworks. The three other division presidents were ballistic that they hadn't been consulted and did not have the opportunity to write their own part of the plan. They ended up not supporting the spin-off. Ellen told us that she had been thinking, "I know I can do a great job on writing the plan and we really can't wait, so I'm going to go for it."

It turns out that Ellen's plan backfired due to the absence of one critical thing—permission. To her peers, she had neither the direct or implied permission to go at it alone. Without permission, she was perceived as trying to show up her colleagues. Several later commented unfavorably on her pattern of "managing up" rather than "managing laterally." She also made a fateful error by being less than subtle and identifying herself as a possible CEO candidate for the to-be-spun-off company (she also had rather dull political sensitivities as well). So Ellen's bold quest for impact and her killer work product were miscalculated. And now, not surprisingly, this brilliant, talented, and proactive executive has left the company—to the resigned disappointment, we should add, of the CEO. Ellen worked seventy-two hours straight on a high-impact, value-added project, truly believing that she was going to be a hero. But her antennae did not direct her to get the buy-in she needed from her peers before going off on her own change initiative. With her downfall, so too went the proposed spin-off, and it was back to the status quo. Even if it was right answer—and it likely was, according to the CEO—her lack of permission torpedoed her.

Your supervisors can torpedo your plans as well. We are painfully aware of another Fortune 500 company where we worked with a CEO and the board to recruit a COO who was to come in with a predetermined time schedule to become the CEO. Both the CEO and the board were looking to the new executive to lead a major change process. In his first year, the new COO had to walk a fine line between cultivating the CEO, who was going to be retiring, and "auditioning" in front of the board to create enough change to get the nod. In this case, the COO couldn't quite get the balance right. He leaned more heavily toward the change agenda and didn't fully achieve real buy-in from the long-serving CEO and those still loyal to him. So when he made critical management and strategic changes, he did not know where the land mines were and kept getting back-channeled to the outgoing CEO, who often overruled and therefore undermined him. Once this process started, it emboldened both the supposedly retiring CEO and the loyalists, who became more blatant in their whispering campaigns that the COO "doesn't get it," and that "he's a short-timer." Without the ability to gain direct or implied permission to become the CEO, the planned succession never happened. The roots of change planted by the COO never took hold and his agenda never got traction. Finally the board heard enough noise and the company's performance was withering, so the COO was let go and the CEO held on for another year. Astutely, the board took more control the next time and the CEO had a concrete retirement, which allowed us to recruit a new CEO. Learning from its mistakes, the board granted the right designated permissions right from the start.

Are these stories unique? Hardly. As Ron Heifetz, professor at Harvard's Kennedy School of Government and author of *Leadership Without Easy Answers*, pointed out, "[Change leaders] get attacked, dismissed, silenced, and sometimes even assassinated because they come to represent loss, real or perceived, to those members of the community who feel that they have gotten the bad end of a bargain."[2] Even in the best of circumstances, when a leader has attempted to build the right bridges and cultivate the right constituencies, leading change without iron-clad permission can be a dangerous affair. "Leaders are always failing somebody," Heifetz adds. "Even a bright new innovation will meet resistance from those who feel threatened." Gaining appropriate levels of direct and implied permission is critical to succeeding as a leader, making it easier to rally others around you in your quest and ensuring that you are within your rights to act should something go awry.

So before you seek to get the experiences you need by jumping straight in, ask yourself a few questions: Do you have adequate levels of direct and implied permission to proceed? Are others emotionally invested in seeing you succeed, such as your mentors in the organization? Have you developed allies among your co-workers to help you accomplish your goals? How can you share the expanded permission set among colleagues to create a virtuous cycle rather than being undermined by jealousies? If you see potential permission roadblocks coming, you can sidestep them instead of hitting them head-on.

WHEN NO DOESN'T REALLY MEAN NO

Although career success requires political astuteness and working within the accepted limits of behavior, securing permission sometimes requires persistence to keep going, even when the answer the first time is no.

Dick Metzler had been working for Federal Express for five years in middle management and had gained the respect of his co-workers for his creativity and work ethic. But to many of the top executives at the company, Metzler was still an unknown figure. In the spring of 1983, however, he had a feeling all that would soon change.

Metzler had recently made a significant career move by transitioning into marketing from a sales role—something that was very uncommon at the company. His first major assignment was to develop a strategic marketing plan for the company. One day, working with his team on the development of the plan, the competitive intelligence revealed subtle indications that UPS had the potential to become a much larger competitive threat in the future. Both companies offered a second-day delivery service but employed differing approaches to the market.

FedEx was the innovator of "absolutely, positively overnight," with a guaranteed delivery of 10:30 A.M., and also a standard two-day service. UPS was known for its Brown Box ground delivery service, offering slower delivery at a significantly lower price point, and they too had a limited second-day offering. FedEx's next-morning delivery service filled a critical need for time-sensitive deliveries in the marketplace, and required a capital-intensive and costly operational infrastructure to deliver. But the next-morning service also contributed roughly 60 percent of the company's profit at the time. UPS' delivery service had far fewer features and was not as time-definite or reliable. As a result, though, it was much less costly to deliver, and allowed the company to offer this alternative service at a significant discount to the price of FedEx's next-morning service.

The two companies competed to a degree, but in the marketplace, the high-price/high-service FedEx offering was sufficiently differentiated from UPS' Brown Box service, so the two coexisted relatively peacefully.

Without much fanfare or promotion, UPS had recently announced that it would add a next-day product in limited markets, with coverage, service reliability, and convenience features much more limited than those of FedEx, but expected to improve gradually. Very few people took note of these potential changes, and few viewed UPS as a major competitor in express delivery at the time. Some within FedEx had dismissed these moves as a poorly formulated me-too strategy by UPS—certainly not a legitimate threat.

But to Metzler and his team, this was no harmless experiment, but rather a cannonball fired across FedEx's bow. While indeed just an initial move to bring UPS closer to product parity, it did position them much closer to competing with FedEx's premium next-morning service. "What if this is only the beginning?" thought Metzler. "What if UPS' intention is to continue expanding its two-day and next-day offerings, adding features that to date were uniquely offered by FedEx, such as guaranteed delivery, bar code tracking, drop boxes, or on-call pickups? Is UPS taking direct aim at FedEx's coveted next-morning customers?" With UPS' much lower cost of operations (at the time, UPS was already delivering packages to most businesses every day), the implications of this could be devastating. UPS could chip away at FedEx's customer base bit by bit, and at a price point that the company simply could not meet without massive revenue and margin dilution. If UPS was able to successfully execute this strategy, it could quite possibly push FedEx out of the leadership position in the express shipping business.

Metzler was certain the only answer was for FedEx to meet the threat head-on, developing its own lower-cost delivery service focusing on an afternoon product. With the conviction of Paul Revere signaling that the British were coming, Metzler marched into a senior management meeting with Fred Smith, the company's legendary founder and

CEO. Metzler had great respect for Smith and had always felt a bit nervous in his presence, but on this day he was as confident as he had ever been. He led the CEO through his team's analysis and the logic behind his proposition. "Therefore," Metzler's proposal concluded, "we must offer a lower-cost next-afternoon service. If we do nothing, the consequences will certainly be dire." With this, Metzler sat back in the large office chair and waited for a reply. Smith was silent, his hands crossed. After what seemed like an eternity, he stood up and leaned across his desk, looking at Metzler.

"You guys are a bunch of parochial marketers who don't have a clue how this company operates!" he barked. Metzler was promptly escorted out of Fred Smith's office.

Smith had reason to be concerned. Given the structure of FedEx's operations, this type of middle-market service would be extremely difficult to implement and could also have a very negative impact on the next-morning service if not properly executed.

"If I live to be a hundred and six, I will never forget that day!" reflected Metzler. "With Fred—the man who literally invented our industry—telling me that I was nuts, that we just couldn't possibly provide that type of service at a competitive price point given the uniqueness of our business model, well, I guess I was inclined to believe him. He certainly didn't seem to leave any room for negotiation." But Metzler decided not to give up so easily. "I just couldn't let the idea go. I just knew we were right."

Metzler developed a plan. Quietly, he went around to other managers in the company and proposed his idea of developing a next-afternoon service. To his relief, many people agreed with him—including some who had previously worked at UPS. After several months and dozens of conversations, Metzler again set up a meeting with CEO Fred Smith. But this time he brought with him an army of supporters—representatives of finance, IT, sales, operations, airline management, customer service, even a representative of the group that prints the airbills—from every unit of the company that would be impacted.

Metzler again made his case for developing a next-day service as eloquently as he could. And again at the end of the meeting, Fred Smith stood up, leaned across his desk, and proceeded to throw Metzler out of his office, this time with his entire entourage in tow.

With his tail between his legs, and with his group of supporters much less enthusiastic about fighting this battle, Metzler summoned the courage to approach Fred Smith one final time. "Just let us do a test in three markets," Metzler pleaded. "Just three markets—then we will find out once and for all."

To Metzler's astonishment, Smith said yes. "I wasn't sure I heard it correctly the first time, but I certainly didn't want to take my chances and ask him to repeat it. We got out of his office as fast as we could!"

As Metzler had believed all along, the tests of the new service were wildly successful. "I really think that Fred doubted we could pull it off. But we did. Everyone worked together as a cross-functional team to make it happen, and within a year, we were rolling out the service nationwide." Today, FedEx's next-afternoon service generates billions in revenue for the company. More importantly, the company was able to successfully thwart a severe competitive threat.

Metzler and his team went on to other successes within the company, developing a heavyweight service, a COD service, Saturday delivery, and other profitable service offerings for the company by formalizing what he learned into what was known inside FedEx as the New Products Task Force. He left FedEx in 1995 after successfully leading the company's catalog/home delivery and third-party logistics business as general manager. Later, he was named the CEO of APL Logistics, a $1 billion global third-party logistics and supply chain management company.

"Sometimes I wonder what would have happened if I had given up with the first no," Metzler reflects. Fortunately for him and FedEx, he didn't.

THE PERMISSION STRATEGIES

Successful executives gain permission and take charge of their experiences—and therefore their careers—in several effective ways. There are eight different strategies for gaining permission: the direct approach, demonstrated competency, clean the slate, get credentials, barter, masquerade as the leader, strategic mentoring, and playing politics. Each strategy has unique characteristics, likely outcomes, and situations when it is most appropriate. Some permission strategies are more effective for gaining direct permission, and others are better for implied permission. Some can be used for both, and one more commonly used strategy, playing politics, is usually not effective for either. But understanding all of these strategies can open your eyes to the many creative ways to gain access to the most desired opportunities.

The Direct Approach

If you want something, you can always ask. One of the simplest and most underutilized strategies for getting permission to expand your role is to simply ask for it. Nothing ventured, nothing gained. Reach out for the experiences you need in order to move ahead—don't wait for someone to hand them to you on a silver platter. Ask your boss what it will take for you to advance. Then meet or exceed the expectations on what you are assigned to do.

Why is the direct approach underutilized? Perhaps people feel that they need to know which experiences are required for career progression before they ask for the opportunity to get them. And this would be right. But many professionals do not take the time to figure out what the correct next steps are. Without developing a plan for the experiences they want to attain, they simply wait for others to make career choices for them. One clue to doing this effectively is to think about your role from your manager's point of view. What will make him or her successful, and how can you link what you want to do to this?

THE PERMISSION STRATEGIES

	Demonstrated Competency	Direct Approach	Clean the Slate	Get Credentials	Barter	Masquerade as the Leader	Strategic Mentoring	Playing Politics
Direct Permission	🔑	🔑	🔑		🔑		🔑	💣
Implied Permission			🔑	🔑	🔑	🔑		💣

The direct approach is most effective in gaining direct permission, yet can undermine your access to implied permission. Go to your boss and request a promotion, a change in title, or expanded responsibility. If the answer is yes, you have been given a powerful form of permission. If, however, the answer is no, it is difficult to then try to back into the broader levels of responsibility through implied permission. Even the perception that you are trying to leverage implied permission after direct permission was not granted can often result in a significant backlash from your boss. Understand that in some cases, it is better to ask for forgiveness than to ask for permission.

Demonstrate Competence in the Building Blocks

When seeking to fill a specific position, companies look for someone who has successfully done it before. It's not surprising that the square-peg-in-a-square-hole approach is seen as the most logical way to fill an executive position and to mitigate risk. That is why the switch from one functional role, such as sales or finance, to another, such as marketing or operations, can be so difficult. But it can be achieved. One effective approach is to break down the role you desire into the specific competencies required for success and then seek opportunities to get experience in each.

For example, to be a successful strategic alliances executive, you need to combine elements of strategic planning with deal making. If you've never led the business development operation but would like to, you can gain permission to play this role if you break the process into its component parts and gain experience or at least exposure across its multiple steps: corporate strategy, target company identification, competitive analysis, deal proposal, company overtures, financial analysis, negotiation, due diligence, closing, and integration. Take Ross Honey, the vice president of business development for Scholastic Entertainment, the media arm of the giant children's publishing and entertainment company, who was recruited from consulting firm Booz Allen Hamilton. He had been a principal in the firm's media and entertainment group. Although Ross had never been a head of business development, nor had he actually led the execution of a joint venture, merger, or acquisition, he was the right man for the Scholastic job largely because he had had experience in each of the component parts of the job. This experience happened to have been in different consulting engagements for different clients. But strung all together over six years, Ross had done market analysis, company prospecting, deal structuring, negotiating, and other key steps for a wide range of entertainment and media companies. Now two years into the Scholastic role, he has put all of his prior experiences together to seamlessly lead the company's business development function.

Another excellent example of an executive whose demonstrated competence has propelled his career is Richard Nanula, one of the top five executives at biotechnology giant Amgen, with responsibility for finance, strategy, and communications at the company, which has a market value of $65 billion. He is regarded as having brought a new degree of financial expertise to the company, playing a leading role in such notable successes as the acquisition of Immunex and a sophisticated convertible bond offering. Nanula joined the Walt Disney Company after business school in 1986, and his gift for finance, deal making, capital raising, and the linking of finance and corporate strategy became immediately apparent to Disney's executive team. He was promoted to treasurer at age twenty-nine and then chief financial officer at thirty-one.

His deep skills became well known in the talent marketplace, and he was recruited to a top general management position at Starwood Hotels and Resorts Worldwide, and later to the Internet sports media company Broadband Sports. Richard is gifted with people, having an infectious sense of humor and an empathetic yet decisive manner, which, combined with his demonstrated abilities, has made him one of the most sought-after executives in the workforce.

Demonstrating competence is an excellent way to gain direct permission without first having the required experiences. As the Dennis Lacey example demonstrated above, a chief financial officer who wants to move into general management can identify ways to demonstrate competencies beyond the financial arena by playing an organizational leadership role, taking on additional corporate functions such as IT or strategy, thereby contributing more broadly to the company's success. From there he can take a hands-on role in operations, marketing, or even sales in order to demonstrate a working knowledge of important areas of the company. Richard Nanula's demonstrated competence linking finance and strategy made him a strong general management candidate for Starwood and Broadband Sports. This further demonstration of skill and ability made him the top candidate for one of the most important roles at Amgen. Once you have demonstrated many of the underlying competencies required of a different role and made those in a position of authority aware of these experiences, you will be much more likely to be considered for the new role.

Clean the Slate

Over time, you develop many forms of permission that define your role within an organization. But like the fixed grooves on a vinyl LP, habit, routine, and time can etch perceived limits to your competencies that can be difficult to break. As time passes, others will develop specific perceptions of your skills and limitations. In some companies with more lock-step promotion patterns, expanding people's perception of you can be an extremely difficult challenge. The most obvious example is when you are young and inexperienced. Starting out, it is difficult to avoid the perception that you are green, unfamiliar with the ways of business. Though you gain new experiences, learn, and grow, it may be difficult to shake that first impression.

At any point in your career, when you are unhappy with how you have come to be perceived and believe that changing that perception seems all but impossible, starting fresh in a new situation may be the best strategy. When you join a new division or company, you have a relatively clean slate on which to earn your permissions. This is especially true if you are conscious of the various forms of permission on which to build right from the start. You are freed from the baggage of others you have worked with for years.

Cleaning the slate often allows you to rewrite the rules of your own permission, both direct and implied. When we recruit someone from one company to the next, there is usually an upgrade in direct permission, perhaps a bigger title, broader scope of defined responsibility, larger geographic territory, and so on. But though it is an effective tool to improve your direct permission, cleaning the slate is often even more powerful when seeking implied permission. Perhaps the most ingrained perceptions others develop of you over time are those things that you can't do: "He's much too young to do that." "She has only been doing that job for two years. How can she be considered an expert?"

Clean the slate too often, however, and you run the risk of being seen as disloyal and a job hopper. Utilized effectively, cleaning the slate can be an effective strategy to gain critical permission.

Get Credentials

One of the most logical ways to gain associative or expert permission is to get relevant credentials. The right credentials open doors and create access both in the short term and over the long haul. An MBA, JD, or CPA can be effective and appropriate at the earlier stages of your career. What if it's not practical to take a year or two off for a graduate degree? That's when an industry certification or executive education program can add value. Securities analysts often differentiate themselves and gain credentials and expert permission from completing the tortuous work required to earn the designation CFA (chartered financial analyst). Mid- and even top-level executives can similarly add to their permission by attaining an executive degree.

When Chris McCormick was chief marketing officer and a member of the office of the president of L.L. Bean, the renowned catalog and Internet marketer, the company sent him to Harvard Business School for its Advanced Management Program. Not only did that intensive ten-week program deepen McCormick's technical skills and add broader general management perspective, it gave him an important credential from a top school that expanded employees' perceptions about McCormick's experience. This turned out to be a supporting point in the company's board of directors agreeing to name him as president and CEO in May 2001.

Many people embark on a journey to gain credentials, thinking that they will result in direct permission. But in fact, outside of the medical and legal professions, it is rare that credentials immediately result in direct permission. They can, however, afford a significant amount of implied permission. Even if credentials don't automatically give you permission to do a job, they can give you a vital leg up.

Barter

You scratch my back, I'll scratch yours. Oftentimes you want the opportunity to make an impact but don't necessarily have permission. Others may have permission but don't see it or have the time or impetus to exploit it. Barter is a strategy in which you trade something of value for the permission to expand your role. Taking a page from our own experience: Co-author Jim Citrin had an idea in 1997 for a book that would identify, interview, and profile the top fifty CEOs in America to develop and disseminate leadership lessons. But Jim had a significant challenge—he did not have access to a majority of these executives. Having been with Spencer Stuart for only four years at the time, his network of top executives was still developing. On the other hand, his partner and U.S. chairman, Tom Neff, has been the industry's leading CEO recruiter and board consultant for over two decades and has one of the broadest networks of top-level relationships of anyone on earth. It turns out that Tom had been interested in writing a book about leadership for many years but had never found the time. After some up-front legwork, Jim approached Tom about co-authoring a book. Jim offered to do much of the heavy lifting, and Tom would help provide editorial direction and access to the CEOs. The plan worked beautifully, and the resulting book, *Lessons from the Top*, became a best-seller.[3] As a by-product, Jim now has access to the top CEOs in America and has the permission to share research and thinking on leadership and career success. The lesson? Find out who controls access to the permission you need, and offer something of value in exchange.

Barter is an effective tool for gaining both direct permission and implied permission. As Jim demonstrated, barter can lead to powerful and effective associations. Others have found that providing something of value to a boss may result in the granting of specific direct permission. Determine what permission you need, and then identify what you can provide in return to get that permission.

Masquerade as the Leader

Another strategy, albeit one with significant risks, can be referred to as the "stealth land grab." There are many situations that arise in business that clearly are in need of leadership, yet there is no one within the organization with obvious authority. Often if you provide the leadership that is needed, doing the things you would do if you had the specific authority, others will quickly assume that you have the permission.

Consider a situation in which a management role that you are interested in opens up, but the company says it will take time to initiate a search. Sometimes an internal executive is appointed to the role on an interim basis. Or just as often, the role is simply left vacant for the two to four months it takes to make a new appointment. If you are designated as the interim manager (a minor form of direct permission), you obviously have an opportunity to show your stuff. But if no one is designated the leader, the opportunity to lead may still exist. Think what you would do if you were designated the leader of the group. You may be surprised that even without full-blown or permanent direct permission, many of the things you would do as the leader can still be initiated. You can start to build bridges between impacted groups, perhaps calling a meeting to frame the discussion of the challenges that exist. You can aggregate all relevant domain expertise, so that it is subtly known that you have as good an understanding of the situation as possible. The key is to contribute in an obvious and effective way to the problem while not being seen by your peers as merely "sucking up" to get the job. The more you can do to really begin to solve the problems that exist, the much higher the likelihood that you will be called upon when a formal appointment is made.

In many ways the amount of permission you are granted is a function of the amount of permission you take. If you act subtly—building bridges between likely team members, developing and then demonstrating expertise in the relevant area, and simply showing interest, effort, and enthusiasm for the task at hand—you can quietly position yourself as the most likely choice. In the end, if you have applied this approach in a sensible way, you will have still gained permission to act in a role that's beneficial to you, whether or not you are formally designated as the new manager.

Rick Rodriguez was an up-and-coming international executive at Discovery Communications, parent company of the Discovery Channel, TLC, Animal Planet, and other cable networks around the world. He was playing a specialized functional role providing centralized direction for the acquisition and development of programming for various Discovery networks. But he passionately wanted to move into a network general management position within the company to broaden his experience and really show what he could do. Getting that first general management position within Discovery, or within any company, always requires a leap of faith. Rodriguez got an opportunity when he was tapped to become Acting General Manager of the company's new EMEA region (Europe, Middle East, and Africa), a unit that was created following the restructuring of Discovery Networks Europe. That international business had been dominated by the UK operation, whose activities dwarfed those in its remaining markets. The creation of EMEA gave Rodriguez his first full-blown P&L to manage. And rather than just act as a caretaker for this strategically critical region during an interim period, Rodriguez was determined to make measurable progress on both the top and bottom line while he had the opportunity. Rodriguez set the stage for the establishment of five regional businesses located throughout the EMEA footprint, which would be better positioned to generate local revenues from a far-flung and diverse customer base. His action-orientation, sound decision making, and concrete progress, even in a six-month time frame, gave the company the confidence that he had the right stuff. Shortly thereafter, Rodriguez was appointed to the coveted position of Executive Vice President, General Manager, The Travel Channel. Discovery had acquired the Travel Channel several years earlier from Landmark Communications but it hadn't found a consistent way to generate a large audience for the network.

Rodriguez's challenge was to devise a new programming formula that built upon the success of a diverse slate of programs ranging from "World's Best" to the smash-hit "World Poker Tour" and to more consistently deliver a large, demographically desirable audience.

Rodriguez's international content perspective and background lent volumes of relevance and innovation to the Travel Channel's platform and promise—and his deep knowledge of Discovery's brands and his credibility and relationships across the organization, coupled with his interim GM experience, turned out to make Rodriguez just the right person on which to take the general management gamble.

This strategy for gaining permission is not without its risks. Rodriguez's EMEA strategy or actions could have been off the mark. Or if he had tried to assume responsibility before being granted the temporary role, people could have turned on him. If you go for a role that others also clearly desire, you can expect a real and immediate backlash. One way around this is to combine the direct approach with a dose of patience—make your interest known and then wait for your shot. Another is to look for opportunities that others don't want, such as the areas with the biggest problems. Armed with a clear understanding of the experiences you need to get, you can look for opportunities that others haven't identified or don't want responsibility for where you can gain these experiences. Then take the lead. If the problems are real and complex, there is a good chance you will meet with little internal resistance in assuming responsibility for them.

Two-Way Mentoring

There's a particular power of psychology in the mentoring process. You certainly get something out of being mentored, but so does the mentor herself. People grow by helping others grow. And you can cultivate a mentor by genuinely seeking and appreciating her advice and expertise. People generally respond well when you put them in a position of power and experience. If you ask someone for advice, she will often be willing to help. If you happen to be looking for a job, keep this two-way mentoring dynamic in mind. Rather than ask someone for a job, seek to have an informational interview. An important goal is to learn how your mentor got to where she is today. If your mentor were in your shoes, what would that person do with her career? What companies, roles, and sectors provide the most opportunity? What advice does your mentor have for your career? If you connect with someone on a mentor basis, making the person feel comfortable with you and feel that such generosity is not a waste of time, the person just might take you under his wing and look for that all-important introduction.

A mentoring relationship can work the same way. The key is for both parties to get something out of the relationship. You get someone who will invest time and knowledge in you, look out for your success, and increase your scope of influence through access to new contacts. But mentors also want to get a return on their investment. You can mentor up as well as down, by offering to help mentors with research, legwork, or contacts in an area that's unfamiliar to them. If you look out for their success, a mentor will have a reason to look out for yours.

Jack Welch gave new meaning to the idea of mentoring up when he instituted a novel program at General Electric.[4] He asked his top executives to find an expert in the organization to mentor them in e-business. Welch chose Pam Wickham, head of GE's Web site, to teach him the ins and outs of doing business on the Internet. Those who were mentored reported that they learned a lot about the Internet and grew more comfortable seeking out feedback from below, while mentors said they were emboldened to feed ideas and suggestions to their superiors.[5] While this is a more structured form of mentoring than normally occurs in the workplace, it illustrates that with two-way mentoring, both sides can be substantially better off. Perhaps most notably, those more junior in the organization who provided something valuable to their superiors developed personal relationships with them and expanded their network of people looking out for their best interest. Extending these powerful and positive relationships with superiors in your organization is a critical element to gaining permission, for when the next great opportunity emerges, having a team of supporters in your corner can be the deciding straw.

Playing Politics

Certainly *not* a success pattern followed by extraordinary executives, playing politics has long been a common form of gaining permission. Mastered by courtiers in the service of monarchs over the centuries, and refined by minions under the spell of corporate executives over the decades, leveraging political power can indeed result in gaining defined or implied permission. However, this strategy is difficult to sustain over time because the foundation upon which the permission is built is not solid. Gaining permission by politics generally entails linking your identity to someone else in power and deriving your influence from that person's position.

Rather than follow this strategy, our research confirmed that extraordinary executives add value to their own roles. They do work with and through other people, whether in a mentoring, barter, or associative relationship to expand their permission, but there is a difference between this and playing politics. The latter is more calculating, and people in the organization know it.

You will recall that the different styles of leadership reviewed in the benevolent leadership chapter include the pirate and the narcissist. Typically it is these two who most commonly attract politics players because they care about their own success more than the success of those around them. Therefore, to get ahead in this working environment, people feel the need to ride the coattails of the person in charge. And if you look carefully at the most extreme cases (many of whom were later accused of fraud or unceremoniously fired by their companies), you will find a coterie of hangers-on who form or formed the inner circle of power. Examples? Al "Chainsaw" Dunlap, the cost-cutting former CEO of Sunbeam accused of accounting fraud; Dennis Kozlowski, the disgraced CEO of Tyco International; and Jeff Skilling, the infamous president and CEO of Enron—all had their political courts supporting their pirate and narcissistic leadership approaches. Less extreme examples include former Mattel CEO Jill Barad, AOL Time Warner's former COO Bob Pittman, and any number of business unit managers or division presidents who had a close group of associates with extensive organizational permission when they were in charge but found themselves on the outs when their chief was gone. The point is that it may be fine to base your power on another executive's ascent temporarily, but as soon as that person stumbles, the rest of the organization reacts forcefully to strip the hangers-on of their permissions. When Kozlowski was riding high at Tyco, building the conglomerate through hundreds of acquisitions over a ten-year period, no one was perceived to be more powerful than the company's chief financial officer and consigliere, Mark Schwartz. And Schwartz was loyal in return. However, as soon as the CEO's transgressions came to light, the company wasted no time turning on the CFO, looking for (and finding) ways to bring his role in the goings-on to the authorities.

Of course, when you are in the moment, it is not always apparent where the line is drawn between seeking to expand your permission through mentoring and other effective forms and attempting to do so by playing politics with an important or powerful executive. Inevitably, at some point, your internal warning bells go off and you have the opportunity to shift to a more productive approach.

In a more general sense, it pays to remember a few different scenarios that create the conditions or temptation for politics. There are cases when people get named to a position because someone owes them a favor, or because a superior feels somehow obligated to provide it, either because of friendship, loyalty, or (worse) the threat of adverse consequences (i.e., blackmail). But make no mistake: When permission is gained through these methods, it is almost always evident to co-workers that the permission was not earned. If direct permission is granted due to politics, co-workers will limit the things the role implies you can do. If implied permission is received through politics, they will seek to box in authority by pointing out the lack of direct permission. In either case, permission received this way is rarely perceived as having been earned legitimately, and often will result in co-workers downplaying the permission, and in some cases even conspiring to see that you fail. No matter which strategy is used to gain permission, without the perception of legitimacy, the chances that you will be able to translate this permission into positive impact are greatly diminished.

"IF I CAN MAKE IT THERE, I'LL MAKE IT ANYWHERE"

One of the clearest examples of someone who found diverse ways to gain the permission he needed, overcoming obstacles to success much greater than most of us will ever have to face, is a Wall Street executive named David Berman.

On CNBC's morning show on December 26, 2002, David Berman was the special co-host, commenting on the holiday shopping season and the implications for retail stocks.[6] He was a natural special guest. After all, Berman is known as one of the savviest investors in the retailing sector and manages his own highly successful hedge fund dedicated to the retailing industry. But what viewers couldn't possibly have known was how long and arduous a journey Berman had made to get to the Fort Lee, New Jersey, studios on that particular morning.

Berman grew up in Durban, a tropical paradise of a city in the sports-frenzied country of South Africa. At the University of Cape Town, he graduated in accounting near the top of his class, motivated less by the academics and more by the realization that he would be off to the army if he failed. "I was so afraid, I just worked and worked in class, against my natural being," Berman said. "I stunned even myself with my grades." His performance and credentials earned him a coveted spot at Arthur Andersen, then the most prestigious of firms.

Berman's father, once one of the top CEOs in South Africa, employing thousands and leading one of the country's top furniture companies, emigrated to the United States but was not allowed to take much of his savings with him. Berman later had to witness his father's tragic ten-year slide from vibrancy and passion to a relentless mental deterioration that caused him to take his own life at the age of sixty-one.

Berman followed his parents to America, also arriving as an immigrant at the age of twenty-three with $1,500 to his name. After spending a few months in Houston, where his folks and younger brothers had recently moved, he flew to Los Angeles, where he knew not a soul and was forced to spend several nights sleeping in his car. He then started his job as an entry-level accountant at the firm of BDO Seidman, for a salary of $18,500. In South Africa, being an accountant was the pathway to power, the African dream, and the route to being a CEO. As Berman would quickly learn, this was not the case in the United States.

Passing his CPA exams, Berman worked fifteen-hour days at the accounting firm but wasn't thrilled. "The quality of my peers did not seem the same as they had been during my stint at Andersen," Berman relayed. Despite both liking Arthur Andersen and performing extremely well, he had not been allowed a transfer from the South African office to a U.S. branch, as it would have set an unwelcome precedent. So he had to content himself with BDO Seidman, which at that time was the number thirteen firm.

Soon Berman was confronted with a serious ethical dilemma. "I was asked to sign off on an audit where I believed some funny stuff was going on," Berman confided. "The company I was auditing leased a generator plant that by my estimates should definitely have been cap-italized according to FASB but was not. I told the manager and then the partner on the job, and they threatened me to sign or else. It was clear that the client wanted the plant off the balance sheet. And, being on a temporary work visa, I was naturally seriously concerned about being kicked out the country. Nonetheless, I took the risk and took a stand, refusing to sign the audit. It created a quiet scandal. My future at BDO Seidman was clearly in question." Desperate, Berman tele-phoned the head of Arthur Andersen in the United States, sent him his degrees, thesis, and evaluations from the South African office, and basically begged him for a job back at the firm. "For me, calling such an esteemed man was like me now calling the president," Berman said. But to his surprise, the direct approach worked. "Within a few days, and after an interview with the top tax partner, I landed the job. I was ecstatic. I was back with the brightest, or so it seemed. But it was only through sheer desperation that I got the job. And how very ironic that I would leave BDO Seidman for moral reasons to go to Andersen, then the best and staunchly moral accounting firm, where the ethics manual was as big and sacred as the Bible, and where we were even compelled to wear dark suits as a sign of our professionalism and integrity."

Berman performed well at Andersen, but it soon dawned on him that the accounting firms were not attracting the best and the bright-est. A cover story in *Forbes* about the consulting firm McKinsey & Company attracted his attention, so he naively applied for a job, only to be told that he must either be a Rhodes scholar or get his MBA from a top school to be considered.[7] This was the first he had heard of doing an MBA as a door opener—that it was a form of permission. He was restless and feeling trapped as an accountant, so he concluded that an MBA might be a logical next step.

But first, Berman wanted a shot at working for Michael Milken. Berman was a huge fan of the world's most well known financier at the time, not for his fame or his money but for the effect he was having on making America more efficient and for his relatively humble lifestyle and hard work. But before he could call Milken (and just getting his phone number was an effort), he had to wait for his green card so he would be a "free man." "The day I got my green card," Berman said, "I went into Andy Kane's office, the partner in charge, and resigned." Quitting without a job, with only a few months' worth of money saved, was certainly a dramatic way to clean the slate and a risky thing to do, but Berman knew that he needed the pressure of not having a job to get him going, to force himself to make the change that he felt he so desperately needed. He also knew he would feel guilty looking for another job while being employed at Andersen. He simultaneously pursued an appointment with Milken while going through the long and ultimately successful process of applying to the best school that did not require the GMAT exam at that time, Harvard Business School (Berman had a low score on the exam).

Taking a page from the movie *Wall Street*, Berman called Milken's office virtually every day, speaking with a different secretary each time. "When one of the secretaries finally said she would put me down for an appointment with him—after calling every day for over a month—I went crazy with delight," Berman said. "He may have been in trouble, having just left Drexel to set up his own firm, ICAG, but he was innocent to me and, it seemed, to most of those in L.A., and to all those reputable CEOs who signed a newspaper petition on his behalf." Berman related the story of his interview. "After a half hour of chatter with the soft-spoken Milken, I took him aside on my way out, frightened that my chance had gone by, and said, 'Mike, I'll lick stamps for you. All I want to do is be near you, and I will work without any pay. It would be my honor and privilege to work with you before going to Harvard.'" Offering to work for free just to benefit from the experience is certainly an unusual use of bartering to gain permission, but once again the strategy worked. "Before I knew it, I had a marathon interview with his right-hand man, Steve Fink, and got the job."

Working for Michael Milken, albeit just a summer job, was a formative experience for Berman. "Being at this level, it was as if I was in a dream. I worked nineteen-hour days and slept four hours. This was the Milken way. I would wake up at four-thirty in the morning and drive to work in Beverly Hills to work side by side with the smartest man in the world in my book. There were only four of us, yet we were meeting with CEOs from everywhere all day long. And the world seemed to want to work with us. We were primarily evaluating distressed and venture businesses, which in itself was exciting. I was pushing the envelope (as opposed to licking it). It was thrilling. I was learning from the best in meeting after meeting and using my brain to such a degree that I learned an important lesson firsthand: *The brain is no different from the legs in that it is just another muscle, and with exercise can get stronger, quicker, and better.* My brain soon went into focus mode. I became like a mental machine. It was an incredibly exhilarating feeling, and it was just the thing to get my brain ready for business school."

When it came time to leave Milken, it wasn't an easy decision for Berman, as they wanted him to stay, but he kept to his plan. And when they offered to pay Berman for the summer of work, he declined, despite being in tremendous debt even before starting school. "Even though my family was bankrupt [due largely to his father's medical bills and inability to work], I turned down the money," Berman told us proudly. "I am a man of my word, and I truly felt that I had gained so much, just as I thought I would, that I didn't deserve to be paid. If anything, I should have had to pay them for the best learning experience imaginable."

Having gained permission to attend one of the world's most prestigious business schools, he now needed to execute. Yet serious challenges arose. Berman went to see the school counselor halfway through his first year. "I wasn't sure I could make it through the grueling program. My only asset, my uninsured car, had been stolen, I was hugely in debt, my dad was in serious trouble, and I had been reading cases until two or three every morning because I am a slow reader. It was simply too much. I thought I was having a breakdown of sorts." Despite this, Berman pulled through, and in his second year he found himself in the top 10 percent in nine of eleven classes, making him one of the top students of the 850 or so that year. "It was one of my greatest achievements," Berman recounted, beaming, "because I was not naturally an academic, but I learned the system and had fun at the same time." Berman was then awarded his degree with distinction (top 10 percent of the class).

For Berman, business school was another formative experience. But what he *didn't* learn there was what he wanted to do with his life. "I was still just as confused as I was when I left accounting," Berman said. Even after landing a plum summer job with the then-hot investment bank Wasserstein Perella between his first and second years, he realized that banking wasn't for him either. He didn't find it stimulating or active enough, and it was too similar to accounting. Interestingly, again Berman had gained permission for this highly sought-after job using the direct approach: He had directly contacted the head of the L.A. office late in the recruiting season. He was still confused about his career: "Desperate, I even took a second-year course called Self-Development. I had come to school wanting to be a consultant. However, I applied to be a consultant with McKinsey, the very firm that essentially got me to go to HBS in the first place, and was turned down. I was shocked. I had done what they had requested of me, and still I couldn't get in. To my growing dismay, every other consulting firm turned me down too. I didn't have a pedigreed Ivy League background like so many others."

Two things happened during his job search that would test Berman's character. First, his father's situation was getting progressively worse, and his intensity and ambition, driven by survival, must have been clear in interviewing. The second effect was his relationship with Milken, which out of principle he refused to hide. "In my second year at HBS, he was found guilty and sent to prison. Now, not only did many of my peers vilify me, but so did potential employers. Inevitably it would come up, and I refused to distance myself from him, despite the dire consequences it seemed to be having on my career. Even though I was never even paid by Milken, nor did I even work at Drexel, I was tainted. Interestingly, I didn't even need to put this short stint on my resume." Berman was learning fast the power of association and one's reputation, and the impact they can have on gaining permission.

Berman needed a job where he could make money quickly to pay back nearly $80,000 in debt and to help his father live. As the eldest son, he felt all the responsibility. He was one of the last in his class to finalize his job, accepting a position with his previous boss, Steve Fink, in a venture capital firm in Los Angeles, a position he was offered based on the demonstrated competency he had gained working for free two summers earlier. He decided to accept this rather than take a hedge fund job with Michael Steinhardt, despite the fact that the latter offered Berman a $50,000 signing bonus, unheard of at the time. "I simply did not think I could work in the rigorous New York City environment for a hedge fund like this, which was famous not just for its spectacular returns but also for firing its employees every other month," Berman said. "Further, I had not prepared myself for the stock market world while at HBS. I never even took the stock market course. So I chickened out and moved to L.A., to the easier but less risky and less lucrative job."

Berman quickly learned that this job too came with risks. A year later, when it became clear to Berman that the venture firm was going nowhere—it was closed shortly thereafter—he left for the hedge fund job in New York, expecting to be gone in a year.

Now that Berman had permission to ensure his success and execute, he outlined a detailed game plan. "I knew that in order to excel in picking stocks in a relatively efficient market, I needed to have an edge. I realized I had to know an industry better than anyone else. To accomplish this, I met with every sell-side analyst, with buy-side analysts, and with almost every retail management team. I walked the malls of America, went to conferences, and sucked in everything. I learned about trading by observing Steinhardt, one of the best traders of all time. He had promised to mentor me." And so, while sharing a New York city studio apartment in order to save as much as possible to help his parents and pay off debt, Berman traveled extensively and worked around the clock. He had put himself in the deep end and had created huge pressure to succeed.

And succeed he has. In his nine years of investing, Berman has achieved an enviable track record, generating an annualized return before fees of 30 percent while suffering just four down months. Berman got to know his sector of specialization very well. He worked long hours and applied the lesson that knowledge is power. He developed his knowledge base further, and confidently and humbly began to build his investment fund, which has given him just the right mix of professional satisfaction, lifestyle freedom with time to devote to his family, and compensation. "Life can be exciting, and it is new experiences and challenges like this, where we test and push ourselves, that surely bring true happiness," Berman concluded. And as he has demonstrated over and over again, finding a way to gain access to these career-building experiences is a critical part of the equation for success.

TURNING PERMISSION INTO ACTION:
RICH BRAY, MICROSOFT MSN

Another person who has earned permission using some of the effective and enduring approaches outlined here is Rich Bray, who runs Microsoft's $2 billion MSN Internet business in North America. Throughout his career, Bray, who is a thoroughly grounded person and thoughtful about how his words and actions impact others around him, has gained access to critical experiences and then delivered results, making him a natural choice for consistently more senior positions.

Bray graduated from Stanford University with a degree in chemical engineering in 1985 with a strong academic track record, a quick-thinking nature, and a clear communication style. Bray therefore represented tremendous future value to prospective employees. Recognizing this potential value, consulting firm Bain & Company offered him a position as an associate consultant after a series of rigorous interviews. Once in the door, he was able to quickly develop skills and know-how in various types of analysis techniques and critical thinking, and as a result, his experiential value increased at a rapid clip. Although Bray realized after a few years that he did not want to pursue a career as a management consultant, he had already gained exposure to a dozen companies in several industries across three continents. This breadth provided him with perspectives, reference points, and a network of relationships already much richer than that of many executives even ten years more experienced. And the permission associated with the Bain credential, even ten years later gave him credit for strategic experience when it came time to be considered for a general management position.

In the fall of 1988, Bray wanted to maximize his career opportunities, and decided to enter business school. Bray knew that in addition to the professional training and new relationships, an MBA from a top school would provide incremental associative permission and open doors for him now and in the future. He was therefore excited when he was accepted to Harvard Business School. When he graduated in 1990, Bray joined Microsoft, where he has been for the past thirteen years in increasingly responsible positions.

At Microsoft, Bray first spent two years working in the Multimedia Systems Division, when they were trying to encourage business partners to develop software to run on the new CD-ROM-powered multimedia PCs. In 1992, Bray went over to the consumer division as an associate product manager on Microsoft Money, which at the time was in a very weak competitive position relative to Quicken, Check Free, and other incumbents. Moving through more senior marketing and planning positions, Bray was promoted to product manager and group product manager through 1993 and 1994 and was finally tapped to become the product unit manager of the Microsoft Money business in late 1995, which is a general management position overseeing marketing, development, design, testing, and user education. These moves were largely a testimony to his experience in the personal finance category, his understanding of the competitive landscape, and his insight into the emerging online banking and bill payment industry. But at this stage of Bray's development, something else came into play as well. Bray had gained some implied permissions to help garner his first general management appointment, which is often the most difficult to secure. Due to his expertise in the personal finance area, he developed the credentials around the key value-added area for the business. And he also demonstrated competency in some key component areas required for a successful general management position—especially marketing, planning, and strategy—that made it logical, or in other words, gave Microsoft management permission to appoint Bray into the GM role of the finance product group. And having gained access, Bray delivered results, which would open access to new opportunities and allow him to deliver results yet again.

One of his decisions was to move the finance business into the Money Central area on MSN, which gave Bray exposure to that business and its management. Bray's team developed a strategy to go after the bill payment market, and then the Money Central team was merged with the MSN division. Now as an insider in MSN, but with relevant non-MSN or "external" experience, Bray was promoted to general manager of the Desktop Finance division of MSN in 1999, managing all of Microsoft's personal finance efforts—Microsoft Money software, the MSN Money Central Web site, and Microsoft TaxSaver. Having gained access to this opportunity, he delivered once again, managing the Microsoft Money business to profitability and winning strong critical praise in the category. Bray moved quickly to shut down the TaxSaver business and reallocate resources to the growing Internet segment on MSN. From here, he was asked to head up marketing and business development for MSN in North America, core functions for the business, and when it came time to designate a new leader for the overall operation, Bray was once again the logical choice, in large part because of the combination of prior general management experience (admittedly at the smaller scale of a product group) and his strategy experience prior to Microsoft. Since 2001, Bray has been leading this strategically critical and highly visible MSN business for Microsoft, with ultimate responsibility for the P&L, direct oversight for marketing, advertising sales, business development, and network programming, and indirect accountability for product development, operations, customer service, human resources, and finance. In addition, Bray has been increasingly serving as the external spokesman for Microsoft on its Internet business, which is giving him additional visibility in the technology industry and in the business press, which will in turn provide access to critical future opportunities.

TRANSFORMING IMPLIED INTO DIRECT PERMISSION

One way to identify successful professionals is to look at their job description when they arrived and compare that to the job they were actually doing when they left. Among extraordinary executives, you will find a consistent occurrence that the scope of their responsibilities, including the things they have direct permission to do, increases over the tenure of their jobs. These most successful professionals view their job description as merely a starting point—a platform on which to build.

This expansion of permission is often accomplished by constantly extending their scope through implied permission, performing well, and then ultimately being granted direct permission. In real estate, this is the equivalent of "squatter's rights," which states that if you openly use property for a certain period of time, it becomes your legal possession. In business, if you maintain responsibility for the performance of an activity or an area, over time it will inevitably become yours. Those tasks you take on through implied permission therefore become direct over time. Extraordinary executives use this process of expanding scope through implied permission and turning it into direct permission as a key strategy for success.

David Hood is a successful general manager who oversaw the growth of Dell Computer's Internet division from $300 million to more than $4 billion in revenue over a period of three years. When he was recruited away from Dell in 2000, his division was still growing at a nearly 40 percent compound annual rate. Much of this success was attributable to the power of the Dell brand, product line, and direct business model. But it was also a testament to Hood's management and leadership skills. Viewing his performance from a distance, one may be tempted to assume that Hood was simply in the right place at the right time. "If only I could be given such a great opportunity, I could perform just as well," you might think. But before you assume too much, you need to recognize that Hood was not given this opportunity on a silver platter. Rather, it was his keen implementation of numerous strategies for permission that allowed him to continually broaden and redefine his role. Specifically, he applied the strategies of masquerading as the leader and demonstrating competency in key areas as his means to successfully increase his implied and then direct permission. And he combined these with the success pattern that we will see in the next chapter, the 20/80 principle of performance, to reprioritize his job against the key creators of value for the broader organization.

In 1997, Hood was recruited from AT&T to join Dell in the position of vice president of Dell Home Systems. His job description was focused on increasing revenue within the emerging Internet division—essentially a job focused on revenue generation through sales and marketing. While a critical and senior position, it was by no means a full P&L role. There were several other similar positions within the company, and his current and former peers seemed to have defined the limits of the role fairly tightly. But from early on in his tenure, Hood decided not to be limited by his job description, discounting the boundaries of the role predefined by others. Instead, at the right time and with the right signal from the CEO, he chose to create a different definition of his scope of responsibilities.

At the time, Michael Dell had given his senior team the mandate of relentlessly seeking ways to increase profitability. While many felt this was principally the agenda of the CEO, Hood quickly made this his agenda as well. "Something as simple as the language you use can have a powerful impact on what you are empowered to do," Hood told us. "Had I talked only about trying to increase revenue in our division, my fellow executives would have likely boxed me into that role. But by talking about the broader message of increasing earnings per share and explaining the linkage between that and what we were doing, it was much more acceptable for me to get involved in other activities across the company." In essence, Dell's stated objective of increasing earnings per share gave Hood the implied permission to expand his role. (It should be pointed out that this gave other managers the same implied permission if they sought to act on it.) Had Hood stuck to his direct responsibilities of sales and marketing, he would have had a more limited opportunity for impact. But with the mandate of increasing profit any way he could, his scope of opportunity increased dramatically. How, specifically, did he do that?

First, Hood reached out to the customer service teams, working to better link the insights gained from customer feedback into marketing strategy and to eliminate hurdles that were affecting customer service. He came to realize that inefficient delivery policies were impacting sales, and made constructive suggestions directly to the customer services group. These changes turned out to be so effective and were presented in such a productive manner that Hood was later given direct responsibility for this organization. Similarly, he worked constructively with manufacturing, which also resulted in bold and positive changes there, and this led to that group being absorbed into his organization as well. By the time Hood left Dell to become the CEO of BeVocal, revenues in his group approached $4 billion, and he had earned full P&L and general management responsibility for sales, marketing, manufacturing, customer service, human resources, and finance.

What Hood demonstrated so successfully is that your job description as initially defined can be dramatically changed to include more responsibility and scope, and by using the appropriate permission strategies to gain access and then having a positive impact, this can be accomplished without being perceived as overly threatening to others in the organization. What's more, Hood demonstrated that permission is not just something that is defined or reshaped early on when you take on a new role—it is something that must be actively managed all the time, while you seek to identify additional levers in the organization that could allow you to have greater positive impact and give you access to the most career advancing opportunities.

By understanding and implementing the strategies for resolving the permission paradox, you should be able to get the permission you seek. But by doing so, you've won only half the battle of achieving extraordinary success. As previewed by David Hood, and as we'll see in the next chapter, permission puts you in the best position to perform.

DIFFERENTIATE USING THE 20/80 PRINCIPLE OF PERFORMANCE

The art of being wise is the art of knowing what to overlook.
—WILLIAM JAMES

Today's workplace demands that you focus not just on what's merely important, but what's wildly important.
—STEPHEN COVEY

WINNING THE MAJORS

In 2002, after his fourth straight Tour de France victory, Lance Armstrong decided to stop racing in the United States—except for one or two special events. Why? In bike racing, the big events—the worthwhile events—occur in Europe, not in the States. Sorry, Uncle Sam.

Armstrong's decision is not unusual for high-performance athletes who succeed at the world-class level. They channel their energies into the competitions that matter most. Insatiable golf fans would love to see Tiger Woods play every PGA tournament, and television producers would like that even more. But Tiger plays fewer tournaments over the course of the year than his PGA brethren and champions of yore, such as Arnold Palmer and Jack Nicklaus. His focus is on the four majors—

the Masters, British Open, U.S. Open, and PGA Championship. And while he does not apologize for passing up tournaments of lesser prestige, Woods' practice regimen and discipline around preparing for the majors are legendary.

Could these athletes tally up additional wins and earn even more prize money if they played more? Yes. But that's not the point. Not only are the other tournaments less important for their definition of success, but they can be a distraction in the pursuit of the ultimate goal: winning as many majors as possible.

Most people know of the 80/20 principle, the observation of Italian economist Vilfredo Pareto (1848–1923) that in many situations it's the first 20 percent of the effort that contributes 80 percent of the benefit. Focusing first on the 20 percent of your customers that are most desirable often yields 80 percent of the profit. In effect, Woods and Armstrong have determined that focusing on the events that are the most important—the majors—will allow them to reap the most benefit. The lesson is simple but powerful: *The quality of your impact often matters much more than the quantity of your activities.* The same principle applies to your career.

But unlike professional athletics, the tasks and objectives that are required as a part of business careers are not all glory. In fact, the 80 percent of our jobs that offer little chance for differentiation are usually narrowly defined and on the surface quite inflexible. But as with Woods and Armstrong, success ultimately requires winning the majors in our careers. It is the ability to get beyond merely achieving what others want you to do and break through to deliver unanticipated impact that will give you—and your company—the most return, creating results that can truly distinguish you. Unlike the 80/20 principle, in business it is usually the *last* 20 percent of what you accomplish (beyond your predefined objectives) that allows you to truly differentiate yourself. The fourth pattern of extraordinary careers is the 20/80 principle of performance—keeping the 20 percent that is under your control foremost in your and your boss's mind, and it is the successful application of this principle that allows you to play and win the majors in your career.

A CAUTIONARY TALE

To better understand this concept, it's instructive to see how failing to apply it can work against you. Consider a disenchanted professional, whom we will call Jerry Martin, as an example of how failure to apply the 20/80 principle can result in torturous mediocrity. Not unlike millions of businesspeople, Martin had suffered several setbacks during 2001 and 2002. At first, it was easy for him to blame the declining economy. But as time passed, Martin became more and more concerned that his downfall may actually have been the result of something he had or had not done.

Early in his career, Martin had joined a large manufacturing company, first as an accountant, soon moving into supervisory and management roles within the finance department. As the company grew, Martin felt that his career was prospering, and he was promoted into middle management right on schedule. Soon he was leading a financial planning and analysis team for one of the company's largest divisions. He consistently was able to close the books on time, and when asked by senior management, he promptly generated the desired financial reports with accuracy.

But slowly and surely, he developed an uncomfortable and almost helpless feeling that his career was losing momentum, and he couldn't explain why. While he was consistently called upon to provide standard financial information, he felt that his input was included in critical strategic decisions less and less. He was not being invited to attend key management meetings as he had been earlier. He tried working visibly harder, logging longer hours than his peers, but even this did not seem to help Martin regain his momentum. Martin was very proud of his track record, always delivering what was asked of him, but he was becoming increasingly frustrated that he was failing to be recognized for his contributions. His hunches were painfully confirmed as he watched younger co-workers get promoted right past him.

"I was doing everything my bosses asked me to do," he told us. "I can't ever remember a time that I didn't meet my objectives. But I was never singled out for what I accomplished. They would say thanks to me in private, but they would celebrate others publicly. Then when it was promotion time, they gave it to someone else."

During a downsizing last year, Martin was let go from his company. As we go to press, Martin remains unemployed, incredulous as to why he went off the tracks, and desperately looking for a job.

So what happened to Martin?

There is no certainty in today's environment of career upheaval, but a critical part of the path toward success and security is through adding value in the most important areas and by differentiating yourself from others. Martin went to work, did his job, and was a solid performer. But somehow the big breaks didn't come his way. When it came time for his company to cut back, he was not viewed as a must-keep employee. He was the equivalent of the athlete who played all the tournaments yet never won a major. Martin was hardworking but undifferentiated—and ultimately expendable.

How is it that some professionals stand out from the pack and others just don't?

It's a factor of the 20/80 principle of performance.

The reality is that you can do what you are told at work—and do a good job of it—and still not have success or security in your position. Although you should absolutely seek to meet the objectives outlined for your job, you should have no illusion that this is enough. Nearly everyone believes he meets the job's goals. Specifically, 95 percent of the professionals participating in our survey for this book said they "consistently meet their objectives."

Like Martin, you can meet your goals, get decent performance reviews, even get the occasional raise, and still not have a stellar career. So much of what we do at work is ordinary work that almost any of our peers can accomplish. Truly. Studying numerous executives, we estimate that nearly 80 percent of effort and resources are spent achieving the predefined objectives set by a boss. But what really allows the extraordinary executives to separate themselves from the pack is where they focus the remaining 20 percent that can be used at their discretion. And top-performing individuals think long and hard about the opportunity costs associated with channeling their energies one way versus another. Somehow they find a way to focus on the majors.

Early in his career, co-author Rick Smith was a marketing analyst for EDS. His job was to gather and analyze competitive information that was given to top executives at EDS. Working month after month with volumes of information at his disposal, Rick gained a valuable perspective on how EDS really delivered value to its customers. Although he would give an occasional presentation to a sales team or be called in to support a critical business development opportunity against a top competitor, his primary role was research. This was the 80 percent of his job from which there was no deviation—and this task filled up most of his days.

Then one day Rick had a breakthrough thought that changed his entire career. With a time-consuming monthly report just completed, Rick sifted through the numerous reports and spreadsheets provided to him by the finance department. One particular file contained the financial performance of all of EDS' significant contracts signed in the last fifteen years, with descriptive details about each. Out of curiosity, he wondered whether the larger contracts were more profitable than the smallest ones, and did a quick analysis. Indeed, there were substantial differences in profitability, revenue recognition, risk, rate of return, repeat sales, and other areas. Fascinated by the results, he stayed at work until after midnight to see where the analysis might lead him. The next day, he cleaned up his work and presented a compelling executive summary of his findings to his boss. "I know this may seem a bit outside of my job description," Rick confided to his boss, "but I thought you would find this interesting." As his boss looked over the work with growing interest, Rick offered, "What if our role as competitive analysts is not just to help win *more* customers, but to help win the *right customers?*" Within a week, the report he had put together made it all the way to the CEO's office.

From there, things really started to happen. In addition to his regular competitive research responsibilities, Rick was asked to conduct further analyses of EDS' business. Over the next year and a half, Rick's findings were presented regularly to the top leadership team of EDS, and on one occasion even to the board of directors of General Motors, EDS' parent at the time. Given the broad interest in the analysis around the organization, Rick was able to develop a powerful network of executives that helped him maximize the impact of his findings. His work sparked a flurry of activity within EDS and eventually led to wholesale changes in how the company went to market, including a reprioritization of the type of business the company pursued and a fundamental restructuring of the way it compensated and managed its salespeople, to ensure the company was focused on winning the right customers.

During this period, Rick's primary responsibilities as an analyst doing competitive research never changed, and he was evaluated positively on his core job responsibility. But over time, he was able to triage his regular tasks, freeing up valuable time and resources which were redirected toward his corporate performance analysis. He worked with the executives who received his standard competitive reports to understand what information was most important and which reports offered little value and could be simplified or eliminated. He trained others on his team and was gradually able to delegate many noncritical activities. He worked with the IT department to automate some research and report generation, reducing the time required to produce the reports from days to hours. This relentless pursuit of efficiency in meeting his required tasks freed up precious time that could be allocated to what Rick felt would add value.

Effectively and efficiently completing his predefined objectives was notable, but it was his efforts beyond his defined job responsibilities that reshaped the trajectory of his career. In effect, he was able to redefine his role from "helping win business" to "helping win the *right* business," highlighting the types of opportunities that were most beneficial for the company, and improving the likelihood of success in these deals. From that point on, Rick was often asked to participate in additional career-building corporate initiatives well beyond his scope of responsibilities—affording him access to opportunities and experiences typical of professionals many years his senior.

In this application of the 20/80 principle, it is important to understand what actions were and were not taken. Achieving this differentiated level of success did not require that Rick log longer hours than his peers or superiors—working harder and longer is not nearly as differentiating as working smarter. And in no way did Rick abandon the primary responsibilities that his boss was counting on him to deliver.

It was the 20 percent of Rick's objectives that *he* was able to define that allowed him to deliver substantial positive impact and which ultimately mattered most. Extraordinary executives understand this and put this 20 percent at the fore.

Senator Elizabeth Dole, one of the most admired women in America, is a well-known public service leader, having served as president of the American Red Cross from 1991 to 1999, secretary of the U.S. Department of Labor from 1988 to 1989, and secretary of transportation from 1981 to 1983. But sitting down with Dole provided a powerful example of the benefits of achieving well beyond the status quo by focusing on the majors.

In both government and not-for-profit organizations, maintaining the status quo is often the primary although unstated objective. Seeking to create abnormal impact is more often met with skepticism and caution. The operating mantra is usually "If it ain't broke, don't fix it." But Dole viewed each role as an opportunity to differentiate herself through her performance and create impact.

"When I became secretary of transportation," Dole shared with us, "my predecessor, Drew Lewis, beseeched me to identify no more than five things that you feel are really important, where you can make a difference, and go for it. If you spread yourself across too many initiatives, years later you will have been working night and day and you'll wonder what you have accomplished. You will have dissipated your efforts."

She added, "I think that's such good advice. It's something that I've tried to do in each of my positions. I try to concentrate on where I really can make a difference, and then I put a lot of energy into making sure that those things happen."

This clear focus has paid off in each of the major phases of Dole's career. In some cases it has allowed her to set the agenda and work on accomplishing goals far beyond expectations; in other cases it's allowed her to positively impact constituencies well beyond her own organization.

One such situation occurred during her tenure as the head of the Department of Transportation, an organization where the performance of one leader was typically indistinguishable from that of the next. At the top of Dole's list of majors was safety. "One of the toughest things that I was ever involved with from a public policy standpoint was Rule 208. This proposed rule, which had been discussed and debated by the federal government for over twenty years, had to do with air bags and safety belts in automobiles. At the time, in the early 1980s, no states had safety belt laws, and it was very difficult to get a car with air bags. Rule 208 provided that passive restraints for all new cars would be phased in over a four-year period unless two-thirds of the population of the United States was covered by state safety belt laws that met stringent federal requirements." Rather than distancing herself from what seemed a futile objective, Dole attacked this visible and politically charged issue head on. She spawned a competition between the automobile industry, which wanted safety belt laws, and insurance companies, which favored air bags, which eventually led to breaking the logjam. "We ended up getting both, which is what we wanted so that we could have the most far-reaching impact in terms of lives saved and injuries prevented." According to the National Highway Safety Transportation Authority, over a hundred thousand lives have been saved as a result of Rule 208, and the climate for auto safety has been changed dramatically.[1]

Dole put all of her work in perspective: "By the end of my days, the question is going to be, 'What did I stand for? Did I make a positive difference for others?' That is what is going to matter, not all of the other more shallow things." These words ring true in our careers, and in life—inspiring to us all.

THE DIMINISHING RETURNS OF OVERDELIVERING

The 20/80 principle requires adding value in surprising ways that make people take notice. Average employees will frequently continue working to exceed preset expectations—achieving more than quota, producing additional reports, or reducing costs by some incremental percentage. While laudatory, this approach rarely creates distinctive positive differentiation. The reason is that success in a given task is usually considered relatively black or white: Either you met the objective or you didn't. While you will likely be singled out for not meeting the objective, exceeding it by 5 percent or even 15 percent will rarely win you more than a basic "Good job." Translated to the normally sterile performance evaluation form, the rating will likely remain "Met expectations" or, at best, "Exceeded expectations." Achieving the highest levels of career success requires more than mere applause; it demands a level of differentiated performance that changes the very perception of your professional talent and worth.

The extraordinary executive takes a different approach. He consistently meets objectives and then starts down a different path—to use his precious remaining resources to impact the company in other ways, with objectives he has created and in areas that generate the most value to the companies. Had Rick Smith focused all of his efforts on overdelivering on the competitive analysis work outlined for him at EDS, he may have produced an extra report or increased the frequency of communications, but in the end, he would have been viewed as just another qualified professional doing his job. It was the impact he was able to have outside of his predefined job description that mattered most.

The beauty of this success pattern is that you have a lot of control in applying it. The key is to use your judgment to determine those particular tasks that are important, timely, and appropriate, and secure the buy-in of your management and others invested in your success. Real differentiation and success are achieved when you are able to accomplish extremely important tasks beyond those that are outlined for you.

READY . . . AIM . . . FIRE!

In the lesser-known Olympic sport of the biathlon, becoming a champion requires a combination of speed, endurance, and precision. Equipped with cross-country skis and a rifle strapped over the shoulders, each participant sets out across a winding course of hills and valleys, typical of other cross-country skiing courses. But along the way, the athlete must stop at predefined target sites and hit targets up to a hundred yards away. Each competitor has a certain number of shots, and each is critical, for the farther away each shot is from the bull's-eye, the greater the time penalty that is added to the person's race time.

World-class endurance is valuable, as is precision marksmanship, but neither is enough by itself. Success requires both. When coming upon a target, contestants must first get *ready*, properly balancing and positioning themselves and slowing down their heart rate so they can shoot accurately, often decreasing from levels of more than two hundred beats per minute. Once ready, they take *aim*, focusing clearly on the target, and then *fire* by steadily pulling back on the trigger.

Careers are comparable, for it is neither the quantity of activities nor the speed of completion that creates differentiation, but the quality of impact. Successfully implementing the 20/80 principle similarly requires that you get ready . . . aim . . . and fire.

Smith got ready to create differentiated impact by first gaining a strong perspective of what was most valuable to EDS' business, then

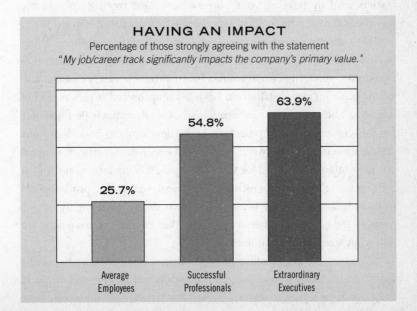

HAVING AN IMPACT

Percentage of those strongly agreeing with the statement
"My job/career track significantly impacts the company's primary value."

63.9% — Extraordinary Executives

54.8% — Successful Professionals

25.7% — Average Employees

triaging his preset activities. He worked with his management team to reprioritize his objectives, keeping those tasks that were important to his boss, such as facilitating quarterly field presentations to various business units. He then took aim, setting his sights high with the breakthrough idea of focusing on increasing the quality of EDS' competitive wins, not just the quantity. This lofty redefinition of his role was motivating to him and others, and helped align resources around him. And then he fired, executing on the opportunities identified while constantly communicating with his chain of management, letting them know of the results he was generating, and reassuring them that his redefined activities were bearing real fruit. And he maximized the impact through a network of executives who became involved in his work and who helped to increase his visibility and greatly leverage his work across the entire organization.

Ready . . .

Before implementing the 20/80 principle, you must get ready by gaining an understanding of what really creates value within your organization, and by triaging your current activities, freeing up valuable resources that can be focused on creating differentiated impact.

How does your organization create value for its customers? What is viewed as its most valuable skill? For example, at Coca-Cola, it is marketing, since the core formulas for its products rarely change, and manufacturing and distribution have been optimized over a period of decades. The success of marketing is what really impacts performance for this company. For Microsoft, it is the development and ubiquitous distribution of great software; for GE and Emerson Electric, it is rigorous general management; for Cisco Systems, it is customer impact; for Starbucks, it is field operations. The most successful professionals intuitively know and are inexorably drawn to the most highly valued parts of the company. They truly know what customers are paying for and what stockholders value most.

Not surprisingly, extraordinary executives are more than two and a half times as likely to feel that their position and career track impacts their company's primary value compared with average employees.

While it is easier to have a large impact if you are on the front lines of how your company creates value, the 20/80 principle can be effective for you even if you work behind the scenes. Think of a pyramid that has your customers at the top. Now think of the different units within your company: finance, operations, field delivery, information technology, marketing, research and development. Place each function as a building block within the pyramid, with the higher levels being those most closely tied to the products and services customers value most.

The further away you are from the apex of the pyramid, the more you can differentiate yourself by linking your activities directly to what creates value. If you're an accountant, you can differentiate yourself by coming up with customer metrics that allow a marketing-driven organization to make better decisions. If you are in systems design, you can break through by helping create a tool that provides better real-time information that helps the sales force convert more prospects into profitable clients. In biotech, it's all about creating the next blockbuster drug. So if you work in finance, for example, you can try to help devise better ways to manage the company's product development portfolio so that the R&D team can make the kind of investment decisions that lie behind creating those next blockbuster drugs. Once you figure out what the true value creator is for your company and industry, invest the 20 percent of your effort that you are able to direct in the highest-priority areas.

Next, you need to carefully consider how successful performance is really defined within your organization. Beyond quantitative metrics, performance is always measured through the filter of how well your activities fit into the corporate culture. Cultural standards impact how you and others communicate, how much risk taking is considered appropriate, and how decisions are made. Take the time to observe how your company rewards and punishes different kinds of performance. Really listen and learn what makes your company tick, who gets the plum assignments, what types of behaviors and impact lead to promotion, who stands out from the crowd.

You also need to understand how adding value is defined at each stage of your career. There is a fine line between being perceived as proactive and a go-getter versus arrogant or out of your league. A new associate at the Boston Consulting Group, one of the most prestigious global strategy consulting firms, might think that being a strong performer means bringing in a new client. But the associate might very well be overstepping her bounds and actually be subtly penalized for not focusing on detailed analysis and problem solving, which is considered most important during that early career stage. At the managerial level, the value might move from solving individual problems to integrating discrete pieces of the analysis into a big-picture solution and working on a day-to-day basis with the client to develop the overall recommendations. Only after reaching the partner level would one have the organizational permission and expectation to bring in new business.

Knowing what constitutes great performance within your organization and relative to your current position is critical to implementing the 20/80 principle. Before you can deliver differentiated levels of performance, you must have the proper context. For extraordinary executive Denys Gounot, this means beginning each assignment with his "feet in the mud."

Frenchman Denys Gounot learned just how valuable the 20/80 principle can be very early in his career. He was born in Besançon, a small town in France, and grew up in Lyon. A very bright student, he excelled in school and was admitted to L'Ecole Polytechnique in Paris, the country's most respected engineering program, and then went on to complete graduate engineering work at L'Ecole Nationale des Ponts et Chaussées. In France, top students follow the career principle "Go blue chip early" by accepting prestigious roles within the government, more so than they do in America. Gounot was excited to accept one of these coveted roles working for the state, but rather than starting in a top agency role or working within the Cabinet in Paris, as did most of his high-performing peers, he opted to start first with some field experience. He chose to take an assignment as a field project engineer for the Department of Highways. "I thought it would be valuable to get my hands dirty out in the field. Little did I realize that within six months, I would literally be standing in the middle of a field with my feet submerged in mud!" Gounot successfully negotiated highway rights of way and learned real-world negotiating skills by dealing with average French citizens and municipalities. In this role, he gained a perspective as to what was and was not achievable, and why. He was surprised when several ambitious projects were completed with much fewer complications than expected, thanks to hands-on involvement and commitment, and he learned the importance of providing very specific care, such as the preservation of a single tree.

When his assignment in the field ended, he then accepted a position in Paris as a deputy in the National Motorways Department, where he was singled out for his performance. To the surprise of many of his peers and mentors, he credited his later success to what he had learned in the field. "What I took from that first assignment was far from anything I ever learned at the university. It is easy to sit back and discuss theories, but unless you have an understanding of what can really be implemented, it doesn't mean much." From that point on, Gounot never forgot the value of perspective that comes from starting with your feet in the mud.

Gounot later entered the private sector, joining Alcatel Cable, and was assigned to a plant in Burgundy. Although everyone considered the (very modern) unit as a model, Gounot felt an urgency to move it to a new level to keep pace with the competitive environment. He discovered that the management team had been there a long time, and that over time he would have to replace most of these professionals. But rather than immediately replacing everyone, he thought it best to upgrade the team gradually, initially replacing each manager with himself, taking on the added responsibility. During his first year at the plant, Gounot assumed the role in marketing, finance, and floor operations in turn, over and above his general manager duties, before a permanent replacement was hired in each function.

Taking on each role directly, even for short periods, once again allowed him the valuable experience of getting his feet in the mud, gaining an intimate understanding of how value is created and the potential opportunities that may exist. Though Alcatel Cable's expectation for Gounot in this assignment was to maintain the status quo in the plant and for him to simply gain field experience before returning for a corporate job (the factory was already operating at full speed), he surprised them. He worked with the plant floor to streamline production processes, instilling a culture of continuous improvement. He built bridges with corporate to get critical inventory and sales information in the hands of the operations managers. And he worked with his finance team to make sure incentives for production workers would have maximum effect on productivity. Having gained a broad perspective on how every position could work together to improve performance, Gounot was able to double the throughput of the factory in under two years.

Gounot continued his career ascent, successfully integrating a major acquisition for Alcatel, running the $7 billion cable operations worldwide, and later heading another business group of Alcatel Althom. He then joined Lucent, where he ultimately led Lucent's optical fiber unit, which he grew to more than $2 billion, turning a losing division into a fast-growing jewel, enabling its successful carve-out and divestiture. To this day, Gounot attributes his many career successes to his strategy of understanding the most important priorities and the real opportunities by getting his feet in the mud. His accomplishments ultimately stood in clear contrast to others who had a lesser understanding of how value was really created. Gaining the perspective of how value is really created in your organization is the first step to delivering differentiated performance.

Triage Your Predefined Objectives

Getting ready also requires freeing up sufficient resources to deliver results beyond your predefined objectives. The 20/80 principle certainly does not imply that the predefined objectives set out for you are unimportant. On the contrary, failing to execute these objectives successfully virtually eliminates the possibility of breakthrough positive differentiation. And in fact, working to execute these predefined tasks usually helps you develop the fundamentals required to succeed in your profession. Finally, completing predefined goals can give you valuable perspective that is required before you can uncover breakthrough ideas. But succeeding at the 20/80 principle means getting beyond these objectives, and if fulfilling them takes up all your time and resources, you will at best meet expectations. You must learn to triage your activities and reprioritize to maximize the impact of your efforts.

Let's assume you are a marketing manager overseeing one of your company's key brands, and your boss, the chief marketing officer, has highlighted three primary objectives for you to accomplish: (1) produce monthly competitive reporting on marketing activities, (2) oversee the implementation of corporate marketing's various initiatives, working with the staff functions and field operations, and (3) lead the market research to help determine the most appropriate positioning and messaging for your brand. Rather than treating them as equally important, initiate a discussion about their relative impact on your business unit and the organization overall. You can apply a scale of 1 to 3, where 1 represents the lowest level of impact, 2 represents more significant impact, but still within your unit, and 3 represents the highest level of impact across a large part of the organization.

Of the three objectives, there is one that is most critical to your business unit and therefore visible to your boss: leading the work to determine the most appropriate positioning and messaging for your brand, which is a 2. The remaining objectives can be described as a mix of tasks and projects, and although necessary, both have an impact level of 1. This represents a total impact of 4 $((1 \times 2) + (2 \times 1))$. Now, if through a constructive problem-solving approach you can reduce or refocus the resources required for certain objectives, you may be able to more broadly impact the organization. For example, to achieve the objective of the implementation of corporate initiatives, you get managers in finance, operations, and sales more directly involved, convincing them that they each need to take ownership of the marketing initiatives, such as consistency of corporate message across all brands and functions, to reach full impact to the organization. Not only does this enable you to share the responsibilities, reducing the direct resources required by you, but you also have the opportunity to practice benevolent leadership, giving the opportunity to others to achieve success and recognition. Doing so actually increases the impact of your predefined objective, raising it from an impact level of 1 to 2. For your objective of monthly reporting of marketing activities, you work with an analyst in your division to standardize and automate the reporting process, requiring that you now only have to proof the output, essentially eliminating the resources required by you for this objective. With the additional time and resources that you have created, you now create a task force across multiple business units, identifying best practices for marketing that can be shared across the organization.

Your boss is thrilled, as you have met all three of the original objectives and have positioned the team as a thought leader for the company. For you, the benefits are clear. Your primary objective of doing the foundation work on brand positioning is met, with an impact level of 2; your secondary objectives of corporate initiatives and reporting have been met, but with more impact in the corporate initiative and less resources required for reporting. And you have added the impact of initiating and leading a cross division task force, with an impact level of 3. Proactively managing the objectives laid out for you has allowed you to double your impact to the organization, from 4 to 8!

This example may seem overly simplistic—most people have much longer lists of tasks and objectives in their jobs. But it does illustrate the power of maximizing the total impact with the resources at your disposal. Extraordinary executives know this and can usually be quickly identified by comparing what they were originally asked to accomplish in a role with the level of impact they ultimately achieved. Reprioritizing your objectives is a way to accomplish a greater impact on your organization and therefore your career.

Presentation Paralysis

While technology has helped us make great strides toward more efficient manufacturing, such as Six Sigma production perfection and just-in-time (JIT) inventory management, new technologies have also decreased productivity in some areas. When pondering the most impactful technologies since the dawn of mankind, *Business 2.0* identified the presentation management software program Microsoft PowerPoint as one of the most influential innovations.[2] But in reviewing the net effect of this new technology, it may also be labeled as having minimal impact on business productivity, and a negative influence on "Quality of Life." The reason is that with presentation software now within nearly everyone's reach, much more time is often spent on the presentation itself rather than on the content. Trying to make the messenger as beautiful as possible through endless iterations in many cases has resulted in much less attention placed on the message itself. It is not unusual for a project team of four or five people to spend weeks in the development of a twenty-page PowerPoint presentation to a client or top management, constantly debating slide titles and chart formats. But the application of the 20/80 principle can help you keep on track. Appealing images can be impressive, but only powerful content can result in true positive differentiation.

For example, in management consulting, a profession in which presentation wizardry seems almost a price of entry, we have found that some of the very best consultants utilize surprisingly simple presentations, or abandon them altogether in favor of a succinct, compelling message delivered directly absent any props. Tom Warren, a successful and engaging technology consulting executive now with Hewlett-Packard, prefers the direct approach. When competing for a large contract several years ago, he expected his competitors to deliver their pitch via a visually appealing presentation, likely to have taken hundreds of consultant hours to put together. Tom tried a different approach, asking only that he be equipped with three standard flip charts. When he and his team arrived to deliver their sales pitch, he began by writing three titles at the top of the three flip charts: *Your Problem. Our Solution. Costs, Benefits, and Timing.*

For the rest of the two-hour meeting, he filled in the pages with his team's understanding of the situation, their solution, and the details of the project. Tom stuck to high-level points but allowed a great deal of interaction with the potential client, in effect letting them direct the flow of the conversation toward what they felt was most important. The lead client executive called Tom shortly after their meeting to award his team the contract. "Actually," said the executive, "you won it not by showing up with an elaborate presentation, but rather by just talking to us in English about our problem and how we could work together to solve it." In the market for professional services, executives like Tom Warren are often the most coveted. They are the ones focusing on the real work at hand—the problem and the solution.

. . . Aim . . .

Once you have gained a sense of how value is really created within your organization, and have triaged your preset objectives to enable a focus on priorities you select, you must set your sights on creating maximum impact, ultimately changing the assumptions of your expected performance. For Pat Byrne, this requires getting well beyond objectives others have set for you—it involves *breakthrough thinking*.

Byrne, former chief operating officer of the global management consultancy A. T. Kearney, who helped the firm grow from $65 million to more than $1.4 billion in revenues, has clearly led an extraordinary career. He was born in Dublin (Glen-in-the-Downs), Ireland, where he lived until the age of eight. His family then relocated to Cleveland, Ohio, where his father was an electrician with the Ford Motor Company. Byrne worked his way through college as a laborer in a Ford plant. Graduating from Kent State University in 1975, he felt that anything but an extraordinary career lay in front of him.

Byrne began his professional career as a distribution manager for a consumer products company, Hormel Foods, and had impressed his boss with his work ethic, intelligence, and ambition. When his boss was recruited to join Schneider National, Inc., Byrne was asked to join as well. He had never contemplated entering the trucking industry, but, given his boss' confidence in him, Schneider's reputation for functioning more like a consumer products firm than a traditional trucking company, and the growth prospects under deregulation, he decided to follow his boss.

Soon thereafter, however, Byrne was not so sure he had made the right move. Although Schneider was indeed innovative, Byrne felt he had entered the most mundane and staid industry in all of business. Byrne started with Schneider as a commerce manager, responsible for tariff filings and company representation in operating authority cases and other related regulatory matters. He soon progressed into the role of pricing manager, responsible for developing pricing strategies and maintaining regulatory compliance. On the surface, the role seemed critical, impacting the profitability of the entire company. But as he settled into his new job, he realized that the organization's expectations for his performance encompassed little more than administration.

At the time, the trucking industry operated under a policy of collective rate making, based on an exemption from the Robinson-Patman Act that prohibited companies within an industry from colluding on price. Byrne would spend his days sorting through long lists of tariffs—pricing rates based on industrywide averages that were put together by rate bureaus and filed with the Interstate Commerce Commission. His two primary responsibilities were to correctly interpret these tariffs to set pricing for trucking services, and to make sure that Schneider filed its request for ordinary rate increases in compliance with regulations. Byrne quickly mastered these straightforward tasks and then began to wonder what else could be done, particularly in view of the pending deregulation of the trucking industry in 1980.

Byrne studied the underlying economics of the industry. He realized that while the rates set by the industry bureaus were based on national averages, actual profitability per shipment varied dramatically around these averages. Essentially, prices on many traffic lanes (origin/destination pairs) didn't reflect the underlying economics and operating conditions. There were many traffic lanes where truckers had excess demand, yet the prices didn't reflect this condition. The prices were predicated on national averages without consideration for carrier-specific traffic lane imbalances and operating costs.

Byrne proposed a radical new system for pricing, based not on averages but rather on the real cost and underlying operating conditions of each traffic lane. For routes where demand was lower, he dropped prices, increasing utilization of trucks. For routes where demand was high, he increased prices, significantly improving the profitability per trip. As his new pricing model and business practices were implemented in the organization, Schneider's revenues and profitability increased dramatically. From an $85 million operation in the late 1970s, Schneider has grown to one of the leading transportation companies in the world and the largest in its sector, with annual revenue in excess of $2 billion. Byrne's method of traffic lane pricing has become the standard pricing practice in the industry.

Byrne credits much of his career success to this type of breakthrough thinking. He added, "Many people believe success comes from doing what is asked, or that exceeding expectations can be achieved by just doing more of what is asked. But if you follow this path, you will only end up doing things the same way they have always been done. Real impact," explained Byrne, "requires breaking away from the old ways of thinking to implement new ideas, challenging old assumptions and fundamentally changing or rethinking the way an organization does business."

In his roles at Kearney as chief operating officer and previous to that as managing director for North America, Byrne again worked with his team to deliver breakthrough thinking and change in a consulting industry that had long since settled on a standard mode of operation. His team implemented innovative, value-based pricing techniques in which some fees were variable based on project impact. He was instrumental in branding one of Kearney's service offerings, Strategic Sourcing, helping his firm quickly assume the leadership position in procurement consulting. During his tenor as chief operating officer (1999 to 2000) and prior to that as managing director for North America (1993 to 1999), Byrne had overseen compounded annual revenue growth of 25 percent and 45 percent, respectively. Operating contribution and overall profitability grew at a much faster rate than revenue during this period. Byrne helped orchestrate the sale of A. T. Kearney to EDS in 1995 for well in excess of $600 million—at the time, the largest sale ever of a professional services company. He remained with the company, facilitating its growth to over $1 billion in global service revenues. It is now one of the largest high-value-added management consulting companies in the world.

The Stuff Around the Edges

Byrne's philosophy of breakthrough thinking is not unique among extraordinary executives. In business, we do not normally have the luxury Woods and Armstrong do to play a limited tournament schedule, focusing on the majors; therefore we need to find our own way to apply the principle. So it is that extraordinarily successful executives focus on what many people think of as the work around the edges, those undefined tasks that no one specifically told them to do but which help to set them apart. On a day-to-day basis, they may actually seem like relatively inconsequential things—a marketing manager going on customer visits, a sales manager taking some calls in the customer support center, a strategic planning director writing an article, a manufacturing manager volunteering for a cross-functional quality project. But in time, these activities compound, such that over the course of months and years, exceptional, differentiated results are achieved. People who follow this pattern are typically referred to in the context of questions such as "How did she find time to do that?" or "If you want to get something important done, give it to the busiest person."

It frequently turns out that the marketing manager who visits customers happens to be the one who develops the promotional campaign with the best feel for the customer base. The sales manager who sits in at the support center is best able to take the feedback from the customer service calls and channel that insight along with what she knows from her field sales team into the product development department—thus becoming known as a strategic thinker and therefore the natural choice for moving into general management. The strategic planner who writes the article becomes known as a thought leader in the industry and is invited to represent the company at industry conferences, creating additional visibility and hence differentiation for himself. And the manufacturing manager builds important awareness and relationship bridges into other departments that differentiate him from others at the same level who are not as well known. The work around the edges is a critical element of the 20/80 principle, resulting in a much broader perspective in your job, the expansion of your critical network, and maximization of the impact of each role.

The Value of Changing the Assumptions

Successfully applying the 20/80 principle of performance requires that successful executives aim extremely high, with the goal of dramatically increasing the rate of positive change within an organization. In the unstable and constantly changing world of business today, leaders able to positively redefine performance expectations are critical to achieving and maintaining market leadership. These astute professionals deemphasize or eliminate make-work tasks such as preparation of noninfluential reports and presentations or process approval steps created years ago that have lost their relevance. Professionals who are able to focus energies and stress opportunities that may materially impact growth, profits, and brand are highly rewarded.

Focusing resources directly on the real but often hidden problem/solution at hand can help to change the assumptions—and positively impact how you are valued. The stock market is an example of a highly efficient marketplace that places a premium on a company's ability to create a positive rate of change. Investors value stocks based on the perceived growth of future earnings. Companies that simply meet these expectations of future earnings, no small feat in the first years of the twenty-first century, generally have relatively stable stock prices. Their revenues and profits may stay on track, but unless the assumptions about performance change, its stock price will not likely change. The expectation of future earnings and growth are already factored into their prices. In other words, in the world of securities, value cannot be created by maintaining the status quo. Rather, value is created—or destroyed—when assumptions change. For public companies, the market price for their stock is based on a series of assumptions related to future profitability, growth, competitive position, strength of balance sheet, management quality, and other factors. If the company continues to evolve but is not able to alter the underlying assumptions of the market, the stock price will generally not move.

For example, in the second quarter of 2000, Intel recorded a 79 percent increase in profits, thanks to an extraordinary gain from its investments. Intel's stock, however, did not budge on the news. The reason is that even though this was a positive and unexpected event, it did not change the market assumptions about its future, which were focused on the underlying demand for semiconductors and the company's resulting growth and profitability in its core business. Conversely, when Intel announced an unexpected underperformance in revenue growth for the third quarter of 2000—a mere 6 percent shortfall versus the market's expectations—its stock dropped 20 percent in a single day. In business, positive and negative changes in expectations are what move markets.

The same principle can be applied to your career. Just doing your job, meeting your predefined objectives, is analogous to a company meeting its performance expectations; in either case the value does not increase. It is only when you meet your preset objectives and in addition add value in other ways, creating positive impact in areas not expected, that your professional value truly increases. Like business, positive changes in expectations are what move careers.

The Language of Successful Risk Taking

Changing the assumptions often requires taking calculated risks. One way for individuals (and managers) to encourage appropriate risk taking is to make it safer to take risks. But how do you actually do that? One simple but powerful way is to change the language you use. For example, the word, *experiment* is much safer than *business plan*. Properly set up, experiments should never fail. Rather, they should prove or disprove a hypothesis. The learning from an experiment can be adjusted and cycled back into the thinking so that over time assumptions are changed. Business plans, on the other hand, are much riskier, because they are either met or not met. Business plans that do not meet their objectives are usually killed—especially in the current economic climate. The key is to help your organization gain as much learning (and as much calculated risk) as possible before formal go/no-go decisions are made. When trying to sell your breakthrough idea to your management team, using the right language can help you increase the likelihood that your idea will be accepted, and mitigate the risks if for some reason your "experiment" doesn't succeed. Proper use of language can help you effectively become a positive change leader.

To illustrate in the extreme, some of the most spectacular successes in business history, Coca-Cola, Levi's blue jeans, and the 3M Post-it, for example, came from experiments gone awry. And one of the most successful new companies formed in the 1990s, eBay, has institutionalized the experimental approach to product development. They use the feedback loop of testing out new ideas on their customers, getting feedback, adapting based on their input, putting new features on the site, getting more feedback, and adapting again. It's a powerful process of sensing and testing for needs and responding accordingly. The chief executive officer of eBay, Meg Whitman, told us, "One of the philosophies of eBay has always been to watch the marketplace, see what is evolving, and then take a small step into it." She added, "We have a program called Voice of the Customer, which is our formalized customer feedback group with which we test out new ideas. They get to vote on all the things that happen on eBay."

. . . FIRE!

As you move from grandiose vision to implementation of specific objectives, it is important to remember to communicate early and often with your management and all related constituencies about the progress of your efforts. Figuring out what to do is really only half the battle. You then need to let your boss know why your energies will be spent on activity X instead of Y. That's not always as easy as it seems, and you need to have a prepared and logical reasoning for reconfiguring your job. Approach it as you would if you were trying to get funding for a new project. Try to stick to the business case of why you are doing what you are doing—that the benefits greatly outweigh the costs. What is the return to your boss of investing your resources in the way that you suggest? Use language to make it safer for your management to support nontraditional or assumption-questioning initiatives. Make sure as well that this reallocation of your efforts is aligned with the goals of your manager and will not neglect the priorities that will make him or her look good in favor of the ones that make you look good.

The more your ambitions veer away from your preset objectives, the greater the need to communicate—in both frequency and content. If you have identified new objectives and reprioritized them, your manager may not feel as much ownership and will need to be diligently kept in the loop to ensure total buy-in. With a change in priorities and expectations, it is critical that you communicate often with your boss to ensure that expectations on both sides remain consistent.

While delegation is difficult when you are getting ready, gaining context and triaging your job, or when you are aiming high with a breakthrough idea, turning your plan into action does not require doing everything alone. In fact, achieving the ultimate level of positive impact possible almost always requires leveraging a broad network of professionals. As we detailed in the pattern of benevolent leadership, achieving impact by your actions alone is not enough. The most successful people focus on succeeding through others on their team. But they are able to do something else as well—leverage their relationships, or more accurately their interconnectedness, to create even greater impact than they can alone.

More than ever, our increasingly interlinked business world depends on networks to make things happen. Contrast the famous story of Paul Revere with his historically anonymous counterpart, William Dawes. David Hackett Fisher, in his book *Paul Revere's Ride*, tells the story of Revere and Dawes setting out from Boston in different directions to warn the revolutionaries of approaching British soldiers.[3] But only Revere managed to inspire the colonists to take up arms. Down through the generations, few have ever heard about Dawes' ride, even though he rode with as much passion and speed as Paul Revere. The reason is that Revere was incredibly networked in towns dozens and even hundreds of miles away from Boston. He had the credibility of his network to get people to spring into action. Dawes, on the other hand, lacked a strong network of friends and associates. When he rode into a town with his message of crisis, he was met with disbelief and had to convince people one at a time. Starting with the same resources but vastly different networks, Revere was able to mobilize thousands more citizens around his cause than Dawes.[4]

Had Paul Revere not been so well connected, he would never have generated such a huge impact, and we might be writing this book in the King's English. Should you come upon an urgent need to mobilize resources around you, how effective would you be?

A more contemporary but perhaps no less successful example of leveraging a network to create impact and value is the case of John Doerr, senior partner of one of the world's best-known venture capital firms, Kleiner, Perkins, Caufield & Byers. Doerr is legendary for two things: (1) spending roughly 50 percent of his time recruiting CEOs and board members to Kleiner Perkins companies, and (2) weaving together his companies and his professional and personal relationships into a veritable *keiretsu* of interconnected mutually assured success. Almost everything he does, from leading an exploratory recruiting meeting to working with a management team, from reviewing investment opportunities to commenting in the press, is related to other company priorities, essentially amortizing any actions and time investment across multiple opportunities to create value.

Bringing this concept to life by making it even more approachable, consider the case of various senior functional roles across a company. If you are a treasurer or CFO, your ability to leverage your relationships with senior professionals in the financial services industry can help you raise funds for your company or put you in a position to review attractive investment opportunities before they are put out to auction. If you are a salesperson, your capacity to build on relationships that help to secure a sales meeting with a very busy potential customer or ensure that your company's products are at the top of your customer's list of budgeted purchases will help you be a higher performer. And if you are a purchasing manager, navigating and optimizing the set of vendor relationships will reduce costs, improve supply, and thereby add greater value to your organization.

The 20/80 principle requires a focus on things that are most important, and leverage of any available resources, such as a well-established professional network, to maximize that impact. Great value is placed on executives who can build influential relationships and make connections for the benefit of their firm—with customers, suppliers, partners, regulators, the financial community, and the business press. There is value at every point you touch in the network. The fact is that if you've achieved broad visibility and influence, you are much more valuable—and more secure in your position—than if you are known only within a small part of your company.

One criterion we often look for when doing an executive or board search is the extent of a candidate's network of professional relationships. In the case of two recent board director searches, we assessed prospective candidates partially based on the breadth of their network in media in one case, technology in the other. In the former case, our client company was looking to the new board director to be a catalyst for extending the company's consumer brands across different media platforms, such as television, radio, and online, through the right top-level introductions. In the latter case, the board concluded that it needed a member of the Silicon Valley community to keep it in the flow of new technology developments, attractive early-stage investment opportunities, and partnership possibilities. In both cases, the searches were successfully consummated, with directors bringing their networks of relationships with them for the benefit of their new companies.

At a personal level, your network of professional relationships can also serve as a sounding board or "personal board of directors" that can provide critical advice and support at key decision times. Scott Flanders, the CEO of $1 billion Columbia House, the world's largest direct marketer of music, videos, and DVDs, was a chief executive at age thirty. After an early career as a tax accountant, he rose up through the trade publishing field, becoming president of Macmillan Publishing Company and then founding an Internet firm called Telstreet before being recruited to Columbia House. Over his highly successful career, Flanders has cultivated a small senior-level brain trust, which has supported him increasingly over the past decade. His network includes several of his former bosses, who offer widely divergent counsel that he harmonizes with inputs from two close advisors. The advisors, who have a tight relationship with him, are a top-level human resources chief of a major corporation and a business consultant he has worked with for almost twenty years.

Flanders has relied on input and support from his advisors to make decisions, including whether to accept the offer to join Columbia House when it was a joint venture of Sony and Warner Music, whether to pursue a leveraged buyout for the company, and how to structure the board of directors for the now privately owned company. Columbia House went private in a major LBO led by the Blackstone Group in mid-2002. When discussing his supporting network, Flanders, a voracious student of corporate strategy, business history, and business philosophy, pointed to Napoleon Hill, the renowned author and motivator. Hill detailed the concept of a "master mind group" in his influential book, *Think and Grow Rich,* written in the 1930s. Working closely for twenty years with legendary mogul Andrew Carnegie in the later years of his life, Hill concluded that one of the keys to Carnegie's success was creating a small group of trusted people to serve as his personal network. The job of the "master mind group," according to Hill, is to help you think through important issues, challenge you and support you. As Flanders emphasized, the advantages from such a group are both economic and psychological, with these influential participants becoming invested in your success.

When cultivating your network, there is an important principle to understand: *It's not only what you know or whom you know, but also who knows what you know that counts.*[5] Traditionally, an executive's network consisted largely of others within the organization. To be successful today, you must build a network that consists of numerous contacts inside and outside your direct working environment. You certainly don't have to become a regular commentator on CNN or an invitee at the World Economic Forum in Davos, Switzerland. But the principle to follow is to network with the *right* people and make sure they think positively about you.

In every community and every industry there are those known as "power networkers" who seem to know everyone and everything that is going on, and revel in the perception that they are the center of attention. But although their networks of contacts are often quite large, few have relationships that are deep and trusting. What others think about you, in the end, is much more important that just knowing you. Any network can be valuable in a career, and a network in which relationships are deeper, built on trust and respect earned over time, is one of the most valuable career resources of all.

Know that only a small minority of those you network with are likely to impact your career meaningfully. Identify those most likely to be influential, and get to know them. The key is quality of contacts, not quantity. Who are the five most respected analysts who cover your industry? How can you be helpful to them so they can in turn be supportive of you? Who are the beat reporters covering your industry for the major trade journals and business press? How can you assist them as a knowledgeable and reliable source of insight (ideally with the coordination of your company's corporate communications department)? Who are the executive recruiters who deal directly with your industry or functional specialty? If you refer attractive candidates for their searches, would they be more likely to help you when the time comes for you to be open about new opportunities? Who are the few people whom you should make aware of your recent successes? Find them, meet them, cultivate them, and become valuable to them. They will, in turn, become invaluable to you.

Another important lesson about building networks while in a leadership position is that trade-offs are often required. As Dale Carnegie's famous book accurately stated, success usually necessitates "winning friends" and "influencing people."[6] But in a leadership role, it is quite often impossible to do both. Getting along with others is critical in any job setting. However, leadership usually requires making tough decisions, upsetting the applecart, and disappointing people. If everyone likes you, you have probably had little impact on the organization. High impact performance requires making tough calls, differentiating performance among peers, and choosing winners and losers. Avoiding these tough decisions will ultimately lead to complacency. Staying in the middle is mediocrity.

MAKING THE COMPLEX SIMPLE

On June 3, 2002, Greg Brenneman became CEO and president of PricewaterhouseCoopers Consulting (PwC Consulting). Due to the SEC requirement that accounting firms such as PwC separate their consulting businesses to eliminate conflicts of interest, PwC Consulting recruited Brenneman to lead a spin-off of the firm. In only a few short months, Brenneman put in place a plan to restructure the business, brought in a new management team, and prepared for an IPO with credible financial projections and operating plans reviewed by several of Wall Street's top financial analysts. In the face of a very difficult business environment with revenues declining across the entire industry, he quickly focused the organization and was able to increase profits 80 percent. The efforts led to a strategic sale to industry leader IBM for $3.5 billion, a significant premium over the anticipated IPO value. The merger of IBM Global Services and PwC Consulting created the largest IT services business in the world, with over $100 billion in revenues, and resulted in a more attractive career path for the partners and staff of PwC Consulting. In October 2002, Brenneman returned to his firm, TurnWorks, Inc., a Houston-based private equity firm that focuses on corporate turnarounds. Brenneman's story of squeezing the equivalent of years of work into mere months at PwC Consulting, quickly bringing focus to a complex, global organization, is an extraordinary example of implementing the 20/80 principle of performance.

Brenneman had earned his stripes and a national reputation as an extraordinary business executive by co-leading one of the most dramatic and successful corporate turnarounds in American business history. From May 1995 to May 2001, Brenneman was president and chief operating officer of Continental Airlines, and together with chairman and chief executive officer Gordon Bethune, Brenneman led the airline back from the brink of what would have been an unprecedented third bankruptcy to a position of market leadership. During his tenure, the carrier turned sixteen years of losses into twenty-four straight profitable quarters, lifting the stock price from $6.25 per share to over $120 (pre-split). Continental also turned an operation that consistently ranked last in Department of Transportation measures of on-time performance, baggage handling, and customer complaints into the most consistent, reliable carrier in the United States. Under Brenneman's leadership, Continental earned numerous awards, including the J. D. Power and Associates award as the best airline for four out of five years and the Freddie Award for the best frequent flyer program for four years in a row. In addition, Continental went from being one of the least admired companies in the United States, ranking 499th out of 500 on *Fortune*'s list of the most admired companies, to being ranked as one of the 100 best companies to work for by *Fortune* in 1999, 2000, and 2001.[7] The carrier finished eighteenth on the list in Brenneman's final year.

Brenneman went to Continental from the consulting firm Bain & Company at the tender age of thirty-three, but already he had been the youngest vice president (partner) ever to be elected to the firm's Worldwide Policy Committee (Executive Committee of the Bain board of directors). He was co-founder of the firm's Dallas office, which was considered one of the most successful office start-ups in Bain history. At Bain, one of his major clients became Continental Airlines. His impact serving Continental (in the aircraft maintenance area) was so significant that legendary investor David Bonderman, the company's lead investor, through his firm, Texas Pacific Group, and Gordon Bethune recruited Greg to come over as president.

The story of how Brenneman and Bethune turned around Continental Airlines has been well told elsewhere.[8] To summarize, Brenneman brought focus and discipline to a very complex environment. He and Bethune created and implemented their "Go Forward Plan," a straightforward but powerful action plan that had four key priority areas: the market plan, the financial plan, the product plan, and the organization plan. They and the company's management team followed the plan to the letter.

After his remarkable Continental tenure, Brenneman wanted to do it again and demonstrate that the principle of focusing on the right value-adding priorities and implementing the right plan works not only in airlines but in other industries as well. Joining PwC Consulting, he could not have chosen a more different type of company to lead. Instead of a heavily capital-intensive, fixed-cost company subject to economic and oil price cyclicity, he now was leading a talent-driven professional services organization where the main variables were people and clients. The story of Brenneman's leadership of PwC Consulting has not generally been told, but as we learned in our interviews, he applied the 20/80 principle of performance to extraordinary effect.

With approximately $5.5 billion in revenues, PwC Consulting was an organization operating in fifty-three countries with thirty-four thousand employees, twelve hundred of whom were partners. While all was on track for the IPO, the firm was approached by IBM, and after several weeks of intense negotiations, the IPO was scrapped and the IBM deal was signed. The ultimate price of $3.5 billion when the deal closed in October 2002 compared very favorably to the IPO estimated price, or "price talk," of $2 billion to $2.5 billion. More importantly, it was the end value favored by the partners, who approved the deal with a vote of over 99 percent.

Brenneman told us understatedly, "We got a pretty good premium on the sale." Some analysts compared the price unfavorably to a previously announced but not consummated deal by Hewlett-Packard to acquire PwC Consulting at the height of the technology bubble in 2000. Despite the fact that HP ultimately rejected the deal as too pricey, this still sounds like quite a comedown, but as Brenneman said, "If you adjust the offer for the decline in HP's stock, since a lot of the proposed deal was for stock, the deal today would have been valued at under $2 billion."

So whether it was six years at Continental Airlines or less than six months at PwC Consulting, how does Brenneman approach turnarounds or business problems in general? What could he have possibly done in such a short time at PwC Consulting? "Whether it was at Bain, Continental, or PwC," Brenneman said, "my approach is basically the same. I think about the business by dissecting the problem into the most important component parts. Then I work on creating a plan for each component. In order to be a great company, you need to develop and implement a great but simple plan anyone can understand." Of course, the plan needs to be tailored to the company, the industry, and the situation, but in Brenneman's view, any good plan has four cornerstones:

1. **The market plan:** What are the issues facing the company? What are the markets you serve? Where are you going? What do you have to do to be successful?

2. **The financial plan:** How do you fund your efforts?

3. **The product plan:** How are you going to deliver a service that customers value and want to buy?

4. **The people plan:** How are you going to create a place where people like coming to work every day?

And critical to the plan is to measure it. Every part of the plan has associated metrics. "What gets measured gets managed," Brenneman said, "At PwC Consulting, we essentially did the same thing as we did at Continental. I had a great management team, and we wrote the plan even more quickly, in the first three weeks. When IBM called, I was in Amsterdam with the top hundred and seventy partners, and we had just finished rolling out PwC's version of the 'Go Forward Plan.'" It read as follows:

1. The market plan was "Grow Our Business." The end goal there was top-quartile revenue growth.

2. The product plan was "Deliver Results for Clients." The ultimate goal was to create a superior reputation with clients versus peers.

3. The organizational and people plan was "Working Together." Here the aim was to create a place where people like coming to work.

4. The financial plan was "Fund the Future." This called for the company to achieve top-quartile profit margins.

A simple, straightforward plan, to be sure. But you may think it seems too simple. A focus on growth, quality performance, teamwork, and profits—surely every company must consider these factors in management. But as happens within so many large, complex organizations, PwC Consulting had simply lost focus. In effect, it was the clarity of this straightforward plan that made it so powerful, allowing the organization to become aligned around it so quickly, and resulting in numerous creative, breakthrough approaches to these classic objectives.

The firm was able to energize and grow current client relationships and also establish and renew critical relationships within the broader organization, mapping consulting partners to the corresponding audit partners on the PwC side to maintain a powerful network. The management team developed action plans for pursuing new markets, new clients, strategically investing capital, and rebranding the firm. And they spent a good deal of time stressing a new focus on a culture of open, honest communications with all employees, and then creating and aligning meaningful incentives around all of these initiatives.

One of the specific goals was to achieve best-in-class client satisfaction, which meant on-time and on-budget projects that delivered the promised results. "We implemented measurements that included getting external client feedback in the form of independent client surveys. I knew that as a consultant, if we delivered on-time and on-budget projects that did what we said we'd do, we'd win, because so few do." The firm even took the unusual step of linking compensation directly to the results of the client surveys. Neither Brenneman nor we are aware of any other professional services firm that so directly links pay to a client's view of performance.

The executive team also relentlessly pursued profits. "When I got there, one of the first things we did was to reevaluate marketing expenditures," Brenneman said. "It became immediately clear that the marketing dollars weren't being spent well. They weren't going toward value-added or thought creation pieces; it was just getting squirreled away in small places where it had no impact. We were spending one dollar in sixty million places versus spending fifteen million dollars in one or two places to really drive value."

Brenneman's attitude and approach to marketing expenditures is significant in that it underscores the point of the 20/80 principal of performance. The key is to figure out where the value is and put the focus and the resource against that.

"We finished the quarter ending September thirtieth, 2002, which would have been our first quarter as a public company, with revenues flat to down about five percent. But our profits were up eighty percent. This was all based on just bringing focus and discipline to drive business and deliver value to clients, but also managing costs to match the revenue stream of the business. Rather than simply reacting to staff utilization metrics, often with surprise, as had historically been done, we started looking out three or four months ahead, more diligently figuring out what our stream of business was going to be and then proactively managing our capacity to the business. That is what allowed us to dramatically increase profits."

If it sounds like Brenneman crammed a couple of years of work into four months, it's true. "Yes, you wouldn't get much debate about that," Brenneman added. But he wasn't the first talented leader of PwC Consulting; there were a lot of other smart people at the helm over time. How did he manage to get some of the most fundamental things done that eluded others?

One of the keys was Brenneman's ability to quickly provide focus, challenging previous assumptions and creating an environment where breakthrough thinking around critical objectives can flourish. He has a keen ability to make the complex simple. It is important to emphasize that simple is not the same thing as simplistic. "Making it simple is the key," Brenneman said. "Here is a good Continental example. If we asked, 'How do we make Continental profitable again?' people would take you through mind-numbing detail, route by route, on the yield, the load factor, the average fare, and how to get these up. You could spend days in meetings like that. Or you could simply say, 'We're going to stop doing anything that loses money,' and you draw some lines in the sand. You know what? Everyone understands that the fastest way to make money is to stop losing money. All of a sudden, the complex becomes simple. However complex an issue is, if you step back and simplify it so that anyone in the company, from the CEO on down, can understand it, then put it in words and a format so that people can remember it, then it can be addressed. The value is in the simplicity. But just because the thoughts end up being simple doesn't mean that the thoughts always start simple. As a manager, you know the issues are complicated; you have a million things going on in your mind, and there are a hundred variables and assumptions. But you have to keep asking, 'How do you cut through it to get all thirty-five thousand people to do something?' And doing something that is directionally correct, even if it isn't perfect, is much better than having a perfect plan that doesn't get done." Perhaps Justice Oliver Wendell Holmes said it best when he commented, "I wouldn't give a fig for the simplicity this side of complexity, but I'd give my life for the simplicity on the far side of complexity." Working with highly skilled team members, Greg Brenneman has been able to break down complex business situations into simple, understandable, and manageable objectives, with dramatic results, time after time.

THE VALUE OF 20/80 MANAGEMENT

Knowing how to implement the 20/80 principle of performance within your career is indeed one of the key patterns of extraordinary careers. Applying this pattern can help steer your career in a desired direction, akin to steering a ship at sea. After you get out of port and start steaming along, it takes a great deal of effort to change course. Tremendous momentum and inertia build up over time. Similarly within a career, there is only so much you can do to change this in the short term. Keeping the engines running and the ship on course is like the 80 percent of your job that's focused on accomplishing your required and predefined objectives. It's the 20 percent that can be freed up and focused on adding the greatest value—the majors of your job— that will allow you ultimately to steer your career in one direction or another.

Throughout this chapter, we have illustrated how the 20/80 principle works in conjunction with the pattern of benevolent leadership. But the 20/80 principle also works with resolving the permission paradox to achieve your desired level of success. Consistently execute the 20/80 principle, and people's perception of you will be enhanced. You will become known as someone who thinks strategically about how to increase the value of your company. Performance isn't just a quantitative measure—who gets the most work done, or even who has generated the greatest sales, profits, or cost savings. Success is built equally upon qualitative judgments, such as being perceived as the person to go to when there are tough problems to be tackled. It's the basketball equivalent of having three seconds to play in the game: Do you want the ball? If you are able to earn this perception of credibility, permission for critical roles will usually follow.

In the late 1980s, Lynn Martin, then secretary of labor, led an effort called the Glass Ceiling Initiative, studying if and why there were limits to women's careers in business. "Not surprisingly," she told us, "the study did find limitations. One of the primary factors found for the lack of promotion among women was that in many cases they were perceived by their superiors as not desiring a promotion. It was assumed—or inferred—that women would not be willing to do what it took to get ahead, such as relocate, take an international assignment, or make the necessary personal trade-offs. These presumptions turned out to be incorrect, as many of the women passed over had actually been very interested in the opportunities—they were just never asked." Martin's work helped to educate many in corporate America to not let stereotypes influence who is and is not given access to critical opportunities. But we strongly encourage you not to leave access to these opportunities to fate. Let others know of your interest for such assignments. Before someone will offer you a big opportunity, you must be perceived as wanting it.

USING THE 20/80 PRINCIPLE TO BREAK INTO TOP MANAGEMENT

Through our professional experience in the recruiting and promotion of hundreds of top executives, we have distilled four governing principles about switching positions: (1) it is relatively easy to move from one company to another company in the same function (especially in the momentum phase of your career, where you are drawing on your experiential value); (2) it is relatively easy to move from one function to another within the same company (especially if you are a strong performer and the next role builds on the prior one); (3) it is more difficult to move from one company to another in a new function (since neither your track record nor relationships and trust have yet been established); and (4) it is very challenging to break from a functional role into general management (because, as described in "Overcome the Permission Paradox," most companies want general managers who have been general managers before).

So how do you branch out from a functional area into general management? Apply the 20/80 principle of performance by freeing up capacity to broaden your responsibility and finding ways to have impact on the most value-adding priorities for your company. Let's take sales as an example. While it seems notoriously difficult for a salesperson to become a general manager, sales professionals actually have an advantage. Revenue growth is always an overriding concern in business, especially in difficult times, and success ensures you'll get a disproportionate share of attention from top executives. But breaking out of sales into general management is still a challenge because top management usually considers sales leaders top-line-focused versus bottom-line-oriented, or lacking the strategic skills to lead the organization. However, a pattern we've observed starts with strong salespeople being awarded a sales team or region to manage. After that, we've seen heads of sales make the case to add customer service to their fold. Then they start thinking about marketing, which is one of the most common launchpads for general management. A clear example of this is George Conrades, the chairman and CEO of the Massachusetts-based software company Akamai Technologies. Conrades, one of the most talented—and persuasive—executives in the technology industry, rose through the sales ranks at IBM to become the head of the company's North American business. Over time he used the opportunity to garner customer and market feedback and cycled it through the product development, marketing, and customer service operations. Known as a strategic market and people leader who made things happen, he added function after function on the way to running the multi-billion-dollar P&L. With his IBM general management card punched, he was a natural choice to become CEO of two high-growth technology companies, culminating with his current role at Akamai.

However, if you are the sales chief or any other functional head, you are presumably not the only person in the company who wants a shot at running the marketing department. Given all the competition, there are several ways you can expand your purview. Even without a formal expansion of responsibility, you can steer the focus of your activities, applying the 20/80 principle to start thinking and acting like a top manager. Become known inside your company, as did Conrades, for helping the marketing and product development teams get the best insights from the marketplace. You already have a great vantage point if you're in sales. Use your customer-facing platform to help your company transform from a "make and sell" operation, which tends to operate in a more linear fashion, into a "sense and respond" organization that is more market-sensitive than your competitors.

If you can help make this work, you will have not only a better opportunity to join the general management ranks, but also more confidence to meet the next challenge and succeed.

With the 20/80 principle of performance now squarely in hand, let's move on to putting this pattern together with the others to think differently about success itself. We want you to find the right fit in a role that plays to your strengths and passions and enables you to work with people whom you like and respect.

FIND THE RIGHT FIT (STRENGTHS, PASSIONS, AND PEOPLE)

Failure's hard, but success is far more dangerous. If you're successful at the wrong thing, the mix of praise and money and opportunity can lock you in forever.
—Po Bronson

When love and skill work together, expect a masterpiece.
—John Ruskin

THE EXTRAORDINARY CAREER DEFINED

What does it mean to achieve an extraordinary career? We've been throwing that term around quite a bit. Part of the mission of this book is to give you tools for success. But another important task is to define and expand what it means to have an extraordinary career.

After thousands of interviews and countless hours of analysis, we've developed our own idea of what constitutes career success. Here's a hint: It's nothing like what many people imagine. For many folks, getting top dollar for a top position is about as far as they think. We're talking about something else. For us, an extraordinary career depends on three critical elements:

You must:

1. Play to your strengths
2. Set your passions free
3. Fit in naturally and comfortably with your work culture

Attain these three things in your working life and contentment will reign within your borders. Our research revealed that extraordinary executives lead careers that leverage both their strengths and their passions *more than six times as often* as average employees. The implication of these findings is profound: Not only is it possible to leverage both your strengths and passions in the same job, but success actually requires it.

Of course, it's not all that easy to find the perfect workplace where you fit in, love what you do, and were born for the job. Many people spend a lifetime looking for it. That's all right. In fact, just knowing that this is what makes a successful executive gives you a leg up on the competition.

Jim Head was blessed with exceptional intelligence and interpersonal skills, but he felt as though he had almost been cursed by his competencies. Head graduated from Vanderbilt University with a liberal arts degree, near the top of his class. Soon after, he completed Vanderbilt Law School, again finishing near the top of his class and making the prestigious law review. He was a shoe-in for a job at a topnotch law firm.

"Graduating from law school, I felt as if my career was on a conveyor belt. It was all too easy to get seduced into the cutthroat competition for positions with the best law firms. And given the opportunity, it would have seemed like lunacy to not accept one of the most coveted

Extraordinarily successful executives lead careers that fully leverage both their strengths and their passions *more than six times as often* as the average employee.

spots. The most successful among us felt as if we were destined for a big firm in a major metropolitan area. It is ironic that in retrospect, the better you performed and the more talented you were, the fewer options you felt you had."

So Head got on the track and joined a prestigious law firm. After two years toiling away on "important" cases that positioned him squarely on the partner path, he began to have second thoughts about his work and his direction. It wasn't until a friend pointed out his visible lack of enthusiasm for the law that he considered whether there were indeed other, more exciting career alternatives. After some reflection, he concluded that his seven years of academic training and two years of sixteen-hour days made starting over from scratch not a viable option. All the same, he longed for a job that drew on a long-suppressed interest—creative businesses. So he left the large firm for a smaller, regional law firm that had a strong media practice. He actively sought to work with media clients and eventually got his turn to work with several of the firm's most prominent clients on the West Coast.

It wasn't long before Head developed an expertise in copyright law, business affairs, and contracts—the core of the media business. After a few years, with skills and reputation established, he was offered a permanent position as in-house counsel for Atlanta-based Turner Broadcasting, the giant cable programming company with networks from CNN to TNT. Once at Turner, Head was able to reorient his work and complete his major career refocus with a move into production. "Fortunately, through aggressive cajoling I managed to convince an amazingly enlightened programming executive that I was actually a budding programmer trapped in a lawyer's body," he told us. Head became a programming executive for one of the Turner networks, and he displayed a natural talent for the role. His knack for developing and scheduling programs immediately showed results, increasing the network's target audiences, which helped him evolve from a role in scheduling to one in acquisitions to the head of nonfiction original programming, and finally to developing and producing original movies, series, and TV specials. "I met with success, largely because I was finally following my heart in my career," he says. "With my strengths and passions coinciding, my career really took off."

Jim Head's story marks a common trajectory shared among the extraordinary executives we know and have studied. In fact, finding the right fit is perhaps the most common of all the patterns of extraordinary careers. If you think back to the varied individuals profiled throughout this book, from the panel of college alumni in the introduction to Lou Gerstner, Greg Brenneman, Elizabeth Dole, Dan Rosensweig, Dennis Lacey, Dick Metzler, Dennis Gouyout, Rich Bray, David Hood, Michael Reene, and Arthur Levitt, each and every one has found a way to migrate toward situations that play to their strengths and interests.

But true success and satisfaction, in the end, are goals that need to be defined by each of us in a way that is consistent with our own aspirations and values. We are confident that applying the first four success patterns outlined in the book so far will help you improve your value significantly in the marketplace. But it is how you use this value, how you invest the career capital that you will accumulate, that really counts.

SO CLOSE, YET SO FAR

Find your strengths, passions, and cultural fit and you will be happier and more successful in your career. How simple indeed.

Yes, the logic behind this pattern for success is simple and straightforward. So with its simplicity, it would be safe to assume that the majority of competent and thoughtful professionals would be able to navigate their way to desired strengths, passions, and people, as did Jim Head. Given the clear-cut nature of this principle, what percentage of professionals do you think are in jobs that maximize their

"I don't know Al. On the one hand, there's no doubt that it's a make work, dead-end job, but, on the other hand, it's also a vice-presidency."

©2003 *The New Yorker* Collection from cartoonbank.com. All Rights Reserved.

strengths and where they are passionate about their work and the people they work with? How many professionals have replicated this critical pattern of extraordinary careers?

Nine percent! Yes, only 9 percent of those we surveyed believe they are in jobs that fully leverage their strengths, performing activities that they are passionate about in an energizing environment and with people that they like and respect. And remember once again that our survey was strongly biased toward professionals who had succeeded greatly in their careers. Therefore, they are in positions of influence, presumably with a much greater ability to navigate their careers toward their strengths, passions, and people than an average professional. Yet even in this group of successful executives, fewer than one in ten had managed to replicate this success pattern in their own career. This ratio, it should be pointed out, is generally consistent with what we've observed in our professional recruiting practice, which has allowed us to interview roughly three thousand executives over the past ten years.

For most people, understanding the logic of finding the right fit for your career—focusing on strengths, passions, and people—is intuitive, even obvious. Virtually everyone desires such a career. And as the statistics have played out, finding your ideal fit will result in improved performance and higher levels of success. However, it is how you go about trying to put this pattern into action that becomes much more challenging.

CAREER PUSH VERSUS CAREER PULL

The statistics that link success and satisfaction to finding your ideal career fit are motivating. But before you can embark on the task of getting there, you need to understand better the reasons that the great majority of working people never succeed in this journey. If you are like many of the professionals we have researched, success may require forgetting some of what you have learned.

A common way that many people think about managing their careers—either consciously or subconsciously—is something we call career push. This entails pushing to climb from one step on the career ladder to the next, and the next, and the next. Knowing the pitfalls of this approach will help explain why so many people are unable to implement the straightforward pattern for success and satisfaction.

In a typical professional progression, it is common for people to try to push their careers along the customary advancement track, from manager to director to vice president to president, or from analyst to associate to principal to managing director. This is all fine and well; however, many people find, partway up the ascent, that their ladders were leaning against the wrong wall. They find themselves in a career that was never meant to be—one defined by others or followed for the wrong reasons. "My grandfather was a lawyer, my father was a lawyer, so there was never any discussion about whether I would become a lawyer." Or "I wanted to make money so I followed the advice to go to where the money is, Wall Street." But all too often, this leaves you stuck in a rut or feeling locked into a path that is carrying you further and further away from your true desires. In the words of Johann Wolfgang von Goethe, "People are so constituted that everybody would rather undertake what they see others do, whether they have an aptitude for it or not."

Sometimes, in coming to the realization they are climbing the wrong career ladder, people abruptly jump toward a different path that seems as if it will be more fulfilling. If you're lucky, this may help solve the problem, but it's more often just a desperate grasp at straws. The bottom line is that following the career push approach risks leading you to one of two treacherous outcomes: staying stuck on the wrong track or becoming derailed altogether.

The seductive influence of pay, prestige, and peer influence can lead you to evaluate these opportunities based on the wrong criteria and push your career off course. During the height of the economic euphoria of the late nineties, many considered leaving stable and secure positions with blue-chip companies to take their shot with a start-up company that supposedly was bound for glory. The stories of success and wealth creation were almost blinding, and looking back, it seems that in just this short period of time, there were more misguided career decisions made than had occurred in decades prior. But one such career disaster was avoided.

John Lemming, as we have renamed him at his request, was being highly recruited to Realestate.com, a pre-IPO company that was planning to go public within the next three months. As a typical dot-com, it had a catchy name, a $40 million marketing budget, and almost no revenue. It was even suggested that Goldman Sachs and Morgan Stanley were fighting over the opportunity to take the company public. John loved his current job, earned excellent compensation, and was on a fast track with a well-known and respected company. Yet he was being aggressively recruited to join Realestate.com as executive vice president of business development, with an equivalent salary and stock options that by all accounts were likely to be worth millions on paper in only a few months. Up until that point, he had been very cautious when managing his career, but with such a lucrative offer coming at him, it was hard for him to ignore it.

John was torn. He was already occupying a role that took advantage of his strengths and passions; plus, he was respected by his peers and enjoyed his work environment. Add to that the fact that the new job came with a bevy of question marks. Was the company really as well positioned as the founder and investors said? Were the realtors really going to play ball on the company's terms because they did not have an alternative? Would the major online firms really want to do deals with the company versus getting into the sector themselves? Did he have the right skills to master the business development game? And more importantly, did he really respect and fit into the group of people who had assembled this company from almost nothing overnight? The more he asked for people's advice, the more he was told that these questions were normal for someone getting ready to make the leap. He was told that if he didn't do it now, he might never do it and would live to regret it his whole career. Did he have what it took to reach for his shot at greatness? And after all, the role was prestigious and the money was good. All told, the pressure to dive headlong into the new opportunity was overwhelming.

So he pushed, verbally accepting the position and giving two weeks' notice to his current employer. Everyone congratulated him on his impending windfall. John felt unusually comforted by the supporting comments of his peers, making it easy to rationalize his internal questions about strengths, passions, and fit for the job. Then, the day before he was to have started in his new position, he froze. In his head, John knew this was a sure thing, but in his heart he wasn't so sure. John delayed his start date for two days, then a week, and ultimately turned down the offer, never able to get completely comfortable with his decision. A few months later, the stock market collapsed, and Realestate.com began its long slide into bankruptcy, ultimately worthless, sued by its major investors, and leaving the reputation of some of its original executives in tatters. Instead of a sure thing, taking that job would have resulted in a major setback in John's career. "I am not really sure what happened," John Lemming told us. "But I do know that God gave me a get-out-of-stupidity-free card. I hope I never need another one!"

This is not to say that any job change John Lemming could have made would have been wrong, but in retrospect, it seems like avoiding this one involved such a simple decision. He was being recruited to a job that was not aligned with his strengths, passions, or cultural fit, so it should have been easy to just say no. But it was compensation, prestige, and peer influence that emerged as the most powerful factors in the evaluation process, clouding his judgment and begging him to take the job. What should have been an easily avoided disaster became a career close call. Far too many manage their career as though they were lemmings. But ultimately, successful people learn an important lesson: *Success through the eyes of others does not equal satisfaction and fulfillment through the eyes in the mirror.*

Although everyone longs to be happy in their career, it is not at all uncommon to succumb to the career advice of other people—well-intentioned advice based on someone else's values. Recruitments and promotions are usually accompanied by more prestige, greater compensation, and the accolades and envy of your peers—itself a form of compensation. And promotions are wonderful if you happen to be on the right path for you. Otherwise they can become tantamount to a harmful addiction. Letting promotions carry you by the hand through your career may lead to positions that are higher on the designated career ladder but which may not represent a best personal fit. This can then actually increase the risk of suboptimal performance and lack of professional fulfillment later on. Like pushing a string across a table, some people struggle to force something to work based on their desire to make it so. With each promotion, they are happy for a moment, but when the drudgery of the new day-to-day reality sets in, they try to rationalize their growing angst. "It's the price of success," they think. Or, even less realistically, they hold on to the notion that with just one more promotion the job will finally become more fulfilling and all their problems will be solved.

Pushing your career in this fashion along a profession's traditional path can easily lead to becoming deeply entrenched in a career that fades farther and farther away from your ideal fit. Alternatively, some become so frustrated with their current career direction that one day they give it all up, abruptly pushing their careers down a completely different path, like the lawyer who quits to become a writer, or the executive who leaves the corner office to start a corner coffeehouse. But although seemingly based on the right intent—the desire to move our careers toward the right fit—this type of career push, abruptly changing direction out of frustration, may have even more adverse consequences.

The problem is that it is easy to know when a job does not leverage your strengths, passions, and cultural fit. But quickly and accurately identifying a better alternative, without sufficient experiences to draw from, is like throwing darts blindfolded. You may admire, even envy others who are passionate about their jobs, having seemingly found their ideal fit, while inside you grow all the more frustrated that this clarity of passion has never emerged in your own career.

In a *Harvard Business Review* article entitled "How to Stay Stuck in the Wrong Career," Herminia Ibarra, a professor at Europe's leading business school, INSEAD, discussed why so many people fail to successfully redirect their careers toward what they are meant to be doing. "We like to think that the key to a successful career change is knowing what we want to do next, and then using that knowledge to guide our actions," she wrote. "But studying people in the throes of the career change process led me to a startling conclusion: Change actually happens the other way around. Doing comes first, knowing second."

Pushing your career in a direction you know is wrong and pushing it in a direction you are not sure is right share the same unfortunate outcome: failing to steer you toward your ideal fit.

CAREER PULL

There is a more effective approach to managing your professional journey—allowing your preferences for strengths, passions, and people to pull your career steadily in a better direction. Using the career pull approach requires allowing your career to migrate, often gradually, to the activities, roles, and environments you know from experience that you prefer and are most passionate about. It requires clear reflection, and in some cases making difficult choices, such as swimming against the current of traditional promotions, or turning down jobs others would envy. It requires taking the long view when managing your career, and thoroughly assessing through a variety of lenses the various career alternatives afforded to you.

The fact is, understanding yourself on a deeper level is very rarely the result of a dramatic epiphany or a brilliant flash of personal insight. Rather, knowing oneself is the result of a journey—success and failures, twists and turns—all the while reading the instruments, taking note of likes and dislikes, and learning to recognize your unique patterns of success. With this self-understanding, you are better positioned to allow your career to be pulled in the direction of greatest personal fit.

Dan Och was a talented young trader at Goldman Sachs. He joined the firm in 1982, straight out of the University of Pennsylvania. After the training program he earned a coveted spot as an apprentice on the firm's risk arbitrage desk, which took proprietary trading positions in announced merger transactions based on highly analytical research. Over the years his successful track record became firmly established, and Och developed into one of the most senior traders in the firm's equities division. But even as he was entrusted with more and more capital to invest, he began to long for the opportunity to strike out on his own.

Could he be as successful without the resources of Goldman? Could he build a great team that would enjoy working together? Could he raise funds with which to invest? After thinking long and hard about these increasingly burning questions, he finally got the right opportunity. In 1994, he was recruited by Ziff Brothers Investments (ZBI), a new firm founded by the three sons of legendary publisher William Ziff, which had $3 billion of capital to invest. The brothers' strategy was to find the very best up-and-coming investors in each type of investing area—equities, convertible bonds, debt, real estate, risk arbitrage, and so on—and put them into business. So Och formed Och-Ziff Capital Management, which was initially funded by ZBI, to invest in risk arbitrage and other heavily research-based trading methodologies. He was finally able to do the hard work of making his dreams a reality. Over the past nine years, Och has successfully built a world-class research, trading, and investment team and has had extraordinarily successful investment returns, which in turn have attracted an enormous amount of other capital to invest. Och's success was the result of being intensely self-aware, knowing what he wanted, knowing what he was great at, and finding the right calling that would put all of this together. While he was proactive at many points along the way, he also allowed himself to be "pulled" from his Goldman Sachs experience over to ZBI, where he could do what he was meant to do.

Och's story is an inspirational one of someone who found his fit by making a single strategic career adjustment. But successfully landing in your ideal career is rarely this pedestrian. Jim Head's story, on the other hand, is about a person who ultimately completed a successful career makeover, step by step. He navigated toward his ideal fit, and success and satisfaction followed. But it is the subtle but concrete way in which he accomplished this shift that holds perhaps the most valuable message of all. First, let's consider what Head did *not* do. As highlighted earlier, he refused to continue pushing his career blindly down a path that was predefined for him based on his strong performance and the educational decisions he made in his early twenties—a path for which he had a promising future but, as he grew to realize, minimal passion. Perpetually following a path that you are convinced is not right for you will certainly yield few extraordinary careers.

But Head did not suddenly abandon his legal career out of frustration based on the gut feeling that he should be doing something else. Sure, we have all heard stories of highly successful people who left a decent job to blindly pursue their dream, such as another former lawyer, John Grisham, who preferred writing about law rather than practicing it, or a young investment banker who gave up a promising early career to start a tiny operation called Martha Stewart Living, or Barry Sternlicht, the young real estate investor who seemingly overnight became the chairman of the world's largest hotel company, Starwood Hotels & Resorts. Such highly publicized stories make it tempting to spontaneously follow your heart via abrupt and dramatic career shifts.

But with this all-or-nothing strategy, successful outcomes are exceedingly rare. For one thing, as Ibarra rightly points out, if you haven't done something before, you truly don't know if you will like it or be good at doing it, especially on the consistent basis that makes something a job. Moreover, even if *you* are thoroughly convinced, you will need to convince others that your new direction makes sense and that you should be given the opportunity. This convincing takes a range of forms, from a job interview all the way up to trying to secure capital to finance your idea. Most people in a position to enable such career transitions evaluate candidates based on what they've done before.

Had Dan Och prematurely started out to build his own investment firm, he would not have had the trading experience, Goldman Sachs credibility, or investment track record to attract capital or other people. Had Jim Head abruptly abandoned his job as a lawyer to become a movie producer, he would have had as much chance of succeeding as the thousands of waiters, drifters, teachers, and others who flock every year to California with the same dream. His strong performance as a lawyer had given him momentum—experiential value—in the marketplace. Abandoning the legal profession entirely would have reset his career momentum at near zero, leaving him to rely solely on his potential to become a movie producer, which at the time, along with $4, would buy a grande mocha latte. And this is to say that at this early juncture in his career, Head was even capable of knowing that movie production was the right career for him. All he really knew was that continuing his career up the predictable ladder of a large law firm was not allowing him to fully leverage his passions, specifically his creative interests.

Instead, Head allowed himself to be pulled toward the right fit—taking incremental steps toward the career path that was uniquely right for him. He didn't reinvent his career overnight, but rather migrated from position to position, from the large law firm to a small boutique, from a job in the legal department within Turner Broadcasting to a support role in programming, and finally from scheduling and nonfiction production to developing and producing original movies, series, and TV specials.

Head also avoided the peer seduction of pushing his career up the structured ladder of the legal profession, and he did not succumb to his frustration and push his career abruptly in a different direction based on speculation about what a better job might be. Instead, he experimented with different roles, each time assessing what he liked and did not like about each position. He allowed his desire and passion for a more creative position to pull his career, step by step, with each move taking him a bit closer to his ideal vocation.

OPPORTUNITIES AND DECISIONS

The reason that people end up on one career path versus another is often a function of dozens, even hundreds of decisions made over time. Some decisions are small: "Do I go to my scheduled class or take the interview? How should I follow up on that introduction?" Some are large: "What industry should I target for my career? Should I focus on the corporate track or professional services? Which job offer should I accept?" The quality of your decision process will impact whether you progress toward or away from your ideal fit.

Through thousands of conversations with executives over the past ten years, we have distilled career decisions into a simple yet powerful framework. We call it the Career Triangle, because inevitably, as you evaluate career alternatives, three different things always come into play: job satisfaction, lifestyle, and compensation.

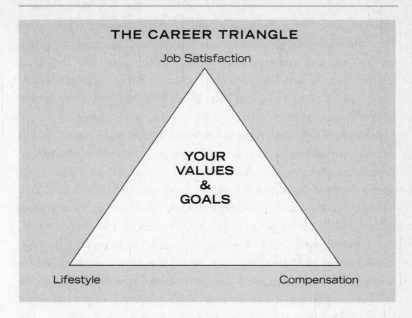

THE CAREER TRIANGLE

Job Satisfaction

YOUR
VALUES
&
GOALS

Lifestyle   Compensation

In our view, job satisfaction has everything to do with the quality of the job itself, how much impact you can have, the quality of the people you work with, the culture of the organization, the professional development opportunities, and the intellectual stimulation. Lifestyle has to do with the raw hours required of the job, of course, but it also incorporates how much control you have over your schedule, the distance and quality of your commute, the frequency, predictability, and class of the necessary travel, the amount of weekend work, and the amount of vacation time. Compensation includes salary, bonus opportunity, stock options, restricted stock, benefits, retirement plans, and perquisites, including social prestige. The reality is that these three elements are generally at odds with one another. It is relatively easy to maximize one of the points of the career triangle at the expense of the other two. It is more challenging but not insurmountable to solve for two of the three competing elements. But of course, the ultimate goal is to try to maximize all three elements of the career triangle simultaneously. We have found that it is a useful exercise to put each major career decision through the sieve of the three factors. For example, a career in journalism may rate very highly on job satisfaction, but this often comes at the expense of lifestyle and compensation. Journalists cover important news stories, have access to the most important people, and can aspire to winning the Pulitzer prize, but they work under intensive deadline pressure and suffer from the unpredictable timing of breaking news, and most of the journalists we know lament about low compensation levels. Other career paths heavy on the job satisfaction but lighter on the other two elements might include public service, the military, science, even the clergy. Careers that rate high on job satisfaction and lifestyle but lower on compensation, for example, might include book publishing or academia, whereas legal, Wall Street, high-tech, and consulting careers tend to rate highly on job satisfaction and compensation but give up severely on the lifestyle front.

How you define and then weigh the different factors is a function of your values (e.g., how do you define impact? What culture is best for you?), your goals (e.g., what do you want to achieve? In what time frame?), and where you are in your life (e.g., are you single with a ton of flexibility or a working parent with extensive demands on your time?). Each career decision will require you to make the best possible trade-offs, weighing one factor against another based on what your goals are, what phase you are at in your career, and where you are in your personal life.

WHAT ABOUT PRESTIGE AND COMPENSATION?

Here and in other areas of this book you have likely picked up on our strong bias against compensation as a factor in navigating your career. But this does beg the question many people ask: "If I make decisions based on strengths, passions, and people and downplay compensation and prestige, will I ever achieve high compensation and prestige in my work?" To answer this important question, let's break it down into pieces. First, we are not suggesting that you ignore compensation and prestige. They are important factors in any career decision. If ultimately they are not at levels you are comfortable with, it will surely impact your motivation and distract you from doing any job. But assuming compensation of different career alternatives is within a similar range (or at least above your perceived minimum), will downplaying compensation really reduce your potential to earn it? Actually, the research indicates quite the opposite. Those professionals from our survey who indicated that the number and quality of career options a position was likely to create was a greater influence on their career decisions than compensation ultimately were nearly 30 percent more satisfied with their compensation. The lesson? To be most satisfied with your compensation over the long run, you will be best served by ignoring it in the short run.

As for prestige, this too can be a seductive factor in a career decision, but often one with only short-term benefits. If you take on a role because it seems prestigious or is met with great peer approval but you are not sure of your strengths, passions, or cultural fit, you are much less likely to succeed in that role. And prestige and position over the long run can quickly become painfully elusive. By contrast, if you identify roles that maximize your personal fit, your natural success in these roles will ultimately lead to the highest possible levels of success for you.

The fact is that both compensation and prestige tend to be trailing indicators of career success. Although you may feel that you earn compensation for the work you are currently doing, in most cases you are paid at your current level based on the work you have done in the past.

As executive recruiters, our searches often result in offering executives increased levels of compensation for taking on new roles based on their previous successes. In most companies, as we discussed, a majority of promotions are experiential and are based on the impact that a professional has already had. But it is important to look more to the success you will likely have in any given role, the value you will create, the lasting positive impact you will have—and know that eventually pay, prestige, and peer approval will follow.

YOU *CAN* FIND THE RIGHT FIT

It turns out that executives such as Turner's Jim Head represent the exception that proves the rule. In every profession at every level, there are professionals who are unskilled, uninspired by their jobs, and unsure how they ever ended up there. But although the path forward at this point may not be obvious, you too, like the majority of extraordinary executives we analyzed, can steer your career in a direction that leverages your strengths, passions, and desired cultural fit.

Finding the right fit is not easily accomplished. But here are four strategies that detail the career pull approach that will get you closer and closer to the mark:

Manage Your Opportunities:

1. Macromanage your career.
2. Create career options.

Make the Right Choices:

3. Watch for career flares.
4. Work with the right people.

Macromanage Your Career

One of the most important things in navigating toward the right fit is keeping your career in the proper perspective. When you steer a sailboat, you always have to keep your eye on the horizon. Focus on the bow of the boat and you'll start veering left and right, trying to correct your course. But if you keep your eye on a fixed point on the horizon and tack now and then in the general direction you need to go, you'll stay on course.

Your career is much like sailing a boat. Many people focus on what's right in front of them, striving for the next raise, the next promotion, the next job. They micromanage their careers. Follow this kind of short-term strategy and you'll not only be constantly distracted but you may ultimately find yourself pointed in the wrong direction.

Successful professionals take a longer view. They *macromanage* their careers, keeping their eyes on the horizon, their long-term goals, while simultaneously navigating short-term conditions. The extraordinary executives in our survey were significantly more likely to focus on long-term goals, while less successful employees focused on the short term. That's not to say that the attention of successful executives isn't intensely focused on the task at hand; adding value to their current assignment is a way that differentiates their performance, of course. But their eyes are just as equally focused on the long-term prize. They understand the fundamental forces that drive their careers, the underlying patterns of success we've identified. They focus on the core values that drive their long-term career path, rather than on the peripheral distractions that influence their short-term career moves.

Larry Bossidy, the recently retired chairman and CEO of Honeywell, commented to us on the challenges that CEOs face in achieving long-term goals and making long-term investments while simultaneously meeting short-term objectives. His views are equally applicable to macromanaging your career. "I don't buy a lot of the crap that you have to meet short-term quarterly earnings at the expense of long-term investment and performance," Bossidy stated bluntly. He said doing either one is easy; accomplishing both simultaneously is more difficult. "The job of the CEO is to do both. You need to find the right balance between creating the right expectations and meeting your short-term quarterly objectives while finding a way to create the right investment for long-term growth." Wise words for the CEO, but also for you as you try to successfully navigate your career.

Macromanaging your career requires taking the long view. Like chess players, successful executives have the ability to think two, three, and four career moves ahead of where they currently are. In fact, when presented with opportunities others might jump at, they often turn them down. In Spencer Stuart's search for the chairman and CEO of AOL in the summer of 2002 (which was led by co-author Jim Citrin), we presented the opportunity to a highly regarded top executive from the technology industry. His comments demonstrate the self-awareness that underscored much of his already achieved success. "Challenging as the situation is, it actually sounds great. What an opportunity to take one of the world's most important companies to the next level. Would I love to have the pay and prestige associated with that job? Yes. Do I think I would be successful at it? Possibly. But I'm not so sure that my specific set of experiences line up with the task at hand and I don't really think I can put all of my heart into it. So I'm going to take a pass, as attractive an opportunity as it is." He was right, because the situation required experience and passion in consumer marketing, programming, and e-commerce, in addition to a strong understanding of technology. Happily for us and for AOL Time Warner, Jonathan Miller, who had been running the $3 billion set of e-commerce businesses for Barry Diller's USA Interactive (including Ticketmaster.com, Hotel Reservation Network, and Expedia.com), agreed that the AOL opportunity lined up beautifully with his strengths, passions, and people he liked and respected.

Why would anyone in their right mind turn down a great job? Because "great" is often a matter of someone else's definition of success, not yours. Successful people position themselves in jobs they know they're going to do exceedingly well at, where they will be excited to come to work nearly every day, rather than situations where they are likely to perform in a mediocre way.

They even allow themselves to drift along in the early stages of their career, gathering experiences in a wide variety of functional areas and naturally gravitating toward the things they do best and like the most. They don't try to force themselves up someone else's career ladder. They "drift strategically," however, testing out different points in the workplace to determine where their true strengths, passions, and fit lie. As we reviewed in "Understand the Value of You," this is one of the objectives for the promise phase of your career.

One executive who did just that is Jennifer Potter-Brotman. She began her career with Little, Brown and Company as an editor in the college textbook division. Although talented in her role, she felt that perhaps she was missing something. "Many of my colleagues seemed to have their career plan already ironed out before they were even thirty. They were intensely focused on holding specific positions by certain ages—rigid and determined about what they were supposed to achieve. At first, I felt that perhaps they knew something that I didn't. I enjoyed certain aspects of my work, but at that point I didn't really know what I wanted from a career," she conceded. "I took a different approach. During my twenties, I learned which capabilities I would need to develop to ultimately succeed at the highest levels within an organization, and I knew that gaining these skills required getting certain experiences. So in the back of my mind, I kept a watch out for these experiences, but I was never really concerned about when these opportunities would present themselves or what form they may take."

After three years with Little, Brown, she accepted an editorial role with the Forum Corporation, a leader in corporate training and education. She excelled within the company, consistently being promoted and loving her work, rising to the level of executive vice president and reporting directly to the president/CEO. Then one day, Potter-Brotman was called in by Forum's chairman, who urged her to consider taking an assignment leading the company's international business. She was flattered but was also concerned that the move was a lateral one at best, with the company's international business representing a small fraction of the company's revenue. In addition, she would no longer report directly to the president and CEO, but to another EVP who reported to the president. "I really wanted to take the job but couldn't help questioning if it was the right decision," she told us. She voiced her concerns to the chairman, who reminded her that a career is a longer-term journey and that being overly concerned with reporting structures or keeping score in the short term added little real value. Potter-Brotman accepted the position. She performed exceptionally well in Europe and was later called back to headquarters to become president, eventually being named CEO.

"People often confuse title and promotion with building competency and capability," she reflected to us wisely—an important distinction, to be sure.

Macromanaging your career successfully also often requires investing in your career when you can most afford it. There is a certain irony in a professional career in that work often requires the greatest personal sacrifices (travel, long hours) right when you are trying to raise a family. Baseball games, birthday parties, and other important family events often fall victim to deadlines and urgent priorities. Conversely, many young people in their twenties place a great emphasis on lifestyle, avoiding high-potential jobs that require an incredible work ethic. But those who make these sacrifices early often reap the rewards later on. They have accelerated their careers even as their peers are forced to later struggle to improve their career trajectory, while at home the kids are looking for time and attention. As best as you can, try to make the key personal investments in your career when you can most afford them.

But by the end of the promise phase you need to "declare a major," so to speak—you need to decide if you're going to pursue a corporate career, go into professional services, or move outside the business arena altogether. You need to determine if you'll shoot for general management, a creative position, functional expertise, and so on. And then you need to develop and master those specialized competencies so that you can pursue opportunities to be the best in your field and to develop skills that are transferable to other industries, which leads in turn to greater options in the future.

Drift, but drift with a focus on the end point—which is to be fulfilled and satisfied. Use your time to figure out what this means to you and which environment best matches that definition. Applying the 20/80 principle of performance can be helpful here. As you recall, this success pattern highlights the importance of the activities outside your predefined objectives on your ability to differentiate. But there is another advantage. What you do beyond your predefined tasks is largely under your control, allowing you an excellent opportunity to experiment. Think you would be happier managing indirect sales rather than direct? Curious whether you should abandon your accounting career for one that stresses strategy formulation? Before taking the plunge completely, use the 20 percent of your time and resources that are under your control to seek out opportunities for direct experience that will give you a much better indication whether your career intuition has any correlation with your real strengths, passions, and interests.

As did Jennifer Potter-Brotman, successful people set long-term, broad goals for success, identifying desired competencies and experiences, and they measure their progress against these goals. Even better than simply setting career goals, detail your aspirations across the key areas of your life and commit to them in writing. The very process of crystallizing what you want to achieve is a powerful first step. And once you write it, you will unleash much of your subconscious power to accomplish what you set out. One effective approach is to write a single page that synthesizes what you hope to achieve, contribute, and become in your key roles and key areas: professional, family member, friend, member of the community. Suggesting a personal mission statement is obviously nothing new. But all good ideas do not have to be new ideas. Use the page as a touchstone to come back to in times of decision making or at regular intervals, such as New Year's Eve or your birthday.

Success Means Creating Options

Now that you have gained insight on career decision making, you should seek to maximize the number of career opportunities available to you. The most successful people don't necessarily have the greatest number of degrees or make the largest amount of money. They have the most career options. An effective test of value comes from putting your major career decisions through the lens of this question: Does the move increase or decrease the number of career options available to you? Not only do successful people understand what drives value at every stage of their career, they have an uncanny ability to create attractive options for themselves.

Bill Matthes utilized a proactive approach to find his right fit. A financial whiz who worked as an analyst at the investment banking firm Morgan Stanley before business school, Matthes had always known he wanted a career in finance, ideally in private equity. When he graduated with an MBA in 1986, the financial services recruiters that came to interview on campus were the national commercial banks and New York–based investment banks. The hot boutique financial firms and the venture capital and LBO firms were noticeably absent, largely because very few MBAs were hired by these firms directly out of school. But Matthes was determined to consider this path and broaden his career alternatives.

First, as did many of his classmates, he interviewed with and secured offers from the top-tier investment banks, including Morgan Stanley and Goldman Sachs. With these offers in hand, he proactively looked beyond the campus recruiting process and approached several boutique firms that worked with smaller clients in equity financing.

Having excellent credentials but also having the validation of offers from the blue-chip firms, Matthes was able to initiate interviews and secure offers from the equity-raising firms Hambrecht & Quist and Alex, Brown. Then, with these other options in hand, Matthes further increased his possible career alternatives by proactively approaching the most relevant venture capital firms, successfully securing interviews and finally offers from two of the leaders, Boston–based Greylock Associates and Los Angeles–based Brentwood Associates.

He may not have even noticed it at the time, but Matthes' approach built on the competitive instincts of the firms themselves, in two directions—both horizontally, as with Morgan Stanley versus Goldman Sachs, and vertically, as with the large firms versus the small firms and then the small firms versus the VCs. Matthes' financial strengths qualified him for any of these positions, but with this many options in hand, he could fully evaluate his career decision based on his passions and preference for environment, beyond just his strengths. Ultimately, this led him to the uncommon opportunity to enter the venture capital industry straight from business school, joining Brentwood Associates. Had he limited his decision set to the opportunities presented to him through on-campus interviewing (as did most of his classmates), he would not have created the various options from which to choose. Only by proactively generating these additional opportunities could he fully explore and pursue his best alternative path. Today he is a highly successful partner with Behrman Capital, another leading private equity firm.

Career Options Have Value

You probably remember someone like Bill Matthes from your class in college or graduate school—someone who seemed to have it all. As others struggled to land a good job with graduation bearing down, these few were seemingly offered jobs from *everyone*. Their multiple offers contained value: The different options gave validation that encouraged other employers to extend offers, and it gave them the ability to choose, to consider various scenarios, and ultimately to align their individual goals and values with a particular job. They knew it, and you knew it. In a career, options have value.

Proactively and creatively generating numerous career options for yourself is hard work, but it can pay off. Happily, this is not always required, as nearly every job that you hold leads to its own set of career options, just as it provides compensation. Yet it is easy to underestimate, if not outright ignore, the value of these options in making career decisions. Far too many people spend painstaking hours evaluating opportunities that come their way, all the while ignoring the impact on career options.

In 1994, Princeton economics professors Avinash Dixit and Robert Pindyck published an insightful book titled *Investment Under Uncertainty*.[2] The book described the flaws in traditional approaches to capital investment, including such decisions as whether to invest in a new plant or product line. Traditional capital investment analysis, they said, stops at a determination of net present value (NPV), the current valuation of the total future revenue generated from undertaking an investment less the total expected costs related to that investment. "In any investment decision," they maintain, "the value of the 'creation or reduction of options' must also be considered."

For example, let's consider a large company that's contemplating a major technology upgrade with a total cost of $50 million. The costs related to the investment are straightforward: hardware purchases, software license fees, installation, and maintenance. The benefits have been painstakingly identified: increased productivity, ability to meet growth demands in existing markets, and reduced network down time. Using the traditional NPV approach, we simply subtract the present value of the costs from the expected benefits and arrive at a clean yes-or-no answer to our investment decision.

Not So Fast

What we have not yet considered is the impact of this investment on a company's *options*. For example, postponing an investment in a new technology platform has value. The value comes from the ability to wait and consider new products entering the market, which is similar to consumers who wait to purchase a new PC in the hopes of getting a better, cheaper product in the future. The moment we make an investment, we forgo the value of the option to wait. We incur an opportunity cost. Most of us live in a world of limited resources, and once resources allotted to a specific area have been spent, they're gone.

Not only does traditional NPV analysis ignore the cost of losing options that are presently available, it ignores the value of creating options as well. In the above example, the assumptions regarding the benefits of an investment ignore the value of any options that are created. This would include the option to expand into new product lines or the ability to more easily integrate an acquisition. These are actions that cannot be anticipated with certainty, and in many cases, cannot be predicted at all. Yet these options have created value, and this value must be considered in the investment decision and so too in a career decision.

A friend named Bill has used the options approach to evaluating career decisions to achieve extraordinary success. Many years ago, Bill was reviewing opportunities as he prepared to graduate from the University of Western Ontario's highly ranked business school. He entertained offers from a wide range of companies: large corporations, entrepreneurial ventures, banks, consulting companies. Of particular interest was an offer from McKinsey, but Bill was a bit concerned that the McKinsey offer paid less than many of his other offers, and considerably less than those of competing consulting firms.

Nevertheless, he valued McKinsey's reputation in the marketplace and felt that his loss of short-term compensation would likely be recouped in the future. He was right. Rather than focus on immediate compensation, Bill factored in the value of the career options that training, experience, and the McKinsey brand association could create. Within only a few years' time, he was being called by recruiters for positions well above those his peers at lesser-known firms were entertaining.

Bill stayed with McKinsey, eventually being promoted to principal and then director (senior partner). Only in his forties, he was not sure that he wanted to remain in consulting for the rest of his career, but he felt that at this stage, the longer he remained at McKinsey the fewer career options would become available. Competitive consulting firms rarely hired from their peers at this very senior level, and with his annual compensation in seven figures, he was priced out of the market for even most senior executive positions.

One day Bill was approached by the CEO of one of his longtime clients, a large industrial company in the Midwest, asking if he would consider joining the organization. Although the position was one of the top in the company, it offered only a fraction of his previous salary. On the surface, it would seem that no job would be worth such a sacrifice. But once again, Bill focused not only on the cash compensation, but on the career options he perceived this move would create. If he performed successfully as a division manager in this highly respected company, he would be well positioned to move up within the organization or to be recruited to larger roles within other, similar companies. And he felt he would retain the option to return to consulting if he so desired. Based on this evaluation of career options, he accepted the position. Ultimately he did succeed, and after building an operating track record of success he was eventually recruited away to become the CEO of a smaller, highly profitable competitor, a position he greatly enjoys, and one for which he would never have been considered had he not left consulting. By some accounts, Bill took a step back to move forward, but such is often required in the creation of an extraordinary career.

This impact of option value should also be a consideration for those who have decided to switch companies or careers. Should you resign first and focus full time on seeking a new employer or conduct a job search while still on the job? If you're still employed, you are not on a timeline and can comfortably wait until an opportunity arises that truly excites you, whereas if you leave, you must consider the lost value of your options the moment you quit. Unless you are independently wealthy, your perspective on a job search changes markedly the moment you *need* a job.

Even if you have a healthy severance package or have money saved up to cover your expenses during a job search, it's simply human nature when in a position of zero compensation to desire to get back on payroll quickly. Each week you are spending money, not earning it. Inevitably, the emotion of this situation will factor into your job decisions. We often hear the following from the temporarily unemployed:

"I know this job is not perfect, but it seems to be the best available, and I really need to get back to work."

In their article, Dixit and Pindyck comment that those investments with particularly high options components, such as investment in research and development, are the most inaccurately evaluated using traditional NPV analysis. Specifically, ignoring the option value results in a dramatic underestimation of the real value created. In a career, there are jobs and experiences that are analogous to R&D investments. These are the jobs and experiences that are likely to create a wealth of options in the future. It might be a management training program early in your career where you are given broad exposure to a number of functional areas and units within a company, or it may be a stint with a leading management consulting firm or investment bank.

Pursuing an MBA or other graduate training can also be viewed as an R&D investment in your career. If prospective students included

CAREER INVESTMENT DECISION: SHOULD I GET AN MBA?

Should you get an MBA? Clearly the costs are high: tuition, lost wages, room and board, etc. Yet the benefits, starting with an expected increase in compensation, are valuable. The traditional approach (chart 1) subtracts the costs from the benefits, with the analysis resulting in a net value of $0 after five years. Using this method, the decision to go or not is a toss-up. The options approach includes the value of the numerous opportunities that are created from earning an MBA. Using this approach, the net value is overwhelmingly positive; *get the MBA!*

the value of the options created by earning an MBA from a top school, the decision would be simple—the benefits are overwhelming.

Can the value of these career options be calculated quantitatively, as with an NPV analysis? In most cases, the answer is no. For a corporation, the benefits of a capital investment are mostly financial. In a career, most of the benefits of a decision are intangible, such as satisfaction with your work, an acceptable lifestyle, personal fulfillment, and so on. In fact, our research points out that the only truly quantitative metric, compensation, is one of the least important elements of career success and satisfaction.

So the next time you're confronted with a career decision, make sure to include the value of options gained and lost in your analysis. It just might lead you in a different direction—and lead to greater satisfaction. In the end, the more options you have, the easier it is to navigate toward jobs that leverage strengths, passions, and people.

Having learned how to maximize opportunities, and view them in the proper perspective, we must turn to the task of properly approaching our career decisions—focusing on strengths, passions, and people. Jim Head was not alone in feeling "cursed by his competencies," when he was a lawyer. The fact is that people who excel in one line of work are actually quite likely to excel in other areas as well. It's just a function of applying those things that you do well in a role and environment in which those strengths are highly valued. So it is actually tricky to make decisions based solely on an evaluation of your strengths. In many cases, therefore, it is easier to steer toward your ideal fit by looking toward your passions and toward people whom you like and respect, and *then* overlaying these factors onto roles that play to your strengths.

Watch for Career Flares

Strengths are relatively easily identified—usually in the form of strong performance. Rarely are we told, "Your performance was acceptable, but boy, did you seem passionate about your work!" Extraordinary success, however, requires steering toward a job that leverages both strengths *and* passions. A valuable tool to help in the process of discovering your passions is to watch for career flares. Commonly used by boaters, motorists, and highway safety personnel as a signal to indicate distress, a flare is a flammable object that emits a very bright light that can be seen from far away. In the professional workplace, a career flare is similar. It is an instance in which a bright, distant light of passion and/or ability can be observed, far away from the tasks currently assigned. For individuals trying to steer their careers, learning to recognize such signals for yourself is important—they are a signpost toward your right fit.

Susan Arnold graduated with a respectable grade point average from Pennsylvania State University and accepted an offer to join Accenture, one of the largest information technology consulting firms. At Accenture, Arnold's work focused on process reengineering, seeking to identify ways to improve the efficiency and effectiveness of a particular business process. Arnold was good at her job but did not distinguish herself relative to her peers. Rather, she was considered a solid, average consultant in the process reengineering group. While reasonably happy with her work, she was not deeply motivated by her role or with her day-to-day activities.

One day, she came up with an idea to reposition one of her clients' products in the marketplace. Over a weekend, she wrote out a marketing plan that described her idea and her rationale about why it would work. The partner managing her at the firm reviewed Arnold's work and was somewhat torn. On one hand, he was convinced that the work itself was truly exceptional—a breakthrough in strategic marketing thinking. But on the other hand, it had nothing to do with the work that Susan was tasked to complete—increasing efficiency and reducing costs in her client's supply chain operations. After thinking about it, the partner disappointingly decided that while the work was excellent, it was unrelated to the work they had been hired to do (which was still incomplete) and to her primary function, and therefore they would not be presenting it to the client. The partner wasn't trying to be small-minded or even overly risk-averse. He just thought it was inappropriate to be doing work off the task at hand at that time. He tried to encourage Arnold by saying that it would be okay to contribute ideas like this in the future, but she should remember what her primary responsibilities were and that she would be evaluated foremost on those, just like everyone else. Not unlike Cinderella, she would be allowed to go to the ball only after she had completed all her chores.

For Arnold, this was a small incident, but she recognized it as an unconscious cry for help that pointed her in the direction of her ideal fit. She was competent in her current job; in fact, there were a great many jobs that Arnold could do very well based on her problem-solving and interpersonal skills. Yet her efforts to develop the marketing plan signaled something important to her. She found herself energized by coming up with the idea for the plan. She enjoyed working all weekend—her personal time—putting the plan together. And when she presented the idea to her boss, she seemed to almost glow with a passion and energy that were palpable. To Arnold, this wasn't work at all. Luckily, she recognized this career flare as a beacon pointing her toward a new and more fulfilling professional direction. Now, nearly ten years later, Susan Arnold is now an extremely successful—and satisfied—marketing executive within a global consumer products company.

What Arnold experienced may seem like an isolated occurrence, but it is actually rather common. Think of a situation where you proactively initiated an activity beyond your current assigned tasks. Evaluate all the aspects of your current job—what things you are most energized about, what you enjoy doing first, what you choose to spend a lot of time on. Given some downtime or a slower period at your job, what activities do you gravitate toward? All of these things are signals that help reveal your true interests—roles you are not only skilled for but also passionate about.

Careers seem to go by quickly and are filled with many distractions. Be sure to take the time to notice that bright light off in the distance—it may actually be your real working passions, buried deep in the rubble of your current job, yearning to be discovered. Watch for them, and let them pull you toward your ideal fit.

Work with the Right People

Just as flares can help you identify a path you are passionate about, trying to migrate your career toward people you like and respect can also move you closer to your ideal fit. In fact, the environment in which you work is critical for maximizing your potential for success in your own career.

Do you have or can you imagine developing strong friendships in the company? While this may seem a trivial question, the Gallup Organization found that the strongest explanatory variable in employee job satisfaction is whether people have one or more close friends in their company.[3] Those who score highest on job satisfaction scales agree strongly with the statement "I feel that I have a best friend in my company." And although it may be surprising on the surface, it makes sense on deeper reflection. People whom we can trust, confide in, relate to, and learn from, with whom we enjoy spending time and sharing common experiences—people with whom we feel comfortable and nurtured, even if the work environment is challenging or unpleasant—are powerful drivers of satisfaction. When asked about the happiest times in their lives, many executives who served in the military relate that those physically and emotionally trying times were the best due to the bonds of friendship and teamwork that were forged in adversity. This is a simple and powerful lesson to keep squarely at the top of your mind as you manage your career and evaluate opportunities.

Finding an organization that is a natural fit for you and in which you like and respect the people is one of the keys to success and satisfaction. A poor people fit can torpedo even a job that's a great match for a person's skills and experience. And on the flip side, a great people fit can overcome major gaps in experience and skills. The reason for this is that when the fit is great, both the individual and the organization are highly motivated to succeed, even if success requires reinforcing the individual with others who have complementary skills and experience.

Different types of companies tend to attract different types of employees. If you can get to the heart of what kinds of people thrive in the company's culture, this will help you sort out whether or not it's a good place for you. But you need to recognize that during the recruiting process, both you and the people you meet tend to be on their best behavior. You are selling, and they are selling, too. So it's often tricky to get an accurate sense of the actual day-to-day working environment and what people are really like. The best approach to get beyond this is to use good questions, have your antennae up, and find ways to talk to people outside the interview process.

Good questions would include the following:

- Who specifically have been the most and least successful individuals to join the company in the last year? What has accounted for their success and failure?

- What does it really take to be successful at the company?

- How are promotion decisions made? What is an example of when something didn't work out despite strong business results?

- What would define success in the first year?

- How will I know if people have bought in, and what are the telltale signs that a new hire is not a strong fit? What do people say behind closed doors?

But don't give short shrift to squishy aspects of interviewing, such as the feel of a place. How does the office environment strike you? Is the physical setup more conducive to privacy and independent work or to open collaboration and communication? Looking out ten or twenty years, would you aspire to become like the company's top people? Do you respect the company's leadership?

One of the most common bonds between professionals is their defined set of personal values. And the environments in which you work can have a profound influence on your personal values and actions, pulling them in one direction or another. The key: *Don't wait until you compromise your values to learn how important they are to you.* People spend a great deal of time setting goals for promotion, compensation, and other tactical issues in their career. Ethics are often in the back of their mind, but they shouldn't be. Your personal values need to be refreshed and updated. Take the time to define the guideposts that you wish to live by in any situation. If you don't, you may unknowingly compromise your values and venture down a slippery slope. Define your boundaries, and you will remain in control. This was learned the hard way, unfortunately, by the thousands of good people who worked for Enron, Tyco, Adelphia Cable, and WorldCom.

THE POWER OF PASSION AND PEOPLE: HOWARD SCHULTZ, STARBUCKS

One of the best cases of someone for whom integrity, ethics, people, and passion all converged to create massive success is Howard Schultz. His story involves the formation of what has become one of the most prominent brands in the world: Starbucks.

Howard Schultz is crazy about coffee. He loves the smell of the beans and the cozy intimacy that swirls around a well-run coffeehouse. So back in 1982 he persuaded a small, one-unit coffee store in San Francisco, Starbucks Coffee Company, to let him join the ranks as head of sales and marketing. A few years later, after spending time in the cappuccino bars of Milan, Italy, he became convinced that the concept of coffee bars would also work well in the United States. But when his partners disagreed, Schultz decided to branch out on his own. He formed a small chain that he called *Il Giornale,* the word for "newspaper" in Italian. Soon thereafter, in 1987, Schultz had enough experience and evidence that his concept could work that he successfully bought out the Starbucks Coffee Company name and the green siren logo. Today the company has become indelibly associated with gourmet coffee, tasty food, and hanging out and has become one of the world's most valuable brands. The chain has nearly six thousand stores and is growing rapidly around the world.

That much most people know. But what's less well known is how Schultz built the strength of the enterprise from the inside, based on empathy and people, and how finding the right fit set him on a career path destined for greatness. Throughout our many conversations with Schultz, he detailed the origins of his belief system and how he tapped into his true calling. After growing up in housing projects in Brooklyn, Schultz became a star quarterback at Canarsie High School, which led to him being recruited on a football scholarship to Northern Michigan University. When he graduated in 1975, he won a spot in the prestigious Xerox sales training program. Friends and family were excited, even envious of Schultz's wonderful opportunity. It seemed an irresistible choice, so he took it. But despite tremendous early success at

Xerox, Schultz sensed that there was something missing. It was obvious that he had a natural talent for sales, but he felt that his true passions were somewhat muted within such a large, complex organization. He thought back to the dreams of his childhood. "I grew up literally on the other side of the tracks," Schultz said. "The odds of me achieving this level of success, if you saw where I came from, were so long, you would never place that bet. But I swore that if I was ever in a position of responsibility, I would want to do something where people would not be left behind. I always wanted to build the kind of company that my father, who as a truck driver and factory worker was injured one day and out of a job the next, never got the chance to work for." Schultz eventually concluded the most likely way for this dream to be fulfilled was in an entrepreneurial setting, working in an evangelistic role.

So after three years with Xerox, he began his transition, joining Hammerplast, a subsidiary of the Swedish-based housewares company Perstorp, which (because they sold coffeepots) ultimately put him in contact with the coffee store. It was the owners' passion for the product that partially inspired Schultz to want to join in. But it was also his conviction that his natural strengths in sales and marketing could help the tiny company do things that the owners could not even dream of. Of course, he would be proven right beyond anyone's wildest dreams.

Eventually, when Schultz acquired the business and really got down to building the company, he paid great attention to the types of people he wanted to recruit—the types of people that would be attracted to his company. This was one of the most important considerations in building the top management team and in establishing the culture of the company. "I believe that the best way to build a company is to have a group of people with shared values and highly complementary skills in an environment of trust and respect," Schultz told us. "This way, people can fit in based on their heart and emotions and people can be organized to play to their strengths."

By any external standard—fame, fortune, philanthropy—Howard Schultz is an incredibly successful person. But what he may be most proud of is achieving his childhood dream—to create a company that impacts people in such a positive way, a company where no one is left behind. At Starbucks, Schultz led the creation of a program called

Bean Stock, where every employee working a minimum of twenty hours a week is covered by health insurance and receives stock options. Not only has this helped form a powerful culture within the company and across the thousands of units in the field, but it has reduced employee turnover to less than 20 percent of the U.S. average for the multiserve restaurant industry.

Schultz has always been driven by his heart, and he has put himself in a position to play to his strengths, passions, and cultural fit. He is truly an inspiring example for the 90 percent of the workforce who haven't found their right fit—just yet.

YOU CAN FIND THE RIGHT FIT

Successful executives focus on finding the right fit, honestly evaluating their strengths, passions, and preferences for people and environment, and then proactively seeking positions and careers that are best suited for them. Jim Head got off the legal-career conveyor belt and worked his way over to pursue his calling—a career in entertainment. Schultz left behind the pay and prestige of a promising sales career at Xerox to pursue his passion for building a small company in an entrepreneurial setting and creating an organization that would leave no employee behind. Each knew that true success results from finding a career track that is personally rewarding and enriching because it leverages the right fit for each of them as individuals—strengths, passions, and people. Ultimately, each achieved significantly more success and satisfaction than would have been possible had they selected only from the logical career options that were presented to them.

Far too many people get caught up in career one-upmanship and lose sight of what success really means. The pitfall is that the trappings of success can catch you off guard. Before too long, you can awaken to find that you have stumbled into a life of financial dependence on and emotional detachment from your daily work. Your job becomes monotonous and life turns dull. The zeal is gone.

But there's a different, more fulfilling way. Instead, you can blend your deepest desires with your strongest skills, allowing yourself to reach untold potential by simply working on what you're *really* intended to be working on. And that's the key. Something almost mystical happens when you are set upon tasks that deeply move you—it's what allows you to step up and contribute something startling and significant to society. Don't forget that your work takes up roughly two-thirds of your waking hours—far too much time to be underutilized or bored. But if you find the right fit and work with the right people in a role that plays to your strengths, then with a little patience and just a little bit of luck, you should attain what everyone longs for—true success and satisfaction.

THE PATTERNS OF EXTRAORDINARY ORGANIZATIONS

No duty the executive had to perform was so trying
as to put the right man in the right place.
—THOMAS JEFFERSON

There is something that is much more scarce,
something finer by far, something rarer than ability.
It is the ability to recognize ability.
—ELBERT HUBBARD

SHATTERING THE ASSUMPTIONS

We wrote *The Five Patterns of Extraordinary Careers* to challenge the most widely held assumptions about professional success. Our intention is that the findings will be provocative, compelling, and actionable—revealing the patterns that lead individuals to long-term career success. But the opportunities for improvement that exist within most organizations may be even more significant. By applying the success patterns at the organizational level, companies should find valuable productivity and performance gains. At the heart of this transformational opportunity is our belief that *the extraordinary organization is not merely a collection of successful individuals, but a creator of them.*

To be extraordinary, a company must seek to fill its ranks with the very best, providing its professionals with the knowledge of success and empowering them to take control over their careers. It must create a culture of success, establishing a strong value system based on empowerment, proactive behavior, and integrity. By rethinking its core approaches to attracting, selecting, developing, assessing, and rewarding its employees, an enterprise can emerge as an extraordinary organization benefiting from the success of its individuals.

A joyful executive turns out to also be a productive executive. As professionals become more successful, our research has shown they are 35 percent more likely to be performing at or near peak productivity levels. They also believe that their value within the organization is growing at above average rates, and they are much less likely to consider external job opportunities. Beyond the tangible, quantitative value to an organization, there are cultural benefits as well. The five patterns rest upon pillars that must exist within your organization if it is to remain competitive and sustaining—namely, trust, creativity, teamwork, customer focus, and self-actualization. Start with these attributes and organizational success is that much easier.

Is your organization extraordinary? How you answer the following questions goes a long way in highlighting the opportunities that may exist.

- Does the culture tend to foster or stifle the success of each individual employee?

- Does the company accurately assess, recognize, and reward employees for accomplishing the right things, achieved through desired behaviors?

- Given the organizational competencies required for success in the marketplace, do sufficient resources exist within the enterprise, and are they properly aligned to meet the challenges?

For years we have been asked to assist in organizational talent audits around these three areas. But now, armed with the depth of research that contributed to *The Five Patterns of Extraordinary Careers,* we can provide a more comprehensive, holistic view of organizational effectiveness. Consequently, for the first time we are now able to close the loop on organizational success, understanding with great clarity what characteristics and behaviors are most desirable in professional talent, and what the makeup is of the organization most able to attract these individuals and allow them to perform to their greatest potential.

Often, we find that executives responsible for maximizing the performance of the organization have committed significant resources toward this objective, but with limited success. Within the enterprise there is not a commonly shared belief about the characteristics and behaviors of the most desired professionals. Although there is a general understanding about the organizational competencies required to win in the marketplace, professionals often are not properly aligned against the most critical objectives or do not exist within the staff at all. And, most unsettling to the executives with whom we have spoken, many organizations have unknowingly created internal barriers that make them unattractive to the most talented professionals and actually limit the potential of those already employed.

The unfortunate truth is this: Today few organizations can answer in the affirmative to the aforementioned questions. Based on our research of more than two thousand executives representing more than a thousand companies, we concluded that a small minority of organizations have succeeded in creating an environment that is attractive to the very best, accurately identifies and rewards them, positions them in the right roles, and allows them to achieve their full potential of success. In fact, we have seen far too many organizations that do not foster a culture of success. Our research shows that fewer than one in ten employees feel that they are in the right jobs for them. And shocking as this figure is, it is easy to understand when you consider that relentless pressure to reduce costs has resulted in many organizations completely abandoning career development activities for their employees, often leaving them to survive or fail entirely on their own. In many cases, mentorship and apprenticeship have become discouraged in favor of producing immediate results, and those who have traditionally played the mentor roles are feeling insecure and demotivated themselves.

But there are exceptions. Some organizations have gone to great lengths to create a culture of success and are benefiting from exceptional productivity, innovation, and performance from their workforce.

Consider the powerful advantages this approach has created for Microsoft.

THE COMPETITIVE ADVANTAGE OF PEOPLE

Many companies demonstrate the five patterns we've discussed thus far in this book, developing a culture of career knowledge and empowerment—General Electric, Shell Oil, Procter & Gamble, McKinsey, Nokia, Goldman Sachs, PepsiCo, Marriott, Toyota, and Amgen, just to name a few. But there's perhaps no better example of the five patterns at play than Microsoft. "Getting our talent and organization right is one of the top priorities on our list," CEO Steve Ballmer told us. Although this may sound like common management-speak, Microsoft has demonstrated that it walks the talk. This is one of the reasons the company was able to recover so swiftly from a seismic shift in its competitive landscape, from desktop computing to the Internet and from the talent raids that confronted the company during the dot-com boom.

Microsoft once again has achieved the dominant position in the rapidly changing and highly competitive software industry. Look closely and you'll see that the value of the company is the sum of the talents under its roof. Microsoft's outstanding price-to-earnings ratio of 32—double that of the S&P 500—is attributable to a number of things, including its market-leading position, its continued rapid growth, its consistent increase in cash flow relative to capital employed, and the power of its brand and product line. But one of the other reasons, for sure, is the quality of the company's people.

Over the years, Microsoft has been highly successful in attracting, developing, and retaining intellectually and interpersonally gifted employees. In addition to exciting professional development prospects and a lucrative stock options program, a primary attraction factor has been Microsoft's strong and competitive culture and its promote-from-within approach balanced by selective additions from the outside.

The quality of its people and its ability to leverage them has won praise, even from skeptical competitors. One top-level executive at rival IBM commented to us, "A lot of people in the technology industry have long demeaned Microsoft's achievements as being based on just copying other companies' technology and driving it through their sales and distribution system. But the fact is that these sour grapes are based on jealousy, fear, and a dose of their own PR. The fact is that Microsoft's people are incredibly impressive and are their biggest competitive advantage."

Our firm has recruited several executives from the outside to join Microsoft's top management group, and the intensity, intelligence, and discipline the company puts into the recruiting process are symptomatic of its success culture and therefore warrant further examination. To begin with, the company's human resource managers are not considered "back office," but rather business partners to the line organization. They bring a strategic orientation and bias for action that would be the envy of other companies' marketing or sales functions. They support the development of the key position requirements that are directly linked to the requirements for the business, but they also drive the interview process, which they call the "loop," in a way that builds rigor and intelligence into the system.

Microsoft policy, but more importantly practice, is that each interviewer does her homework by learning the candidate's background in detail. She has also been made aware of the issues to probe in each successive meeting on the loop. Within minutes of completing each interview the evaluator writes a detailed e-mail to the interview group, assessing the candidate's strengths, weaknesses, and what has been learned about the issues previously identified. We have read these assessments, and indeed, the penetrating quality of the thinking and evaluation comes through loud and clear. Most impressively, each person gives her bottom-line recommendation—hire, no hire, or continue to evaluate—with the assessment. The recruiting manager supporting the process acts as cajoler, or when necessary whip, ensuring that all of the feedback is in. With this process refined to a science, the company is able to make decisions quickly on the basis of both fact and judgment.

Of course, recruiting is just one small piece of Microsoft's overall human capital strategy. Many companies consider it a luxury to address human capital planning on a strategic basis. However, given long-term demographic trends and the changing talent requirements needed to implement its ambitious strategies in a rapidly shifting world, Microsoft's top management has concluded that it is both critical and timely to consider such a proactive and holistic approach in the future. According to MSN's Rich Bray, "I think we are doing a whole lot more than just trying to maintain our position. I know at the highest level, Bill and Steve take a very long-term approach to this business, and to the people and organizational aspects of it." The result is an organization in which many professionals echo the sentiments of Bray, who told us, "It is highly motivating to work with people who are so smart and energetic. Getting our people to work together in a way that takes advantage of their greatest skills allows us all to grow and to put the best products out in the marketplace. Our culture is to want to work on things that you think will have an impact on the economy broadly, help Microsoft, and generate a successful return to shareholders, which is our ultimate goal. We do this by devoting a lot of effort toward building very, very effective teams, establishing strong partnerships, and helping people manage their careers for the long term."

THE CRITICAL ASSUMPTIONS

Attracting, retaining, and developing the very best talent is one of the most critical challenges facing organizations in the twenty-first century. Markets are in a state of continuous change. The battle for success and survival is voracious, with global and now virtual competition occurring at levels that would make even Darwin blush. Employees feel unmoored from their companies and are searching for greater meaning in their work while at the same time expecting to work for an increasing number of different companies over the course of their careers. Talent—the very best talent—now stands as the business world's most valued asset. But although almost every organization states an interest in attracting and retaining the very best, and enabling their most productive levels of performance, we have observed many that unknowingly are structured in a way that actually stifles their success. Often, we observe the following:

- Companies aspire to recruit and retain the most talented professionals... ...but are unable to identify or attract the most desired resources.

- Their employees are frustrated that the organization offers little assistance in managing their careers... ...yet employees also lack the knowledge and tools to become truly empowered.

- Top talents want to be rewarded handsomely for their individual performance... ...but are concerned that performance is not being evaluated fairly or accurately across the organization.

- Companies have a strong understanding of the organizational competencies required to compete and win... ...but are unsure if those talents exist internally, or if so, are properly apportioned toward their most critical use.

Addressing these challenges is no trivial task. But it can be done if those in charge focus on three critical facts of organizational life:

- Individual career success benefits the entire organization.
- The strongest performers contribute a disproportionate amount of the value to a company.

- Performance and productivity are maximized when resources are aligned with the most critical organizational needs.

Are the activities of your organization aligned with these core realities? If so, it can build a business with a leg up on the competition, one that is lasting and very tough for competitors to replicate. Examining these assumptions at a more tactical level reveals actionable insights valuable to any company:

- If individual career success benefits the entire organization, then you should *create a culture of success, providing each employee with the tools, information, and environment to foster his or her own advancement.* This implies giving your employees the career knowledge that will improve their chances of success, and creating an environment where they are emboldened to take action.

- If the strongest performers contribute a disproportionate amount of the value to an organization, then you must *implement the most accurate and effective system of assessing performance, and recognize and reward the highest performers in such a way that they will stay and are motivated to perform up to their highest potential.*

- If performance and productivity are maximized when resources are aligned with the most critical organizational needs, then organizations must continually *evaluate existing resources against current and future competitive challenges and aggressively seek to fill any gaps.* This requires a thorough understanding of the employee skills and capabilities and management competencies required for competitive success.

From these assumptions, three imperatives for the most effective talent management system emerge: (1) *create a success culture,* attracting the very best and providing the knowledge, tools, and an environment that empowers all of your employees to increase their own career success, (2) *assess and reward performance,* instituting the proper blend of differentiated rewards and precise and consistent performance evaluation; and (3) *close the gaps,* periodically reviewing the alignment of resources against market requirements for success, and aggressively taking action to stay ahead of the curve.

Examining and illustrating each of these imperatives in greater detail should allow a better understanding of opportunities that may exist within your organization and the actions you can take to realize them.

IMPERATIVE #1: CREATE A SUCCESS CULTURE

Working with a global telecommunications company in an assessment of its organizational talent, we had completed a review of the most senior executives as well as the company's highest-potential employees. Our efforts resulted in an analysis and presentation to the company's CEO and human resource chief about the strengths, weaknesses, aspirations, and concerns of each employee. This was valuable information, to be sure. But what was most unexpected by the CEO and the HR executive about our findings was that beyond the discussions about each specific person, we synthesized a series of consistently emerging issues into a theme that applied to the entire company. While there were numerous very talented and successful professionals within the organization, many felt they had succeeded not because of the organization but rather *in spite of it*. A majority told us that the organization was too rigidly managed. In effect, many of the highest-performing employees felt they were not being given room to grow or the freedom to make decisions on their own. They were not encouraged to experiment with new approaches to solving problems or exploiting opportunities, instead being told in no uncertain terms that everything different had to "have all the risk managed out before starting." The problem with this approach is that if the risks are managed out, then it is by definition too late to use the new approach—the opportunity has already been taken by the competition. In addition, many expressed frustration that the organization neither provided support for their career growth nor supplied the information and skills to become empowered to achieve their own success. The overall theme, which after some painful reflection the CEO and HR chief acknowledged, was that instead of fostering the success of each individual, the organization unwittingly seemed structured to stifle it.

Distressingly, organizations seem to have abandoned responsibility for their employees' career development. Alignment of goals for success, if at all, is usually haphazard. For decades, many great companies firmly held on to a no-layoff policy and spent millions actively managing the careers of their employees. Then, unable to resist the fierce competitive forces of globalization and profit pressure, they were forced to abandon this policy in the 1980s. Today, less than 5 percent of professionals from our survey believe that their employer actively helps manage their careers. Most companies have determined that it is simply not practical or economic to provide anything close to full-service career management for their employees. The costs are prohibitive, and few employees will be employees for their entire careers. Except in the rarest of organizations, trust in the employer to aid career progress is at a very low level. The pendulum has swung too far. Our research shows that organizations providing the right career management resources reap great benefits in increased productivity, impact, and loyalty.

This is not to say that change was not needed. Decades of coddling employees, managing their every career move for them, resulted in a culture of entitlement within many companies—a culture that was difficult to break. Professionals need to know that career management is still their responsibility, not the company's. What's more, employees who take control of their careers are likely to perform better, not waiting for someone else to do it for them. The best strategy for the organization, then, is to be neither overprotective nor unsupportive. It is a balance that requires providing the information, tools, and framework for career success, while simultaneously permitting and encouraging individual empowerment to achieve career success.

Often, the first step in creating a success culture is to communicate the powerful messages that underlie *The Five Patterns of Extraordinary Careers*. Share the positive principles with your organization. Teach its messages of empowerment, planning, impact, leadership, playing to strengths, fit, and personal values.

To understand how imparting these success principles on employees can positively impact a company, let's explore how increasing the presence of the patterns of extraordinary careers can play out at the organizational level.

• Increasing the career knowledge within your organization—what we call *understanding the value of you*—makes your employees more likely to manage their own careers, proactively doing the right things that add value to themselves and your organization and remaining loyal to your company. In fact, when comparing average employees to our group of extraordinary executives, the extraordinary executives were almost twice as likely to be completely satisfied in their current jobs and unwilling to consider any outside opportunities. Their higher levels of career knowledge help them see that the grass on the other side may not be so green; they will be more rarely disillusioned into changing jobs.

• Encouraging the *practice of benevolent leadership* results in a focus on the success of the team. This in turn leads to the development of both leaders and employees to their full potential. When managers focus on the development of their subordinates, providing career assistance, guidance, and mentoring, an environment is created where everyone can more readily develop and succeed. What's more, this leadership approach, with its underpinning of open and honest communications, reinforces a culture of fairness and integrity that is fundamental to any organization's long-term success. Benevolent leadership also supports the time-honored approach of apprenticeship, in which some of the most positive and enduring lessons are taught—and learned.

• Teaching employees to *overcome the permission paradox* results in an atmosphere of growth, a commitment to equal opportunity, and a workforce that feels proactive and empowered, not helpless. Employees look ahead for what they really desire in their careers and use positive and honest strategies to attain these critical positions. Gaining critical experience increases the depth of the talent pool within the organization. Companies that encourage employees to increase their options rather than penalizing them for it reinforce a culture of healthy risk taking and proactive behavior.

• Fostering the *20/80 principle of performance* results in employees focused on those things that add the most value to the organization. They seek efficiencies in their daily tasks but look for ways to expand beyond their preset expectations and deliver breakthrough value no matter where they are in the organizational hierarchy. And applying this pattern in the most effective way secures buy-in from management and effectiveness working across organizational lines, thereby strengthening the fiber of the entire organization.

- Migrating your employees toward positions of maximum *fit* represents potentially the greatest opportunity for an organization. Employees with jobs that they are passionate about and highly competent in will reward you with a dramatic increase in employee satisfaction and productivity and just as dramatic a decrease in unwanted turnover. In our study, only 9 percent of employees strongly agree that they are in positions that fully leverage both their strengths and their passions. Among those who don't, estimates are that their productivity could increase by an average of 35 percent if their jobs evolved toward positions that represented a better fit with their strengths, passions, and cultural preference. Help them get there, and the benefits to all will be clear.

IMPERATIVE #2: ASSESS AND REWARD PERFORMANCE

Despite our conviction and those of many other experts about the value of talent in business, there are still a number of management prognosticators who question the degree to which top professional resources are valuable to an organization, and query how best to manage them. The talent advocates say that the best organizational performance is derived from an obsession about talent, its identification, recruitment, and retention—and that the very best talent should be rewarded disproportionately well. The great companies mentioned above certainly believe in this position. One of the most prominent articulations of this viewpoint came from Ed Michaels, Helen Handfield-Jones, and Beth Axelrod at McKinsey and Company in their book *The War for Talent*. They argue that the most successful companies have a "talent mind-set," employing specific strategies to attract, develop, and retain the most talented professionals. Their research found that the highest-performing companies were 60 percent more likely to strongly agree they make talent a top priority.[1]

The contrary view was recently expressed by Malcolm Gladwell, author of *The Tipping Point*—that talent may, in fact, be overrated *and substantially overcompensated*.[2] Gladwell pondered whether "some companies fail not for lack of a Talent Mind-set, but *because of it*." Gladwell's argument stems not from the belief that strong performers are not valuable to organizations, but rather from the idea that most companies typically do a very poor job at accurately identifying and assessing the best talent. Because they often fail in their assessment, significant differentiation in compensation and recognition is ultimately random and often detrimental. This, he argues, is due to two things. First is an overreliance by organizations on intelligence as an indicator of talent, which has *not* been shown to strongly correlate with superior performance. And not only do organizations measure and reward the wrong attributes, Gladwell states, but the measurement process itself is unreliable, often evaluating each individual's performance in a broad, highly subjective, and inaccurate manner. Adding to the performance assessment dilemma is the continual movement of designated fast-track employees, who never seem to stick around in a position long enough for their lasting impact to be known. "You can grade someone's performance only if you *know* that person's performance," Gladwell says, and according to him, most organizations don't. Distributing highly unbalanced rewards to employees based on these imprecise assessments of their relative level of talent is a recipe for disaster.

So which side of this debate is correct? The talent advocates, led by McKinsey and others, or the talent-is-overrated contingent, supported by Gladwell? Actually, they may *both* be right. How can this be so? The most effective system of talent management requires both acknowledgment of the best performers and disproportionate recognition *and* a system that consistently and accurately assesses performance. Without both, the results are suboptimal. It's almost impossible to dispute the idea that talented people make a talented organization. We have found that extraordinary executives were much more likely to directly impact a company's core value, to feel that their value within the organization was growing at above average rates, and were able to attract other high-performing professionals to them. In another study conducted by Spencer Stuart of venture-capital-backed entrepreneurial companies, we additionally found that companies with the strongest relative talent were more than twice as likely to meet or exceed their investor's financial objectives.[3]

But Gladwell is also correct, highlighting common flaws in organizational assessment programs and accurately pointing out that differentiation in rewards without a true understanding of real talent or performance risks being random at best and actually destructive to an organization at worst.

Success requires both high-quality assessment and highly differentiated rewards. But as you would expect, not every company is able to achieve both objectives.

Taking both assessment and rewards into account, we have observed four distinct approaches for attempting to put talent management into practice: the socialist stepladder, Pin the Talent on the

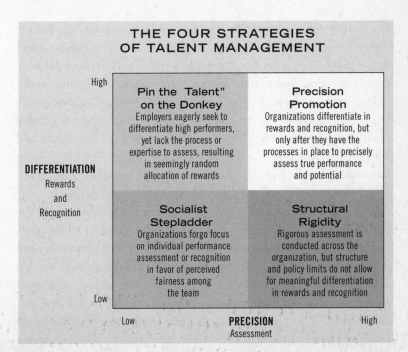

THE FOUR STRATEGIES OF TALENT MANAGEMENT

DIFFERENTIATION
Rewards and Recognition

High

Pin the Talent" on the Donkey
Employers eagerly seek to differentiate high performers, yet lack the process or expertise to assess, resulting in seemingly random allocation of rewards

Precision Promotion
Organizations differentiate in rewards and recognition, but only after they have the processes in place to precisely assess true performance and potential

Socialist Stepladder
Organizations forgo focus on individual performance assessment or recognition in favor of perceived fairness among the team

Structural Rigidity
Rigorous assessment is conducted across the organization, but structure and policy limits do not allow for meaningful differentiation in rewards and recognition

Low

Low   **PRECISION**   High
                        Assessment

Donkey, structural rigidity, and precision promotion. Each approach has its own benefits and challenges. The goal for your organization is to learn from each approach and develop an assessment and reward program that makes sense for your business, organizational structure, and corporate culture.

The Socialist Stepladder

Many companies seek to create an environment of teamwork above everything else. Some refuse to differentiate their pay among different professionals—in extreme cases completely unbundling pay from performance. The belief is that any such disparity in pay, no matter what the level of individual contribution, will damage the cohesiveness of the team. In some instances, companies intentionally forgo measuring performance among individual professionals altogether. This atypical approach to compensation can sometimes be found in large established law firms, management consultancies, and even some executive recruiting firms.

In the highly competitive world of professional services, performance among junior consultants often falls within a fairly narrow range. But as professionals develop, their role usually shifts to client development and sales, and performance among partners can vary greatly, sometimes by a factor of ten or more. What's more, unlike other types of performance that can be tough to measure, sales and profitability contribution in the professional services industry can often be tracked with great clarity down to an individual consultant. For this reason, the majority of the top firms have an incentive model directly tied to actual performance, with resulting compensation varying greatly.

Going against conventional wisdom, there are several firms in the professional services industry who do not differentiate at all based on performance. In the most common application of this approach, each professional enters the firm at approximately the same compensation level, with year-end bonuses sometimes used as a tool to further reduce any variability between individuals. Annual raises are predictable until after a predetermined period of time, usually five to eight years, when each person is considered for entry into the partnership (or not, in which case they are usually asked to leave the firm). From this point on, the profits of the firm are divided up among the partners around the firm primarily based on tenure—how long one has been a partner. With some firms, it actually matters not whether you live in San Francisco or Mexico City, or whether you generate $200,000 or $2,000,000 in fees; you are paid equally with every other partner voted into the partnership during your year. This tenure-based model may seem odd to many, but for some law firms and consultancies, particularly those based in Europe, it has worked fairly well. In theory, the only motivation for any consultant is to maximize the profits of the entire firm—the team is vastly more important than any individual. In addition, some firms applying this approach have historically experienced relatively low levels of partner turnover, as increasing pay for tenure raises employee switching costs over time.

But as you might expect, this model is not without its problems. First of all, in any compensation system, there is always the tendency to view your pay in proportion to how hard you work or how much you contribute. Therefore in this system, the person who works harder, shows more initiative, or produces disproportionately more value than his or her colleagues receives no additional compensation, resulting in the disincentive to do more than expected. Second, while this socialistic model has worked well for some firms in Europe and parts of Asia, it has thus far not proven to be as effective in other highly competitive talent markets such as the United States.

The problem is that as the strongest performers begin to emerge within a firm, the partnership is often unable to hold back aggressive competitors willing to pay their people what they are really worth in the marketplace. Some firms using this model have suffered tremendous defections of top performers, with departing employees in some instances more than doubling or tripling their compensation the day they walk out the door. Unfortunately for these firms, there is a continual struggle to retain the highest-performing consultants, who are so critical to a firm's growth.

Not differentiating compensation, or even not seeking to evaluate performance, does not create barriers to teamwork, to be sure, but it provides no mechanism for the most valuable performers to be recognized and rewarded, and thus the retention of these critical team members is inevitably difficult. In highly competitive marketplaces, organizations with this strategy run the risk of creating cohesive teams of B players acting as a farm league for the industry's top competitors.

Pin the Talent on the Donkey

An alternative approach is one we call Pin the Talent on the Donkey—where an organization attempts to differentiate pay based on performance while maintaining a very fluid organizational structure, moving executives from position to position quickly or even letting them dictate the timing of their rotations. The goal of this strategy is to organize for rapid change, allowing both resources and organizational lines to evolve in real time, while simultaneously retaining those with the highest perceived talent via highly differentiated compensation. An unfortunate outcome of this approach, however, is a lack of accuracy in the assessment of performance, with rewards seeming to many to be doled out almost randomly, or based heavily on subjective criteria of preference—like a blindfolded child attempting to pin a paper tail on a paper donkey.

Differentiating in the recognition and compensation of your top-performing employees is critical to retaining them, but doing so without an accurate understanding of true contribution can be dangerous. Such is the primary argument of Malcom Gladwell in his *New Yorker* article "The Talent Myth."[4] He argued that performance in many cases is subjective and that some companies move people from job to job too quickly. "How do you evaluate someone's performance in a system where no one is in a job long enough to allow such evaluation?" he asked.

Consider Enron's widely publicized star system, where those deemed top performers were compensated dramatically differently than their peers. "We hire smart people and we pay them more than they think they are worth," said one Enron executive to Richard Foster, quoted in his book *Creative Destruction*.[5]

Enron had many problems, but its desire to hire the best people and its efforts to ensure that the company retained them were not among them. In fact, the company did succeed in building an organization with thousands of highly talented professionals that were the envy of its competition. But in addition to the well-chronicled accounting and financial management malfeasance, Enron's problems were exacerbated by its lack of understanding of who the top performers really were. Professionals were free to move around the company from one job to another. Managers actually competed for internal resources, even holding "job fairs" to recruit away employees from other divisions. But with this fluidity came instability. Professionals moved from one role to the next so quickly that it was often impossible to accurately evaluate their performance. And even a clear lack of acceptable performance often did not stop a fast-track career. As Gary Hamel commented in his book *Leading the Revolution*, "At Enron, failure—even the type that ends up on the front page of the *Wall Street Journal*—doesn't necessarily sink a career."[6] Of course, in the end, it ended up sinking the entire company.

In the freewheeling and frenetic environment of the late 1990s, with soaring stock market valuations and adulation in the business press, this chaotic environment seemed to make sense. Looking back, the flaws in this model are clear. A system of aggressive differentiation in compensation and rewards without a corresponding accurate system of assessment or accountability for performance created a destructive environment. To many employees, disproportionate rewards seemed to be handed out almost randomly, creating resentment. In some cases, employees felt that those who were rewarded either had been "anointed" by other executives, an incredibly demotivating belief, or, worse, were succeeding merely by "gaming" the system, substituting perceived success in the place of lasting positive impact.

The case of Enron is well documented, and the reasons for its demise are indeed complex. But there are other successful organizations that suffer from the pitfalls of the Pin the Talent on the Donkey system of talent management, though for different reasons.

AT&T and IBM are two of the most influential corporations of the last century, and over the past ten years, both have developed and attracted some of the most outstanding executives in America, such as Lou Gerstner and Sam Palmisano, former and current CEOs at IBM, and at AT&T, Dave Dorman, CEO, and Betsy Bernard, president. But until relatively recently, both companies relied almost exclusively on their internal management development programs, which, while valuable, contributed to almost bringing the companies down.

Decades ago, both organizations set out to identify those experiences that would be required to develop the high-performing executives of the future. The list included international experience, manufacturing, finance, sales, and marketing. The conclusion was that the only way to have professionals with all these experiences was to develop them—and to start early. Both IBM and AT&T set up leadership development programs for their most promising employees, known at the time as the Executive Leadership Program within IBM and the Leadership Continuity Program at AT&T. In theory, these programs made sense—identify the most talented professionals and deliberately expose them to the most value-building experiences, shaping them in the image of the company.

But over time, three challenges emerged in these programs. The first was that people were selected very early on in their careers to enter these programs, typically in their early to mid-twenties. Few had worked long enough to prove their performance level at all, and as one insider put it, "The criteria for entry was really raw intelligence and how good you looked in a suit." Obviously, performance potential for an entire career could not accurately be assessed at this stage. But over time, after many rotations and documented track records, individuals were rarely thoroughly reevaluated for their fit with these elite programs. Only in the case of outliers, whose performance was so severely lacking, were people removed. The result was a feeling by many inside both companies that entry into these career-building programs was not earned over time but bestowed early on, after which members could do almost no wrong.

The second problem with relying exclusively on leadership development and rotational programs was that they led to a debilitating, internally focused culture. Rather than focusing on what customers were demanding and on how new technologies could be commercialized, the most promising talent became focused on which meetings, programs, and assignments would continue their promotional path within the company. The companies rarely recruited fresh talent from the outside, and in many cases, those who were brought in were not assimilated well and then left. Unchecked, the companies became untethered to their marketplaces, and the internal organizational jockeying was much like rearranging deck chairs on the *Titanic* while it was sinking.

The third major problem with programs such as these is that in order to provide the participants with the broad list of experiences the corporations feel they need, they are rotated from job to job extremely quickly, with many rotations lasting only a year or less. How is it possible for anyone to make an impact in such a short time, or for that matter for the true value of their performance to be accurately measured? Proactively developing internal resources can provide great benefits to an organization. But to have a long-term positive impact, rotations must be long enough so that true performance can be evaluated, and this evaluation must be continued even after professionals gain early acceptance into the programs.

Differentiating rewards and recognition in order to attract and retain the highest-performing professionals is a worthy objective. But without a system—tools to accurately assess performance and selectively complement inside talent with outside perspective—the damage may outweigh the benefits. It may be true that simply having a system of differentiation among employees may attract more talented employees, confident in their abilities to succeed and be rewarded in such an environment. But without accurate performance assessment, these high-performing and undercompensated professionals will be the first to leave.

Structural Rigidity

Many organizations have developed structured programs and policies for managing talent. Created over time, these programs often couple standardized performance review programs with tight policies for compensating employees. People at a specific rung on the organizational ladder who are evaluated as performing in a specific way can expect total compensation to fall within a narrowly defined range. The purpose of these programs is to institute consistency across an organization, taking out as much variability as possible. The thought is that, as with operations management, the less variability in the process, the easier and more predictable it is to manage. But people are not as easily managed as physical assets, and there is often great variability in the value that any one individual may represent to an organization. In such cases, the approach of structural rigidity falls short, as you'll see in the story of Larry Handen.

In the spring of 1997, Larry was excited. He had succeeded greatly as a consultant over a five-year period with Price Waterhouse, and was aggressively being recruited by a competitive firm, Deloitte and Touche. We had been retained by Deloitte to identify and recruit three of the very best professional services partners serving the telecommunications industry. We had presented two senior, seasoned partners from competing firms who seemed like natural fits for Deloitte. But our third candidate took our client by surprise. Larry Handen was only thirty years old and wasn't even a partner at Price Waterhouse. Yet he had led the growth of his firm's information and telecommunications practice from almost nothing to one of the firm's more profitable and fastest-growing sectors, increasing revenues by a factor of thirty. His client list was impressive and his track record unblemished, and his references indicated he was truly the very best in the business, bar none. But the partners at Deloitte had a hard time believing that Handen could be so successful, so early in his career. They brought him in for interviews and were impressed. Still nervous about the accuracy of their assessment, they called him back for an even more rigorous second, and even third, round of interviews. Finally, they became convinced. Handen was indeed one of the best in the business, comparable to nearly any senior partner in their firm.

Then the time came to make him an offer. They eagerly wanted Handen to join the firm but faced the internal dilemma of compensating him as a senior partner, or even as a partner at all, with him not even being a partner in his own firm. In the end, Deloitte made a lowball offer, well below what Handen had indicated would be the minimum he would accept. Disappointed, he promptly rejected their offer and recommitted himself to his current employer. He continued to succeed greatly, dramatically growing his practice. After a year of observing Handen's continued impressive performance in the marketplace, Deloitte decided to go after him again. This time, they doubled their original offer and agreed to hire him in as a full partner. By now, however, Price Waterhouse had also recognized the tremendous contributions he was making, and had promoted him and dramatically increased his compensation—well beyond even Deloitte's second offer. Handen politely thanked Deloitte for their continued interest but again turned down the offer. He went on to become one of the top billing partners within all of Price Waterhouse (even after its merger with Coopers and Lybrand), with his team responsible for a significant percentage of firm billings per year. Deloitte was never ultimately able to recruit him into the firm, and all because of a few thousand dollars.

What seemed ironic to the partners at Deloitte after everything was said and done was that they could have easily recruited Larry Handen the very first time they had interviewed him had they offered a partner title and a compensation package that was a mere 15 percent higher—a 15 percent that they knew he was worth. They had spent an inordinate amount of time assessing him and were sure of his performance potential. Yet the structure of the firm was such that they were not able to make an exception. The rigidity of their hiring process ultimately resulted in their unsuccessful attempts to recruit Handen at more than twice their original offer.

Some organizations do recognize the value of really knowing the true level of talent within their organizations and work painstakingly in their assessment, yet lack the flexibility to reward those with the most talent and highest performance. In certain situations, this is a worst-case scenario, like being cursed to be able to foretell the future but powerless to change it, for you know with some accuracy who your top contributors are, making it that much more obvious and painful as they walk out the door to those organizations with the flexibility to reward them.

Precision Promotion

The fourth approach to talent management, and the one we feel is most positive by far, is precision promotion. It combines the benefits of disproportionately rewarding employees based on performance and aligning incentives with organizational objectives with an accurate and consistent methodology for assessment. With both rewards and assessment in place, increased performance, productivity, morale, and employee retention will naturally result.

The benefits of identifying your top performers and rewarding them disproportionately in order to retain them and keep them motivated are many. But as we've shown, this process must be accompanied by an accurate, consistent, and periodic process of evaluation to be most successful.

McKinsey practices what it preaches when it comes to organizational development and talent management. It has a model for promotion and development of its people that has changed little in many decades. The company is perhaps the most celebrated practitioner of the up-or-out system. The majority of line consultants enter the firm as associates, directly from business school, with roughly the same years of experience (notwithstanding an increasing proportion of consultants being recruited from industry and other graduate disciplines such as law and medicine). From that point, they are constantly and consistently evaluated by their managers and peers, and approximately every two years they are considered for promotion to the next level. Unlike IBM and AT&T, where historically people were whisked between divisions and roles, at McKinsey these advancements are in many ways more promotions in title than in function. For example, an entry-level consultant may be promoted from associate to senior associate, from senior associate to junior engagement manager, and then to engagement manager. As an associate principal, one is expected to assume leadership of two clients.

The criteria for each promotion are standard across the firm, and if someone is not promoted at any step along the way, he is asked to leave the firm. Either they go up, or they're out. Like clockwork, every year McKinsey rigorously evaluates and removes the lowest-performing consultants, making room for the next class of new consultants entering the system. Keeping only the best-performing consultants creates a culture of excellence within the firm, and the perception that the bar is continuously being raised. Although rigid and sometimes daunting, employees across the firm view the process of evaluation and promotion as consistently applied and fair. The firm invests heavily in its most senior partners spending time leading these performance appraisals; they are not delegated to staff. And when it comes to election to the partnership, whether at the junior partner (principal) level senior partner (director) level, the firm spends scores of hours per partner candidate collecting internal and client references.

Rewards and recognition vary significantly among consultants at McKinsey. While compensation at each level may be in defined ranges, because of the up-or-out system those who remain with the firm see their pay compound at approximately 20 percent per year. With the power of compounding, it is not uncommon to have consultants with a mere eight years more tenure with the firm earning five or more times the income of their more junior peers. But the reason that this system works so well is not because the lure of such great pay retains the best and the brightest. It is the differentiation in rewards among individuals, combined with an accurate, standard, and systematic evaluation process, that leads to the success of this model.

Another component to making its up-or-out system work well is the care and support that the company provides to those consultants who are forced to leave. And with built-in turnover at such a high rate, it did not take many years for the number of former firm members to far surpass the number of current ones. Long ago, McKinsey recognized the commercial power of cultivating a loyal alumni network, many of whom go into industry and have the opportunity to retain the firm. When a decision is made that a consultant is leaving, the firm supports the person with aggressive help in strategizing and executing an effective job search. The individual is able to stay on board for many months, contributing to projects or working on pro bono assignments while being able to openly look for a job. The firm retains the services of an executive search firm to be the departing consultants' counselors and advisors and put them into the job market with more power behind the advice than the often depressing outplacement services that other companies offer. As a result, the departing consultants are able to secure better positions. They then feel better about McKinsey because of the way they were treated and are more likely to use or recommend McKinsey when they have to hire consultants. Only recently have their competitors realized that they were missing a major opportunity to treat their departing talent as an asset to be cultivated rather than a liability to be excised. Our own firm, Spencer Stuart, has been working with several of the world's most prominent corporations on similar programs to support the senior managers who are leaving the company due to required reductions in force or after merger consolidation (from this work we developed the Spencer Stuart Job Survival Guide, included at the end of the book). These clients have recognized that they too want their former professionals to think like alumni rather than downsized employees. One of the world's largest technology companies has concluded that it would take only one commercial order by a former employee to pay for the entire cost of the counseling and career support program.

General Electric also uses precision promotion in managing its talent. GE recruits its new employees very early in their careers, many directly from top colleges and universities. They develop and train their own employees and seek to promote from within whenever possible. And like AT&T and IBM, they also seek to identify those professionals with the highest potential early on in their careers, and advance them as fast as they can. In an interview for the McKinsey book *War for Talent*, one GE executive proclaimed, "Bet on the natural athletes, the ones with the strongest intrinsic skills. Don't be afraid to promote stars without specifically relevant experience, seemingly over their heads."[7]

Some would argue that this system is not unlike the old AT&T and IBM approaches and that taking a chance on up-and-coming employees is risky and could lead to resentment from those not selected for such career-expanding opportunities. But for GE, two things have allowed this model to work very well. The first is that the company has a consistent and rigorous evaluation process that incorporates both quantitative performance and values. What was the financial situation when a new manager came into a role—revenues, profits, asset utilization, and so on—and what was it when that manager left? And how did the manager accomplish the results in terms of treating people, developing employees, and building customer relationships?

GE synthesizes these different dimensions into two categories, numbers and values. It then separates its managers into four types and evaluates them and takes action accordingly.

- *Type I*: Shares the values, makes the numbers. Sky's the limit!
- *Type II*: Doesn't share the values, doesn't make the numbers. Gone.
- *Type III*: Shares the values, misses the numbers. Typically gets another chance or two.
- *Type IV*: Doesn't share the values, delivers the numbers. This is the toughest call of all, but at GE, this manager is a goner too, demonstrating how committed the company is to precision promotion and managing for talent.

So while GE may promote people well beyond their experiences, the company does so based on a strong understanding of their track record of performance. They may be taking a chance on introducing a new experience, but not on the competency and potential of an individual—*that* they know fairly well.

The second reason this system works is because each rotation at GE is typically longer than with other companies, in many cases three years or more, and very often within the same business unit. Professionals entering new assignments know that they have a finite amount of time to accomplish their objectives before they are rotated out, but it is enough to put in place new strategies and implement real operational change. They also know that any superficial quick fixes whose benefits fade away quickly over time will do them little good, as they will hope to be around long after these superficial gains are gone. They are measured on lasting impact, evaluated by specific performance metrics, and they know that if they create real value, they will continue to be rewarded handsomely. One senior executive at GE Medical was given a year to turn around the performance of the Southern Europe region. He was right on track in the allotted time, but rather than move him into a new, unrelated role next, he was given the entire

European region to manage, and the results of the Southern Europe turnaround could be read for the entire three-year period.

Implementing a strategy of precision promotion is not easy. There are indeed many situations where evaluation is difficult and subjective, such as in the measurement of performance in marketing, human resources, or business affairs. But just as GE's famed Six Sigma quality program has been tailored to be able to measure and improve even "soft" staff functions, so too has a rigorous, data-driven performance evaluation been implemented for professionals across all company operations and functions.

Unlike GE or McKinsey, however, many organizations are unprepared to implement the best techniques for evaluation of human resources and need to be trained or retrained. There are entire books written on the art and science of performance appraisals, but the keys are that they must be timely, specific, data-driven, and delivered in a constructive yet direct communication style. Many managers find trying to perform such appraisals one of their most unpleasant tasks, and since most companies do not hold them accountable for really doing it well, they end up giving it short shrift. Accurately evaluating the professionals within your organization takes time and investment, but it is obviously critical, for only with a detailed level of evaluation can you really understand the different levels of performance and potential within your employees. And only with this understanding can you effectively put in place a reward structure to recognize and retain the very best.

Malcolm Gladwell's wise words on this issue are: "The best talent management systems focus on the retention of their top performers, but you must first understand who and where they are. Many companies think they have identified top people, but it's much harder than it seems."[8]

IMPERATIVE #3: CLOSE THE GAPS

By identifying and communicating the patterns upon which each employee can better achieve his or her potential, you have taken the first step toward establishing the rules of engagement for career success within your organization. You are then in a position to execute the second step: evaluating and rewarding the true inventory of talent across your entire organization. Armed with this broader assessment, you are then well positioned to execute the third imperative: to close the gaps that exist, by filling or upgrading the talent in critical positions.

Is the deck stacked in your favor with extraordinary executives, or does your organization lack the competencies that will be required for success going forward? Finding out sooner rather than later can reveal a great deal about your likely future success and put you in a position to be proactive and manage your future better than your competitors.

There is a growing recognition of the power and critical importance of understanding the talent within an organization. Specifically:

- What is the quality and depth of your organization's top management talent around the world?

- How do the top managers line up versus the company's key competencies and requirements for success, and versus external benchmarks?

- What is the rate of management turnover around the company and across the globe, and where are the major holes and organizational blockages?

- Where might expatriate managers have become stranded on international assignments, and where are the key geographic holes?

- How does the diversity of your organization's top management group, in terms of gender, racial, and ethnic background, compare with that of other leading companies and key constituencies that the company serves?

- What are the strengths and improvement opportunities in the way your organization recruits and assimilates external senior management hires? How well does the recruiting organization partner with the line organizations? What can be learned from best practices from other companies?

Assessing Organizational Talent

One of the keys to closing the gaps is to implement a successful process for undertaking human capital planning. Such a process should include the following steps:

- Interviewing a cross section of senior managers to gain a deeper view of your organization's long-term strategy and the leadership implications and organizational competencies required to successfully implement the strategy
- Interviewing senior human resources managers to get their input into the company's longer-term human capital needs, to incorporate their thinking on the key business issues, and to refine the understanding of required competencies for key roles and positions
- Interviewing the company's top managers, to assess them against the agreed-on competencies and specific skill requirements
- Developing a detailed analysis to be shared, reviewed, and discussed among the top line and HR executives on:
  - The key findings in terms of critical competencies required for success and organizational themes that emerge
  - Individual feedback versus key competencies and versus external benchmarks
  - Competency assessment by business unit and built up for the organization overall
  - Discussion of and recommendations on future improvements

Consider this scenario: You are an executive within a large organization and have just been assigned the general management responsibilities for a critical, growing division within your company. If successful in this highly visible role, you will be positioned for even greater responsibility within the organization, or in the broader marketplace for talent.

The unit is in a market segment that you know well and which you are convinced will likely continue to grow rapidly, delivering sustained margins for the foreseeable future. You feel that the unit has a competitive advantage in the way it goes to market, its processes, technical advantages, patents, and so on. Overall, you feel the division is poised to deliver on a great opportunity.

However, you are uncertain about the strength of the management team. Even after spending hours with key executives, questions emerge:

- Has my initial evaluation been somehow biased by my excitement for the new position or personal relationships with key managers? If so, to what degree?

- Knowing the market and competitive challenges that exist for the company, how can I predict the likely behaviors and performance of my management team?

- The management team clearly possesses many positive qualities, but how do I know if they are "best of breed," equaling or surpassing the talents of other executives at competing companies or those who are available in the marketplace?

- Will holes in the management team eventually come to light? How soon will I know, and when should I begin planning for succession?

As the pressure to make every career opportunity count rises, professionals today have reason to be concerned. As a result, executives are increasingly spending more time assessing the strength of their teams, seeking additional clarity on the current state and management potential that exists within their organizations.

A formal assessment for each individual, along with a review of the entire management team, can illuminate critical observations, including identification of specific individuals to retain, and assessment areas where gaps in talent may need to be filled—the bar raised. Each executive can be compared against the skills and competencies that will likely be required as the company and market mature, and if possible, can also be compared with general assessments of executives at key competitors.

Competency Curves

One approach that can help with this process involves a rigorous evaluation of existing professional talent compared with the current and future requirements of an organization—something we call competency curves. These competency curves have shown to be particularly powerful in synthesizing huge volumes of information on human capital assets. A competency curve is simply a diagram that lists required organizational or individual competencies across on the horizontal or X axis, and a relative measurement on the vertical or Y axis. Competency curves help illustrate the relative talents required in a marketplace, or those that exist within a competitor—in comparison to those already existing within an organization. In a straightforward manner, they illuminate current and future gaps in talent within a particular division, or throughout an entire organization.

Competency curves can be used to highlight existing and/or required skill levels across the primary functions of an organization. To begin a competency curve analysis, you first develop (from input provided by all required parties) the list of clearly defined competencies in each critical area, such as leadership, business development, operations, and administration. This list should then be provided to key stakeholders, asking them to select the specific competencies most

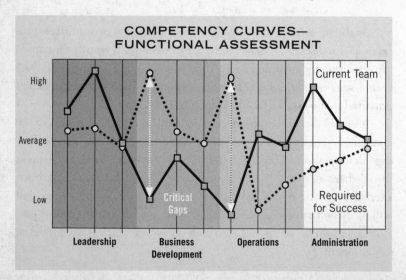

important in each area. For example, within leadership you may list the competencies of change management and turnaround effectiveness; within operations may be just-in-time inventory controls and managing contract manufacturing, and so on. Next, go back and ask participants to rank each competency in terms of its criticality to the current business (or in the near future): "Will strength in, or the lack of, this competency make or break the company/unit competitively?"

Simultaneously, conduct a detailed assessment of the existing management team, incorporating their beliefs and any assessment already conducted by other parties. From this, you can plot both the competency requirements for the business and its current level of capability, highlighting the strengths and critical gaps that exist within management. This information can be used for short- and longer-term planning purposes, key recruiting priorities, when considering an acquisition, or for go/no-go investment decisions.

The Hallmarks of a Good Organizational Assessment

To close the gap and get the full power of developing and applying competency curve analysis, a thorough organizational assessment process is recommended. No matter who leads this process—unit executives, human resource professionals, or external consultants—the approach should have three important attributes: that it be time-sensitive, accurate, and objective.

Time Sensitivity

The context in which an organizational assessment is reviewed must take into consideration the specific time horizon used for evaluation. Two critical questions to answer: Does the current team clearly possess the required competencies necessary for success today? Given the direction of the marketplace, what competencies will be required to win in the future, and how does the team stack up? Over the years, numerous assessments have been conducted without the context of a specific window of time. In today's competitive environment, the time horizon is far more important, requiring an evaluation of management's ability to meet specific, often foreseeable challenges in the near future.

Accuracy

While many consider talent assessment an art, years of developing and measuring the accuracy and relevance of various tools and techniques has resulted in widely recognized best practices. Many professionals are trained specifically in professional assessment and have conducted numerous projects over long periods of time, increasing the accuracy in standard evaluations. Whomever you are using as your assessor (internal or external resources), it is critical that the most relevant and accurate interviewing and assessment techniques are used.

Objectivity

As important as the accuracy of the assessment is being clear what you are assessing against. What business issues are currently faced? How does the management team compare to peers within the industry or in the broader professional workforce? Just as it is almost impossible to describe size, for instance, without common measurements or comparison in relation to something else, so it is difficult to successfully compare management talent without proper context. This critical perspective is often brought to the process by external consultants, who are constantly in the market evaluating and assessing a large number of executives within similar sectors. Talent should always be viewed relative to some agreed-upon benchmark or touchstone to clearly understand its strengths and weaknesses.

The information provided in a comprehensive organizational assessment provides managers with critical data from which to make informed decisions. In most cases, many initial instincts about the management team are corroborated. However, other important information also usually surfaces, such as who is most essential to the operation, what organizational themes emerge, and what the most important gaps are that must be closed.

Having this knowledge in hand allows managers to develop retention plans for key individuals and highlight specific areas in critical need of improvement. The leader is fully aware of the organization and able to keep a close eye on it so that any transition, if and when necessary, can be managed effectively and successfully.

IN CLOSING

For individuals, the five patterns reveal that career success is not random, but can be created over time. For organizations, a similar realization is now apparent. The existence of extraordinary professionals within your company should not be left to chance, but should actually be developed from existing employees. With a focus on creating a culture of success, where the top performers are accurately identified and disproportionately rewarded, and where organizations use a deep understanding of the existing and required talent in order to compete effectively and consistently raise the bar, companies can position themselves to substantially outperform their peers—over time, becoming truly extraordinary organizations.

PUTTING THE PATTERNS INTO PRACTICE

*Destiny is not a matter of chance, it is a matter of choice. It is not
a thing to be waited for, it is a thing to be achieved.*
—WILLIAM JENNINGS BRYAN

*There comes that mysterious meeting in life when someone
acknowledges who we are and what we can be, igniting the
circuits of our highest potential.*
RUSTY BERKUS

Perhaps no lesson in *The Five Patterns of Extraordinary Careers* is
more important than the power of career knowledge and action.
Taking positive actions in a career really does result in positive impact,
allowing the patterns of extraordinary careers to manifest themselves.
But as so many careers have shown, positive outcomes from positive
actions are rarely immediate. This is an idea we call "detached
impact." In your career, if you create real value for yourself or your
organization(s), you will almost always be rewarded for it, but not
always immediately.

So as you now turn to the task of implementing the five patterns of
extraordinary careers in your own professional life, the concept of
detached impact is one of the most critical concepts to keep in mind.
Why? Because otherwise, you may perceive prematurely that your
efforts are not taking hold. Measuring success in a career governed by

the five patterns requires a new scorecard. We have become accustomed in a society of immediate gratification to taking action and immediately looking for an outcome from which we can calibrate. When we miss a target to the left, we aim more to the right. When we fail, we try to identify what (and what not) to repeat to avoid failure in the future.

These are, of course, the right steps to follow, but this cycle of looking for an immediate result from our effort often leads to the belief that we have not succeeded if such a positive outcome does not instantly appear. We work diligently and perform well on key projects, but the person in the next office gets the promotion. We develop a breakthrough idea for a customer, yet receive no recognition. We assist a subordinate in his success, but the effort goes unnoticed. At first glance, you think these are fruitless efforts.

But having no immediate outcome is not the same as failure. The journey of a successful career is similar to chopping down a great tree. You swing the ax countless times, noticing only minor progress—with many swings, none at all. In the end, there is only one swing that is successful in bringing down the tree, but it is the thousand prior that made the achievement possible. Every swing, no matter how immediately visible the impact, is important in the process.

As you change your thinking and begin to take actions to implement the five patterns, you may see little immediate impact. But like each swing of the ax, this is not at all failure. In a career, success must be measured by the positive actions that are taken, not the immediate results. In the short term rewards are not highly correlated with specific actions, but over the long term they are inseparable. Just as compound interest gains accelerating power over time, so too does the impact of following the success patterns—something Harry Totonis has seen play out, time and time again.

Harry Totonis has led a multifaceted and extraordinary career as a consultant and software industry CEO. But ask him to reveal the factors that accounted for his success, and he seems almost speechless. "The only things that come to mind are luck and hard work. I am not the type to overanalyze my career or be concerned with every twist and turn. I have never really expected to be rewarded immediately for the specific actions I have taken. I have just tried to do the right thing and treat people fairly. I really feel fortunate to have been given the opportunity to succeed and to have led a career that is exciting to me."

Given his incredible career success, many may infer that Totonis is likely a portrait of take-no-prisoners ambition. The reality is quite different. And like the members of the college alumni panel in the Tim Reynolds story told at the beginning of this book, Totonis was probably not voted most likely to succeed. But look more closely, and you will discover the clear and consistent occurrence of the five patterns that have led to the extraordinary success of so many professionals.

Harry Totonis was born in Greece, spending his early childhood in Athens. His parents and several of his relatives collectively owned and operated several businesses in Greece and Turkey. When relations between the governments of the two countries deteriorated in the late 1950s, the Turkish government took over all assets in its country owned by the Greeks, and offered to buy the Totonis family's holdings for only a fraction of their worth. Out of pride, the family rejected the offer, surrendering the businesses they had worked so hard to grow, along with their home, receiving nothing in return. In 1965, they packed up everything they had left and emigrated to the United States, where together they started over.

Slowly, the extended Totonis family was able to again start several small restaurants and acquire some real estate. Only in fifth grade at the time, Harry was already expected to pitch in for the family business, working after school and on weekends, for which he was paid 50 cents an hour. Growing up so close to his relatives, business for Totonis was truly a family affair (not unlike *My Big Fat Greek Wedding*). His mother and father owned and operated the businesses, and each of his close relatives helped. "Everyone in my family was a shrewd negotiator, but there was always a level of fairness. Agreements were never made with the help of lawyers, just with handshakes. I learned firsthand that if you treat people fairly, they are likely to treat you fairly in return. It's really just the most efficient way to do business."

Being brought up in a hardworking family business, Totonis learned early on that there are few entitlements. He was schooled in the importance of hard work and how to create value. In a sense, he was given an early education in the "value of you." He had no problem working his way through college, and when he entered the professional workforce, he felt he actually had a stronger grounding in what really adds value—to clients and to himself—than many of his Ivy League co-workers. This knowledge allowed him to consistently maximize his potential and experiential value in the marketplace.

Totonis continued working with his family until he graduated from high school, and then went on to earn a degree from Ohio State University. After graduation, Totonis accepted a position with Goldman Sachs. He was one of the few state-school graduates to be extended an offer by the venerable firm. Although he performed admirably, he was not inspired by his day-to-day activities or by the path that promotion was likely to lead him onto. His longer-term ambition was to learn how to make business run from a CEO's perspective. So, early in his career, Totonis practiced the fifth pattern, finding the right fit for his strengths and passions, and left behind what others would see as a dream career at Goldman Sachs to join the global consulting firm Booz Allen Hamilton. He felt his passion came alive with the ability to execute his potential as both a thought leader and a leader of people.

Even in his earliest assignments at Booz Allen, Totonis' management approach was to treat everyone fairly, from the senior partners he worked under to the lowest-level associate on his team. "To me, taking the time to help develop junior people was at least as important as impressing my superiors. It may sound trite," he admits, "but you touch people every day, and as I have been given opportunities and been treated fairly, so have I tried to treat others as such. No one is perfect. You just try and do the right things." On the wings of exceptional performance, Totonis moved quickly up the ranks from an entry-level consultant to partner and then to senior partner, eventually coming to lead the entire Global Financial Services practice in record time, nearly half the normal rate of progression.

"When I was asked to head the Financial Services practice, I was a bit uncertain about how the team would welcome me in the role. Many of the senior members in the practice were partners even before I joined the firm." But Totonis didn't rely on a title to command respect; he set out to earn it, one colleague at a time. "I took my time to discover what motivated each of the members of my team. For example, one of my partners who was critical to the practice very much enjoyed assuming the role of industry thought leader and dealing with the press, but he was not the very best at writing groundbreaking articles. During the first year, I drafted articles for publication, then handed them over to him to take the ideas to market. Internally, many knew that I had originated the content, but I had no problem letting others take the limelight. I simply helped them find a role on our team where they would be motivated." Totonis' practice of benevolent leadership, working to ensure that every partner had a place, had the powerful consequence of retaining key employees, including every key partner during his tenure—even the partner whose position he assumed.

In 2000, after fifteen successful years with the firm, Totonis left Booz Allen to become CEO of Kinexus, Inc., a software firm targeting the financial services industry. The move to Kinexus is another example of Totonis finding the right fit, migrating from a practice leadership role to the CEO position within Kinexus, with total management responsibility for the organization, the strategy, and the financial results. The CEO role represented his ideal fit, playing to his strengths in leadership, strategy, management, and team building, leveraging his passion for providing solutions to the financial services industry and evangelizing a growth company, and allowing him to build a team of people around a culture that was hand crafted.

He knew the company needed help, but when he arrived, he uncovered problems much more significant than he had expected. Kinexus was burning through cash at a rate of $50 million per year and was generating not a penny of revenue. "There was a group of about fifty people on the operations floor of our building. I asked what they did, and I was told, 'They manage operations, processing transactions for our clients.' This was most disturbing, as I had just learned we had no clients!"

Knowing what was required to turn around the company, Totonis was faced with some hard decisions, needing to significantly reduce costs and lay off nearly 50 percent of the company's employees. "Kinexus had never been through a downsizing. We were at a critical juncture, with a fragile culture being tested by uncertainty. I was gravely concerned that the layoffs would significantly damage our already fragile morale." Of additional concern to Totonis was that the company's severance policy was to provide one week of pay for each year served. For a two-year-old company, this meant that nearly everyone would receive only one or two weeks' pay. As much as Totonis wanted to reduce costs, he felt this was simply unacceptable. He worked with the board to increase the severance packages, seeing to it that most employees received two or three months' pay. In one instance, the position of one of the firm's oldest employees, Sonny Pearson, had become redundant, requiring that he be let go. Knowing this would be particularly hard on Pearson, Totonis worked with the CFO to engineer nearly a year's severance for him. When Pearson was let go, he certainly wasn't happy, but he recognized that the severance went well beyond what the company was obligated to provide. Dealing with Pearson and other employees fairly sent a positive message to the organization, and word spread that they were justly treated.

Totonis did indeed turn around Kinexus, reducing costs and focusing the company's efforts on signing up customers and getting product out the door. Within three months, his company won its first major sale with Chase Manhattan Bank, beating out several other aggressive software vendors for the business. This lighthouse account gave Kinexus credibility, and soon other major customer wins followed: First Union, Wachovia, Merrill Lynch, and J. P. Morgan. These initial sales gave Totonis permission to represent the company as the emerging market leader and positioned him as the industry expert. In only eighteen months, the company grew from $0 to $15 million in sales, and swung from losing more than $50 million per year to nearly breaking even.

At Kinexus, Totonis practiced the 20/80 principle. Although always making sure to meet his predefined objectives, he was able to create visibly differentiated levels in performance not just by bringing life to the company's product line but by changing the product altogether, as well as the target market. In a short period, Kinexus moved from selling outsourced services to small family offices to providing consolidation and aggregation services to the world's most prestigious and largest banks and brokerage firms. Although it was the time of free-flowing capital, Totonis knew that he had to reorient the company's priorities on eliminating the cash burn and turning a profit. Fortunately for all involved, he took the necessary actions to approach profitability before his competitors. With this performance to match its cutting-edge product and technology, the small company became an attractive target for Advent Software, which acquired Kinexus for $180 million in December 2001, well after the values of most of its competitors had waned in the collapse of the stock market bubble. As the CEO of Kinexus, Totonis was rewarded handsomely from the company's sale. But others on his team had not fared quite as well, although they had worked extremely hard together as a team. In a final, unexpected gesture, Totonis took more than $900,000 from his gains and redistributed it to key members of his team who he felt had earned it. Although he is a bit uncomfortable discussing it, this figure represented a meaningful percentage of his proceeds from the sale, and he was never under any obligation to provide it. Once again, for Totonis, it was just "the right thing to do."

THE SUBTLETY OF SUCCESS

Seeing how the dots were connected between Harry Totonis' actions and his extraordinary success requires looking closely at his career. Having to work to help his family and paying his way through a good state school certainly didn't represent a privileged upbringing. At Booz Allen Hamilton, he invested time developing the most junior consultants, efforts certainly unlikely to be rewarded with immediate payback. As CEO of Kinexus, expanding the severance for displaced workers *cost* his company money in the short term.

While not always receiving any immediate positive benefits for his actions, he was able to orchestrate an extraordinary career. His actions did ultimately influence his career in numerous ways. It was the unexpected, often far removed impact of his actions and experiences that caused the five patterns of extraordinary success to appear in his career.

Practice Benevolent Leadership

While he strongly denies that success was ever a motivation for treating others with respect and fairness, Totonis' career is replete with evidence of him succeeding by making others successful.

- Leading the financial services practice at Booz Allen, Totonis worked to ensure that every partner had a place. This had the powerful consequence of retaining key employees. With the team secure and highly motivated, Totonis' team went on to achieve exceptional performance in the marketplace.

- After Kinexus had won its first critical sale with Chase Manhattan's Private Bank, Totonis learned that the chief operating officer of the division, a key decision maker, had actually worked with Totonis at Booz Allen more than ten years earlier, when he was a junior consultant. It was this very positive impression of Totonis from years before that ultimately helped tip the scales in favor of Kinexus, setting it on a course for success.

- When implementing the necessary staff reductions at Kinexus, Totonis later learned that several employees let go during the staff reduction had relayed to remaining employees how fairly they were treated, and how they appreciated and supported Totonis' leadership. What could have been a critical blow to morale turned into a galvanizing event for the company, focusing everyone around the objectives at hand, and performance of the team accelerated.

Overcome the Permission Paradox

While not overly aggressive about gaining permission, numerous actions taken by Totonis resulted in access to critical experiences.

- At Booz Allen Hamilton, Totonis' reputation as a thought leader (gained through drafting articles and other activities) contributed to his gaining the permission to be named as head of the global practice.

- At Kinexus, the first few sales to Chase, Wachovia, and First Union gave Totonis permission to represent the company as the emerging market leader, and positioned him as an industry expert. Additional customers soon followed.

Find the Right Fit (Strengths, Passions, and People)

Totonis' laissez-faire, long-term approach to career management worked to his great benefit, ultimately leading him to a position of strengths, passions, and people that represented his natural fit.

- Early in his career, working for highly respected Goldman Sachs, Totonis took an honest assessment of his strengths and passions and subsequently left behind what others viewed as a dream career to join Booz Allen. It was a relatively subtle move—from working in the financial services industry to consulting to it—yet Totonis felt his passion come alive with the ability to be a thought leader and a people leader. His outstanding performance followed as a direct consequence.

DON'T BURN BRIDGES, BUILD THEM

"Don't burn your bridges" can be a trite axiom, but one that is valuable to revisit nonetheless. We would actually implore you to go a step further and seek to build them as well. As the extraordinary careers of Harry Totonis and so many other professionals in this book have helped illustrate, one of the underlying themes of successful careers is that they are based on interconnected relationships—in other words, bridge building. Some of the bridges are crossed immediately, such as IBM's Lou Gerstner or AOL's Jon Miller being placed through an executive search firm or Greg Brenneman executing his revitalization plan of PwC Consulting and sale to IBM. But others, such as Totonis' Kinexus deal with its landmark customer, Chase Manhattan—thanks to his former Booz Allen associate—are not crossed for a long time. Regardless of when you cross it, every time you take a positive action in your career, you build a bridge. You cannot predict when that bridge will become valuable to you, or even if it ever will. But by taking positive action, you do your part to put it in place.

The power of taking the long view and resisting the impulse for immediate gratification is illustrated by a memorable experiment called the Marshmallow Challenge. Initiated by psychologist Walter Mischel during the 1960s at a preschool on the Stanford University campus, this research involved dozens of four-year-old children of Stanford faculty, graduate students, and university employees. In the experiment, each child was seated at a table. Someone would enter the room and place one marshmallow on the table in front of the child. The child was then offered the following proposal: If the child desired, he or she could immediately eat the marshmallow placed on the table, but if the child could wait until the facilitator returned from an "errand," he or she would be rewarded with an extra marshmallow. This remarkable experiment was detailed by Daniel Goleman in his book *Emotional Intelligence.*[1]

Some four-year-olds were able to wait what must surely have seemed an endless fifteen to twenty minutes for the experimenter to return," Goleman wrote. "These plucky preschoolers got the two-marshmallow reward. But others, more impulsive, grabbed the one marshmallow, almost always within seconds of the experimenter's leaving the room on his "errand."

The diagnostic power of how this moment of impulse was handled became clear some twelve to fourteen years later, when these same children were tracked down as adolescents. Those who had resisted temptation at four were now, as adolescents, more socially competent; they embraced challenges and pursued them instead of giving up even in the face of difficulties. The third or so of the subjects who grabbed for the marshmallow, however, tended to have fewer of these qualities, and instead shared a relatively more troubled psychological portrait.

Even more surprising, when the tested children were evaluated again as they were finishing high school, those who had waited patiently at four were far superior as students to those who had acted on whim. Most astonishingly, they had dramatically higher scores on the SAT tests—a 210-point difference in total score.

At age four, how children do on this test of delay of gratification is twice as powerful a predictor of what their SAT scores will be as is IQ.

Goleman concluded optimistically, "There is ample evidence that emotional skills such as impulse control and accurately reading a social situation can be learned."

For a four-year-old, it is hard to imagine a more challenging test than forgoing the impulse to eat a delicious marshmallow in favor of waiting for two. But in a career, this challenge of delayed gratification is made all the more difficult as you try to manage your success in an environment of great complexity. Any benefit resulting from a positive action is rarely known beforehand, and in many cases completely unforeseeable—we are not even promised an extra marshmallow! At best, we can only assume that our positive actions will eventually lead to positive events in our career, but without any certainty of when these events will occur. Consider the difficulty in passing up a promotion that offers an increase in pay and prestige in favor of the possibility of a move in the future that will represent a better personal fit, or spending your time helping others be successful rather than remaining laser-focused on your own near-term career success. But long-term success requires this focus on positive actions, seemingly untethered but ultimately inexorably linked with success.

Understanding the concept of disconnected impact and practicing its recommended approach of succeeding through positive actions despite unknown benefits has an additional advantage: It is the best path to gain control over your career. Many people grow to believe that the only way to achieve control over the direction of a career is to manage its every turn very tightly. But due to the increased volatility of careers, tactically managing your professional life down to the finite details provides only a false and fleeting sense of control. As singer/songwriter Sting appropriately chorused, "If you love something, set it free."

TAKING CONTROL OF YOUR CAREER

Ultimate control over a career in the long term actually requires letting go of it in the short term. Despite many successes early in his career, Sean Seitzinger ultimately learned what achieving control over your career is really all about.

After being hired to head the Strategic Innovations department at Coca-Cola headquarters in Atlanta, Sean Seitzinger feared that he was living a career catastrophe. He had abandoned the road warrior rigors of a consultant's life for a more stable existence at Coke. But no sooner had he assumed his new role than he was upset to find that the department he headed was on the company's endangered-species list.

Perhaps most unsettling to Seitzinger was the feeling that he was losing control of his career. During his twenties and early thirties, he had steadily ascended the professional ranks, landing a position as a senior principal within the highly successful consulting firm Diamond Cluster International. He had ridden the company's growth through its successful IPO, and in the talent-hungry market of the late '90s, he was constantly called by recruiters tempting him to consider other exciting opportunities. But his exit from the travel-intensive consulting industry coincided with a dramatic decline of the economy. Dreams of stock option windfalls dwindled, and the calls from recruiters stopped altogether. Seitzinger began to realize that what he had perceived to have been control over his career was actually just the effects of a hyperenergized market—one that had actually been controlling him. "Is true control over my career even attainable?" he would ask himself. He thought perhaps he would find the answer by joining a large, stable corporation such as Coca-Cola. But soon he began to question whether being a senior executive of even the most stable company was the recipe for control. "I wasn't quite sure how the game was played within such a large company," he said. "I felt that unless I gained some traction, my career at Coke would end up being frustratingly unimpressive."

So he decided to act. Rather than hope that top management would suddenly take a greater interest in his group's work, he decided that being proactive, even if it meant no foreseeable, immediate reward, was better than doing nothing. With this new attitude, Seitzinger soon learned the game and played each card with care—to his advantage. Seitzinger began by networking and developing relationships broadly within the company, meeting professionals at all levels, grasping their perspective on the organization as well as their rationale for their positions. He reached beyond the borders of his division and formed trusted allies who valued his insight and expertise.

More crucially, he pinpointed precisely how his small, orphan organization could be a strong platform from which to have impact. His unit consisted of disparate groups, all dealing with some aspect of innovation in product merchandising. But many people around the company were dubious about the idea that merchandising was fertile ground for innovation. After all, they believed, it was a practice that had been honed over the course of a century—what more was there to know?

Seitzinger disagreed. Although what his group did was not considered sexy, he knew it could deliver real business impact. To him, merchandising was the last stop before the customer got the product, and therefore innovation was not only possible but absolutely critical to Coke's survival in future competitive markets. "This simple redefinition of my role, even if I created it in my own mind, allowed access to opportunities all over the organization," underscored Seitzinger. "Instead of being confined to a limited and uninfluential role, I became convinced that our group's perspective was needed across the organization. When it was clearly articulated as such, others soon agreed."

Soon, Seitzinger began expanding his role—redefining his direct and implied permission. He managed only a handful of direct reports, but he solicited involvement—and also resources—from both internal and external constituencies with whom he worked. Ultimately, he was indirectly steering the efforts of hundreds of people, leveraging resources for R&D, product development, agency management, and national sales. And then his efforts started to pay off for the organization. That got people to notice. "Early on, my mentor within Coke joked that he would see pieces of our work showing up in strange places around the organization. But now he feels that our small unit has become one of the most influential strategic groups in the company." Through all this, Seitzinger shifted his focus of activities from tactical marketing, in which he was competent but not passionate, to corporate strategy, where he was unquestionably skilled and where his passion was evident to himself and nearly everyone around him in his unquenchable thirst to develop, analyze, and test different strategic options for the company and in his unique insights.

Slowly, in some cases perhaps even subconsciously, Seitzinger began taking positive actions, putting the patterns of extraordinary careers into practice, and started to see the trajectory of his career change. "I was relentlessly patient," Seitzinger recalls. "I balanced an aggressive bias toward action with the patience of knowing that positive results would eventually appear." Executives began to call him into key meetings, ask him to participate in critical initiatives, and raise his name when seeking to fill significant executive positions. In a company filled with longtime veterans, and with a reputation of being incredibly difficult for professionals recruited from the outside to penetrate, Sean Seitzinger had created tangible upward momentum in his career within only a few years. Small, positive actions, over time, proved to have a very large impact on his career.

Throughout *The Five Patterns of Extraordinary Careers*, we have examined many stories like this one—from Denys Gounot's mud-laden trek to the corner office at Lucent Optical to Dan Rosensweig's sure and steady ascent to the COO role at Yahoo! And all of these examples have two things in common: subtlety and pure intentions. Harry Totonis didn't bully his way to the top; for that matter, he never even expected to reach his ultimate level of success. Totonis did not avoid actions that offered no immediate personal gain, nor did he ask for recognition for his acts of goodwill. Sean Seitzinger didn't try to play politics with the CEO or sabotage the work of his peers in his quest for greater and greater power within the company. He did not single-handedly move Coke's stock price upward or stumble onto a new, improved formula for Coca-Cola itself. But both Totonis and Seitzinger took the long view, and both took action. Both learned, helped, expanded, impacted, and demonstrated a passionate competence for their work. And in the process both their success and satisfaction moved significantly upward.

Ultimately, this is another important lesson of *The Five Patterns of Extraordinary Careers:* Small efforts to create the occurrence of the success patterns can have an incredible impact on any professional career over time. Michael Reene volunteered to coordinate office meetings at Accenture and developed a deeper understanding about how the firm functioned, which partners commanded value, and why. Herb Kelleher sought to make others realize their potential by creating an environment of true caring where people could just be themselves, and over time he attracted the best and brightest to his company. Howard Schultz gave up a successful and promising career as a Xerox sales executive to run marketing and sales for a single coffee store because he was passionate about coffee and the idea of building a different kind of company. Totonis was guided by doing the right thing. Seitzinger simply redefined the role of his organization in his head and converted a group on the verge of extinction to one of the most critical units in the company.

For skeptics, the five patterns may seem too simplistic to be truly meaningful in the complex world of careers. We, too, agree that the patterns are simple in concept: Attain career knowledge that is learned only when peering between the lines. Focus on the success of others, who will in turn carry you to the top. Use creative strategies to gain access to critical opportunities, and then deliver breakthrough impact to create lasting differentiation. Follow your true fit in strengths, passions, and people and you will be rewarded with the ultimate levels of success and satisfaction. All very simple notions, to be sure. But it is the rarity of their occurrence that makes these patterns so powerful. Understanding these patterns, in the end, may be relatively easy, but it is the deliberate act of putting these patterns in motion within the context of your own life that can dramatically alter the course of *your* career.

Succeeding via the five patterns requires that we fundamentally change the way in which we look at ourselves as professionals, at our careers, and at our world. We have spent a great deal of time in this book dealing with subtle differences in approach and action, most of which pay no immediate dividends. It is hard to believe that altruism can pay off within an organization. But it can. It is difficult to grasp how expanding our scope of permission ever so slightly or aiming our last ounce of resources toward greater impact for our employers will have a material impact on our careers. But it can. It is overwhelming to accept that sometimes stepping backward, forgoing a perceived "great opportunity" in favor of one that plays more to our strengths and interests, may actually light the way to far greater success and satisfaction. But it most definitely can.

THE POWER OF POSITIVE THOUGHT AND ACTION

The human mind is constantly making associations and distinctions. In a complex world, these act almost like a lighthouse in a foggy and uncertain sea. And that's precisely the role of the five patterns. Yes, it's often hard to see the connection between your actions at work and the long-term payoff, but the patterns we've elucidated in this book illuminate the vital link between positive actions and long-term professional success, reinforcing that, over time, all of your small steps toward success make a huge difference.

Most successful executives we know can identify specific points in time when each of the five patterns has played a significant role in their ultimate success, but none has indicated that he was able to predict these points before they occurred, or that at the time he grasped the ultimate impact of these moments. Only that they happened.

The objective of this book is to provide insight into a new way of thinking about, talking about, and ultimately acting out your career ambitions. By expanding your permission sets, you will broaden your horizons; by focusing on what is most valuable to your employers, you increase your own value; and by migrating toward careers that maximize strengths, passions, and fit, you position yourself for the ultimate success and fulfillment that is attainable.

The Five Patterns of Extraordinary Careers is a testament to the power of positive thought and action, and to the potential that exists within every professional. If successful careers seem random or unattainable, secret or stolen, they are not. From the most subtle and well-intentioned replication of the five patterns in our own careers extraordinary things can emerge, and we truly hope that they do for you.

As you go forth and start testing and implementing the five patterns, we hope you will let us know how it is going. While much research and professional experience have gone into this book, the real test begins right now, with you and your own unique journey. We invite you to visit www.5patterns.com to share what's working and what's not, and any new insights that your experience brings to bear. After all, it is in the action that career knowledge has its greatest value.

THE SPENCER STUART JOB SURVIVAL GUIDE

MANAGING A CAREER TRANSITION

One of your possible courses of action for implementing the five patterns of extraordinary careers is to decide to clean the slate and make a job change. Or, like many thousands of professionals, you may find that this need has been thrust upon you from a downsizing or postmerger integration that has eliminated your job. Whatever the reason, we know that many readers of this book may, at some stage, want to or need to think about finding a new position. This special section is designed to guide you through this process in the most effective way possible, leveraging the lessons of the five patterns.

The material in this guide is the result of nearly two years of work, originally developed on a customized basis for one of Spencer Stuart's largest global clients. We were engaged to provide individualized coaching to departing senior executives following a postmerger rationalization—a value-added layer over and above traditional outplacement services. Our client's objective was simple: Beyond simply doing the right thing for its people, the company calculated that the benefit from having scores of alumni spread throughout the business landscape feeling positive from being treated with so much respect and support would far outweigh the costs of the program. And from the company's perspective and the participants in the program, the feedback has been overwhelming—our client now has scores of ambassadors in the market rather than disgruntled former employees.

With that as background, let us move to share the Spencer Stuart Job Survival Guide with you. There are four phases to developing and implementing a job change strategy. The first phase, the plan, consists of seven steps.

PHASE I: DEVELOP THE PLAN

1. Find Your Strengths

As we discussed in "Find the Right Fit (Strengths, Passions, and People)," a key pattern of extraordinary success is to find yourself in a role that plays to your strengths. We all have an intuitive sense of our strengths and weaknesses, but now is the moment to become very specific. To do so, there are a number of exercises we recommend as well as resources to take advantage of. First, build a skills and accomplishments inventory. Start with a blank sheet of paper and make a chronological list of all your jobs since you began your career. Then next to each job note the things about that role that you did well and not so well. In addition, for each position, note what you believe was your most important accomplishment. Be thoughtful about this and try to get beyond the obvious.

One key to assessing your strengths is to see beyond the functional roles as defined in your workplace. View yourself not as a banker, marketer, manufacturer, or magazine publisher with industry-specific skills, but as a unique person with specific skill sets that can be broadly applied across a number of fields. For each accomplishment and role, list the key skills that were required: problem solving, product design, managing yourself, leading others, team participation, conceptual thinking, written communications, salesmanship, and so on.

After filling up a few sheets of paper, you should notice themes emerging, the themes of the strengths and weaknesses throughout your career. If you are like most professionals, there will be surprising consistency over time.

Brutal honesty helps, even if it's difficult. Are you short-tempered with people but patient with projects? Are you a good motivator but poor at delegation? Do you manage up well but down less well? Are you a good presenter to large groups of people, or do you get stage fright? Are you an off-the-cuff communicator, or do you require detailed preparation and support? Are you led by facts and analysis, or do you lean toward generating ideas and concepts? Are you gifted at complex problem solving? Do you revel in the immediate gratification of checking to-do items off your list? Do you thrive on the thrill of the hunt or perform better servicing existing customers? Do you love the action of the markets or feel trapped being tethered to events out of your control?

There are many forms of self-assessment, most of which can be helpful in identifying strengths and weaknesses and other job-related issues. Of the various other resources we are familiar with, one of the best and longest-standing in self-assessment is a program run by the Johnson O'Connor Research Foundation. This not-for-profit institution, with offices in many major commercial centers, has been conducting research into and measuring aptitudes and their effect on human performance, success, and work satisfaction since 1922. The foundation runs individualized programs in its Human Engineering Laboratory, resulting in the development of an individualized inventory of your aptitudes. After personalized testing, your pattern of strengths and weaknesses is compared to the hundreds of thousands of subjects that have been assessed over the decades from which high-level career implications can be drawn. The people to whom we've recommended this program have come back with incredible enthusiasm for the rigor of the testing and the data-driven feedback of the results. Further information on Johnson O'Connor can be obtained on their Web site, www.jocrf.org, or by calling 212-838-0550.

2. Identify What Gets Your Juices Flowing

You've fallen out of love with your current job, or it looks like layoffs are coming and you will be one of the victims, or you want something more from your career—something the last experience didn't provide. That's normal enough, but you need to define what it is that you will be passionate about. What subjects or industries really get your creative juices flowing? Does high-tech bore you? Do consumer products fascinate you? And how do you like to work? Do you like participating in team goals on a daily basis? Or do you prefer to sift through and analyze information on your own?

If you are hard pressed to identify a potential career path that really intrigues you, here's a simple but effective way to give yourself an informal "interests X ray": Get a pile of newspapers and magazines, both national and local, that cover the last four to six weeks. Go through them and tear out everything that appeals to you. Don't ask yourself why—just put what you've ripped out in a folder. Then separate all of your selections into piles, one pile for each area of interest. What does the landscape tell you? What themes emerge? If you are like most, the tallest piles will be those things that genuinely get your juices flowing.

Another step is to build off your strengths and weaknesses inventory from step one. In reviewing your list of roles and accomplishments, take out another sheet of paper. For each one, list what you liked most and what you disliked most about achieving each accomplishment. Then force-rank them in terms of the enjoyment you derived from them.

3. Build Your Personal Board of Directors

As we discussed in "Differentiate Using the 20/80 Principle of Performance," it helps greatly to have a "master mind group" or "personal board of directors" to provide support and insight into your talents. If you have not yet done this, make a list of trusted, experienced individuals whom you've known for years. They make the best sounding boards. Contact them. Ask them to review your assessment of strengths and weaknesses; if they do not agree with your tally, alter your assessment. Implore them to be straightforward. You may hear things that surprise you, positive and negative. Ideally, you will gain valuable insights and ensure that there will be no unfortunate surprises later on. In addition to corroborating your views, these individuals may also be your professional and character references down the road. You want to ensure that there is no dissonance between the assessment of strengths and weaknesses that you communicate to potential employers and that of references.

4. Identify What You Would Like to Achieve from the New Position

Consistent with the career triangle that we described in "Find the Right Fit," clearly articulate what you must have and what would be nice to have in your new position. Where do you want to live, and in what kind of setting? What compensation package do you require? With what level of responsibility are you comfortable? Thinking hard about these will help you identify acceptable trade-offs early. Maybe you are willing to make a lateral move in terms of money and/or responsibility in order to obtain an opportunity to learn and grow in ways that will be very useful to your long-term plan. Perhaps you are open to other regions of the country.

Beyond the concrete attributes of the specific next job, try to put your thinking into a prioritized list of personal goals. Determine how important the following are to you: achievement, duty, expertise, friendship, self-improvement, independence, leadership, family balance, pleasure, power, prestige, recognition, security, service, wealth. Make a list and force-rank such personal goals.

5. Generate Options from Fact-based Research

It is all too easy to get caught up in career myopia. Recognize that your skills can be applied in many industries. Sit down and stretch your brain. Fixate on those fields that you think might interest you, or that might have similar characteristics to your areas of expertise. Make a list of major industry sectors, dig down and identify specific companies, and develop a preliminary target list.

Review local and national publications. Identify trends, companies of interest, and functional areas of growth, as well as the current thinking and trends in your industry. Staying up to date is important to maintaining your enthusiasm, credibility, and viability.

Also, review the piles of articles you tore out from magazines and newspapers. Certain companies will draw your attention. Then use Yahoo! Finance or Hoover's to identify the competitors to those companies. This will help you build your target list.

6. Develop a Written Plan That Supports Your Job Strategy

Develop a written target list of specific companies that interest you, search firms at which you have contacts, outplacement firms, and associations, as well as friends, colleagues, and acquaintances who may have connections to such organizations. Make a methodical plan for contacting each one.

Devise a realistic timetable. This will give you much-needed structure and tangible goals. Be prepared to make midcourse corrections and/or contingency plans as necessary.

7. Further Educate Yourself

Select one or two books from the supplemental reading list, or visit www.amazon.com or www.bn.com for recommended reading lists. We suggest you review at least one career self-help guide. Some books may espouse different models from what we recommend here, yet there is no single plan for every person or situation.

PHASE II: TAKE ACTION

With the plan now developed, it is time to take action. Executing an effective job search requires discipline and work. Approach this search as a full-time job. Manage yourself as effectively as you have managed your own teammates or employees. Having said this, recognize that job searches take time, and while it's important to keep moving forward, it's also important to be patient. Focusing 100 percent of your waking attention on a job search will make you tiresome company. It is essential to stay refreshed by doing some activities outside of your search. Join a local community board. Spend quality time with the kids. Exercise regularly. Take a little time for yourself.

We recommend that you start by posting the Job Search Survival Mantra on your mirror or the inside of your laptop case. You will need to remind yourself of these axioms regularly.

THE JOB SEARCH SURVIVAL MANTRA

A career transition is:

- A major step
- A full-time job
- A problem to solve—and an opportunity to exploit
- A time to reflect and reprioritize
- The first page in a new life chapter

A successful career transition requires:

- Planning
- Practice
- Humility
- Hard work
- Discipline
- Creativity
- Ability to deal with disappointment, anger, and frustration
- Willingness to see the best in yourself
- Eagerness to market yourself
- Many irons in the fire
- A positive attitude

Four steps constitute the remainder of Phase II.

1. Develop Your Outreach Materials

1.1. Resume Law #1: Omit Needless Words

In their famous little style guide, William Strunk and E. B. White codify the rules of polished writing. Rule #17 is simply: Omit needless words. Never is this rule more applicable than in resume writing.

A good resume conveys the heart and soul of someone at a glance. A tall order, yes. Always describe the company at which you worked. Unless it's a household name, people probably won't recognize it by name alone. Be clear by noting which geographical location you worked in. Be complete and specific with regard to the dates; don't leave time gaps, which will only raise questions. Write in simple, direct language. Don't state your objective—that is what the cover letter or e-mail note is for. Indicate how the company should contact you; if the potential employer shouldn't call your office, state that in the cover letter.

It is not necessary to mention every esoteric project from the beginning of your career, but it is frequently useful to include not-for-profit, volunteer, or extracurricular information, as it provides extra information about you and potentially a hook or link to the reader. However, never embellish. And, as obvious as it seems, never misrepresent your academic credentials. They are easy to check, and the effects of misrepresentation are devastating, as certain top executives learned in 2002.

Both your resume and cover note should communicate how you can be a solution to a given company's need. No company wants to know why this would be a great opportunity for *you*; they want to know why you would be a godsend for *them*. Put your time and skill toward identifying the problems you can solve for the potential employer—do your due diligence. Is the company attempting to grow or exploit a new market? Figure out the company's key challenges and present yourself as the solution. If you can come close to identifying your skills as a solution to that company's needs, it is more likely that your letter will be read and your phone call will be answered.

If you prefer to use a service to help develop your resume, you might try www.careerresumes.com, www.expertresumes.com, or www.

crsresume.com. These services are accredited with the PRWRA (Professional Resume Writing and Research Association) and the NRWA (National Resume Writers' Association).

Once you have put together a solid, up-to-date resume, develop a mailing plan that includes postal mail as well as e-mail. Don't forget to develop a crisp phone message for networking and calls to follow up. Try it out on a friend or two who will give you helpful, honest feedback.

1.2. Adapt Your Cover Letter and Resume for e-mail

In today's wired world, e-mail has become the preferred means to send a cover letter and resume. While this is not as formal as sending a resume by regular mail, some companies prefer e-mail for its convenience and its ability to be easily forwarded to the most relevant person. But it still requires close attention to language, spelling, grammar, and punctuation.

We advise cutting and pasting the text of your resume into the body of the e-mail, as well as attaching it as its own Word document (but not a zip file). Don't forget to include a direct and descriptive subject line, such as "VP of finance seeks new opportunity" or, better yet, "John Kelly suggested I contact you." To the extent that you can find someone whom the recipient will recognize as having suggested you contact them, the more likely it will be that your e-mail will be answered. Be sure to include your complete contact information in the message and the resume attachment.

Begin the e-mail with a brief introduction that includes what you are looking for and whether you are willing to relocate. If you are trying to transition into a new function or industry, address why you are capable of such a transition. Ask for specific advice or direction. If you don't know the recipient, ask them to take a specific action on your behalf: "Can you forward this on to the appropriate person? Can you instruct me as to how I can receive calls or e-mail from your firm? Can you direct my resume to any appropriate colleagues or clients? Can you spend fifteen minutes with me for a courtesy interview?"

But keep your e-mail cover letter brief—the individual reading it may have received hundreds of resumes and rarely has time to read lengthy communiqués. Avoid sending pictures, fancy HTML, or other distractions in your e-mail. Here's a good example of getting to the point: "I am a turnaround executive with strong financial skills, excellent at managing large groups of people."

2. Activate Your Personal Network: Tell and Sell

Now that your presentation materials are ready, it is time to share them with as many well-placed people as possible. This is one of the most important things you can do. Talk to former colleagues, associates, contacts, and friends from college and/or graduate school. Join and mingle in associations, local networking groups, and online networking sites. Ask every contact for additional contacts.

You might be a superstar at your current company, or maybe you are one of the many undervalued overachievers. Either way, the next person you meet hasn't been studying your professional and life history. You need to *tell* and *sell*—tell people the pertinent details of your last job and sell it in the most positive light. This is especially critical if you're looking to reposition yourself in a different industry. You must redefine yourself in terms of the competencies that you possess. Highlight the traits that most hiring executives are seeking: intellect and skills; resourcefulness and problem-solving abilities; flexibility in applying these talents to new areas; leadership and interpersonal qualities; specific industry, process, or functional knowledge relevant to their company.

In your positioning, you should also address two critical issues: what you can personally offer a company, and what you can do to help it advance its cause, build its business, and make it a more competitive and profitable organization. View your skills and talents as leverage, rather than as a means to develop your weak areas. Playing to your strengths will make you more marketable, more successful, and—as we've stressed throughout this book—happier in your next position.

Identify and contact executive recruiters who specialize in your field. In print, the sourcebook for executive recruiting is *The Directory of Executive Recruiters 2001* (30th ed.), edited by Kennedy Information. Known to insiders since 1971 as the "Red Book," the 2001 edition contains detailed information on over thirteen thousand recruiters across North America. Online, try the following Web site: www.recruitersonline.com/match/search.phtml.

Post your resume on executive recruiting and general career Web sites geared toward executives. Spencer Stuart offers candidate registration and job postings at www.spencerstuart.com. Additional free posting sites geared toward executives include www.HotJobs.com, www.6figurejobs.com and www.chiefmonster.com. Several leading sites charge fees for the use of their services, such as www.bluesteps.com, the official resource of the Association of Executive Search Consultants, and www.execunet.com, a career advancement membership organization for executives earning more than $100,000 a year.

Avail yourself of outplacement firms and career counselors. While we can't recommend any one firm, some of the largest and most well known include Drake Beam Morin; Allen & Associates; Challenger, Gray and Christmas; Lee Hecht Harrison; Right Management Consultants; and Spherion.

3. Interviewing: Prepare, Practice; Prepare, Practice; Repeat

Interviewing well is an art. High-performing artists rehearse exhaustively. You should, too. To prepare, thoroughly research the industry, company, job, and culture. If possible, find out how employees dress for work so you can dress accordingly, yet professionally, for your interview. Develop questions and identify anyone you know who works there. Home in on cultural issues to which you should be sensitive.

USA Today recently asked Richard Bolles, author of *What Color Is Your Parachute*, "What is the worst thing a job hunter can do?" His answer: "Going in and knowing absolutely nothing about the place. The basic rule here is that organizations love to be loved, and when a job hunter walks in the door and doesn't know a thing about them, the first thing they say to themselves is this guy doesn't love this place."

Rehearse. Verbal presentation is key. So is Q&A. Become comfortable selling yourself, serving as your own agent. Test your style and presentation out on people who will give you feedback. If the interview is by phone or videoconference, determine what you need to do differently from an in-person interview. Phone interviews are becoming increasingly common, so take them seriously. Make sure you have yourself set up to do it from a land line, not a cell phone; make sure the kids or the pets will not create unprofessional background noise or interruptions. And remember the goal of the phone interview is not to get the job, it is only to move the ball one rotation forward—to get invited for an in-person interview.

Don't overlook the thank-you. It is simply common courtesy to send a thank-you e-mail or letter to anyone who took time to meet with you. While this is rarely what gets you the job, a potential employer will notice if you skip this step. A brief, well-written note reinforces your image of professionalism.

4. Take Stock of the Situation

Allow yourself a realistic timetable, but at a certain point, if things aren't working well, you need to figure out why. How does one discern the difference between discouragement and a real need for a mid-course correction? If you're over six weeks into your search and not getting at least some response, you should look at each item on your list and figure out where you need to make corrections. If you're well over six months into your search and still gaining no traction, perhaps you should explore other alternatives.

Is your net cast wide enough? If your research into a particular industry isn't yielding options, maybe you should expand your geographical limits. Perhaps you want to meet with a career counselor or an outplacement counseling firm. Other options to consider: an entrepreneurial venture, consulting, school, a not-for-profit.

PHASE III: PREPARE FOR THE OFFER

1. Be Prepared to Receive an Offer

Yes, it should happen, and you need to be ready for it. When you receive an offer, the very first thing to do is to thank the potential employer with a call or in a personally written note or even an e-mail. Then you should establish a timetable for decision making with those who have offered you the job.

Develop your follow-up questions. This is your last opportunity to do your own due diligence on your potential employer. If you are relocating to a new community, you might plan to make a special trip to the company's location with your spouse, family, or significant other.

- When will I receive the offer in writing?
- How much time do I have to assess the offer?
- May I please have a copy of the benefits program?
- Now that I have the offer, may I meet with other members of the organization?
- Do you offer relocation benefits?

2. The Offer Is on the Table—Now Reach a Decision

Accepting or turning down a job offer is a critical decision with many factors to consider, and you would be wise to consult with trusted counsel, be it a spouse, a colleague, a mentor, or your search consultant. It's important to know when to seek advice about:

- Negotiating
- Legal matters
- Financial concerns or compensation
- Cultural/international matters

It's not always categorically a good idea to negotiate. Be realistic. Ask yourself—or your consultant—if this is the best offer you're likely to get, based on your skills, experience, the job market, and the terms of the offer. Expect candor from your search consultant, and rely on him or her to advise you. Typically, he or she has perspective on whether the company has put together its best offer, take it or leave it, or whether the company expects to negotiate. In rare circumstances, you may need to reach out for legal advice on consultation or compensation.

3. Be Prepared for a Counteroffer

If you are leaving a job to take a new one, it is not uncommon to receive a counteroffer from your current employer in a last-ditch effort to retain your talents. Don't let this confuse you; if you are ready to leave, stay true to the goals that compelled you to look for a new opportunity in the first place. In our experience, even if an employee accepts a counteroffer, unless the situation that made the job unsatisfactory changes radically, he or she will move on to a new position within a year to eighteen months.

4. Once You Have Decided to Take the Job, Clarify the Employer's Expectations of You for the First Thirty Days, Ninety Days, and One Year

This may happen before you formally accept the job or after you first begin, but it is vital to put your potential employer's expectations into concrete terms early in your tenure. Be clear about what you will need to do to demonstrate your success. The better you understand the targets and the more measurable those targets are, the greater your likelihood of success.

5. Accept Graciously to the Appropriate Person, Both Verbally and in Writing

Relationship building is important at this time—seize this chance to convey your excitement about the new position and build rapport with your soon-to-be colleague(s). If you choose to decline the offer, you should offer an explanation and close the communication gracefully and in such a way that future contact will be welcomed.

6. Resign from Your Current Job

If you are employed, two weeks is the minimum notice you should provide, although you may choose to provide more advance notice than the bare minimum. In any event, set a firm date for leaving and stick to it.

7. Close the Loop with Your Professional Network

This is a particularly crucial step that will enable you to maintain a strong professional network and strong relationships with your contacts. Thank the people who have helped you, and let your contacts know about your new position. Most important, let them know how they can contact you in the future. Completing the communications only strengthens your professional network and ensures that you will hear from and be free to contact colleagues in the future.

PHASE IV: GET OFF TO THE RIGHT START IN YOUR NEW JOB

Once you have landed the job, the next goal is being successful at it. We recommend the following:

1. Do Your Homework

Much of your success during the first hundred days actually comes before you report for work on the first day. Before you begin, you should request materials to review at home on your new duties and learn all that you can about the new company. Ask for information that you don't already have about the company's products, services, and business strategies, and begin to accumulate your knowledge base before you begin. Go to school on all the relevant business plans that have been written, and use them to help assess the company's situation relative to the competition. Expect that your new employer may even want you to participate in a critical meeting in advance of your start date—be flexible and available for that contingency.

2. Be Upbeat and Build Bridges

Keep in mind that right off the bat, you will be watched closely by all with whom you come into contact. It is a virtual certainty that in the first few weeks, people will start rating how you're doing. Your style and comportment will be what people see well before the results. Be enthusiastic without being obsequious. Be as nondefensive as possible. Set realistic commitments and meet them. Be prepared for meetings, knowing the details of whatever it is you are talking about. Be nonpolitical, recognizing that new managers are like flypaper for attracting different people's points of view. Acting like this will keep the honeymoon period alive as long as possible, giving you the time to build your bridges, build your team, and develop your plans.

Don't rely solely on the human resource department or your direct supervisor to manage your orientation. Instead, be proactive. Your integration into the professional network of the organization is your responsibility. Your company will likely do a number of things to bring you up to speed and help you identify key contacts, but different companies vary in their integration processes. Take matters into your own hands. Set up meetings or lunches with key people you will interact with. Find out what departments you will need to work with and begin to forge relationships with them.

3. Listen and Learn

The sooner you master the unwritten rules about how the company operates, the more likely you are to be effective. The way to do this is to listen and to incorporate the feedback. Get to know the corporate culture. But don't just listen, listen intensively—both to the words people use and to the messages below the surface. Make sure to solicit key mentors and protectors by keeping them informed about progress on your priorities, the feedback you are garnering, and the political land mines that seem to be near the surface. Incorporate all of this input into how you behave. How do your colleagues communicate with one another—impromptu face-to-face meetings? Memos? E-mails? How are meetings conducted? Whom do you need to keep in the loop and when? How flexible is your new company when it comes to work arrangements, lunch hours, or time off?

4. Keep Track of Your Short- and Longer-term Objectives on a Monthly Basis

As a manager, your job will inevitably involve accomplishing both short- and long-term objectives. Leverage the process of listening and learning to forge relationships to get broad buy-in to your plan and to the key priorities. Then circle back to your supervisor and your most important mentors to check on your plan every month. The goal here is to track your progress, note accomplishments, and continue to complete your objectives. Set up periodic meetings with your supervisor and mentors to ensure that you are calibrating on performance.

After you have followed these steps and gotten off to the right start, then you can really get to the work at hand and help build a high-performing organization—and a highly successful professional career.

UNDERSTANDING EXECUTIVE SEARCH: HOW IT REALLY WORKS, AND HOW YOU CAN INFLUENCE THE PROCESS

You've probably heard about or possibly even had some direct experience with executive search firms in the past few years, as most of the highest-profile professional positions are filled this way. As you move through the promise phase into the momentum phase and finally the harvest phase of your career, many of the jobs that you will want to get move through executive search firms. But from the outside, the search process may seem difficult to understand. The executive search profession has been around for nearly fifty years, operating with cloak-and-dagger confidentiality, quietly conducting recruiting assignments behind the scenes. To succeed, it is to your advantage to understand how executive search *really* works and, importantly, how to influence the process to your advantage.

Executive searches are typically done in a highly confidential manner, with a process not made public until it culminates with a new executive's appointment. Indeed, a good executive recruiter is nothing if not discreet. But if you want to maximize your chances of landing a top position, it will be helpful to know how to influence the search process. So here are the four key steps in a search, along with some tips to help you on your way.

1. DEFINING THE NEED

Once we are awarded a search assignment, we meet with a search committee in the case of a CEO assignment or the hiring manager and the human resources chief in the case of an executive position to detail what is required from this new employee. This input feedback becomes the foundation for a detailed position and candidate specification, including the key selection criteria against which candidates will be evaluated. We need to describe the industry and competitive position of the company and outline the challenges and opportunities facing the new executive in the position. In these first briefing meetings with our client, we come with a lot of questions: What is the company's competitive strategy and what are the leadership implications of this strategy going forward? What are the organizational relationships for the new position, both formal and informal? What are the must-have skills required in the new individual, and what personal characteristics will it take to be successful? Which companies do you most respect for the particular discipline and which do you not? What types of people have been successful coming into the company from the outside and what has tended not to work? How are decisions really made at the company—does it tend toward data-driven, analytical decision making, or idea- or relationship-based decision making? How would you describe the opportunity if you were trying to sell the ideal candidate if he or she were sitting in front of you?

Tip: Try to get ahead of the search. That may sound tricky, but you might be in a position where you hear about high-level openings that are coming up that could suit your skills. If you can have your interest and relevant skills made known to the hiring manager, the company may try to fill the position without a search. After all, you might be able to help the company save the enormous amount of time (about three months) and money (one-third of first-year base salary plus bonus) typically spent on a professional search.

2. RESEARCHING AND PROSPECTING

Here's where we perform the research to define and develop the appropriate candidate pool. To do that, based on the most desired skills defined in the key selection criteria, we start by identifying the leading companies in the relevant industry sectors. This target list typically comprises about twenty-five to forty companies—enough to generate sufficient potential candidates but concentrated enough to research in a time frame of several weeks. Then we work to identify the managers most responsible for the success of the relevant business. In the case of CEO searches, this is relatively straightforward, but in functional areas or at the middle management level, this is a little trickier. In both cases, we combine the usage of our proprietary database with highly targeted third-party sourcing to analysts or company alumni who would know the identified prospects. Our goal is to learn enough about who a person is and why he or she may be an appropriate prospective candidate before making the first phone call. Our sourcing calls tend to avoid "Whom do you know?" and more toward "We've had a recommendation of Susan Kelly for this particular assignment. Can you tell me if she lines up well against these criteria?" The quality of the question and of the source determines the quality of the insight we are able to generate. The end product of this phase is a list of the most attractive and relevant potential candidates that we will review with the client—the "long list," in search parlance.

Tip: Be a good source. Executive recruiters call a lot of people for references, and helpful sources who give candid, insightful comments about prospective candidates will be contacted by search firms time and time again. At some point, and probably sooner rather than later, a good source will become a candidate for a search. The reason for this is that these types of reference calls build trust with the recruiter and also give an opportunity to demonstrate how you think. Inevitably, conversation turns to things such as "What kinds of positions would be of greatest interest to you?" Also, at the right time, do not hesitate to let the recruiter know the sort of opportunities you might be interested in. Word travels fast.

3. DEVELOPING AND PRESENTING CANDIDATES

Here's where the rubber meets the road in executive searches: approaching a potential candidate, developing her interest, assessing her, and presenting her to the client. When we make the first phone call to a prospect, we typically have three to four minutes to present an opportunity. Our goal here is to open someone's mind to learning more about the search. After all, if there is no interest or if the timing is just not at all right to consider something new, it is not worth the candidate's or our own time to spend going into a deep conversation or assessment. Since we know a lot about the person we are calling, we generally have productive conversations right from the start. Most individuals at the other end of the phone will find our approach logical. And if they are interested, we then go into much greater detail explaining the situation and what we're looking for and arranging to send the position and candidate specification. Let us be clear: Most people generally *enjoy* getting our calls. It is not like trying to sell insurance or push an unwanted product. In fact, Dick Parsons, the CEO of AOL Time Warner, told us, "You guys have a great job—like playing Santa Claus! Who doesn't want to get a call asking you if you're interested in taking on some big new job?" In fact, Dick is right. The way we usually approach one of these initial conversations is to ask if the individual would have a personal interest in exploring this opportunity, or if not, could they make a recommendation. Generally, people will respond to one of those two tracks. After determining a candidate's potential interest, we arrange a meeting to interview her and assess the person against the key selection criteria. These are confidential meetings, often done in one of our fifty-four offices, but sometimes over a lunch or dinner at a discreet location. We then write up detailed reports (often twelve pages long) and organize meetings for the best candidates to meet the client.

Tip: Be honest about whether a situation is of potential interest, but also try to be open-minded. Experience shows that even if it does not initially seem like the right thing at the right time, it could turn out to be a great opportunity. When it comes to interviewing, the process can be a little trickier than it looks. Of course you want to be enthusiastic about the opportunity, and you want to present your talents in the most positive light. But it is to your advantage to play just a little hard to get, to make the search firm and the client recruit you. After all, it is human nature to want what you can't have. Another key point is to analyze why you may be a great match with the job requirements. Prepare for the interviews by writing notes about your relevant responsibilities and achievements against the key selection criteria outlined in the position description. You can then focus your interview on the key points. You may even consider preparing these notes to leave with the search consultant or client.

4. NEGOTIATING AND HIRING

This is the emotional part of the process. You anxiously await an offer, and then, if you're the chosen candidate, you negotiate the terms. If it is a CEO search, a team of lawyers, compensation consultants, and financial advisors gets involved. But in the other 99 percent of searches it is usually a conversation between you, the executive search consultant, the human resources manager, and the hiring executive. As much anxiety as you may have, remember that the company shares your disquiet. At this stage, both sides have a lot at stake. You have invested a lot of time, energy, and emotion getting to this point, and the company has chosen you as the candidate. This is the key point where the search consultant comes in. Our role here is to keep the dialogue open, positive, and moving forward. We're also helping to guide both sides through the tricky compensation issues. But most of all, we're trying to make the deal happen in a way that everyone is pleased about.

Tip: At this delicate stage, it is critical to understand the balance of power. The company has a lot invested in you as the candidate of choice. Should the negotiations break down, it would take a lot of time to find another candidate. But of course the company can always pull away—rescind an offer or find another candidate. And it is the role of the search consultant to have a strong backup candidate ready if this should happen. Most importantly, don't think for a minute that the company will forget the way you conduct yourself during negotiation time. If you go for every last bit of compensation or play hardball, this will likely impact your relationships later on, when you come on board. On the other hand, in some cases the client expects you to negotiate and will be disappointed if you take a first offer. Help figure out where you are with the help of the search consultant. Overall, it pays to keep your eye on the big prize.

NOTES

Introduction

1. David A. Lord, CEO, Executive Search Information Services.
2. *The Organization Man,* William H. Whyte, Joseph Nocera, Jenny Bell Whyte, University of Pennsylvania Press, 2002; *The Man in the Gray Flannel Suit,* Sloan Wilson, Bentley Publishers, 1980.
3. "Why CEOs Are Prone to Leave Their Posts," Samantha Marshall, *Wall Street Journal* (accessed at www.careerjournal.com), and "Turnover at the Top," Drake Beam Morin, June 12, 2002.
4. "Strategic Rewards: Managing Through Uncertain Times," Watson Wyatt Worldwide research report, 2002 (www.watsonwyatt.com).
5. "Tech Advances Raise Job Insecurity," Beth Belton, *USA Today,* February 17, 1999.

Pattern I: Understand the Value of You

1. *It's Not About the Bike: My Journey Back to Life,* Lance Armstrong, Sally Jenkins, Berkley Publishing Group, 2001.
2. *Zoom: How 12 Exceptional Companies Are Navigating the Road to the Next Economy,* James M. Citrin, Currency Doubleday, 2002.
3. *Who Says Elephants Can't Dance? Inside IBM's Historic Turnaround,* Louis V. Gerstner Jr., HarperBusiness, 2002.
4. *The War for Talent,* Ed Michaels, Helen Handfield-Jones, Beth Axelrod, Harvard Business School Press, 2001.
5. Spencer Stuart CEO survey, June 2002.
6. Ibid.
7. *Take on the Street: What Wall Street and Corporate America Don't Want You to Know,* Arthur Levitt, Paula Dwyer, Pantheon Books, 2002.

Pattern 2: Practice Benevolent Leadership

1. *Swim with the Sharks Without Being Eaten Alive: Outsell, Outmanage, Outmotivate, and Outnegotiate Your Competition,* Harvey Mackay, Kenneth H. Blanchard, Fawcett Books, 1989.

2. "Michael Ovitz: Hollywood's Comeback Kid," BusinessWeek Online, April 2000 (http://www.businessweek.com/bwdaily/dnflash/ apr2000 /nf00414e.htm); "Michael Eisner: Mouse in a Gilded Mansion," Forbes.com, April 26, 2001 (http://www.forbes.com/2001/04/26/ eisner.html).
3. "The Dark Side of Charisma," Robert Hogan, Robert Raskin, Dan Fazzini, Leadership Library of America, 1990.
4. *Good to Great: Why Some Companies Make the Leap . . . and Others Don't,* Jim Collins, HarperCollins, 2001.
5. Spencer Stuart CEO survey, June 2001.

Pattern 3: Overcome the Permission Paradox

1. At http://volcanoes.usgs.gov/Hazards/What/Lahars/lahars.html.
2. *Leadership Without Easy Answers,* Ronald A. Heifetz, Belknap Press, 1994.
3. *Lessons from the Top: The 50 Most Successful Business Leaders in America—and What You Can Learn from Them,* Thomas J. Neff, James M. Citrin, Paul B. Brown, Currency/Doubleday, 2001.
4. "GE Mentoring Program Turns Underlings into Teachers of the Web," Matt Murray, *Wall Street Journal,* February 15, 2000.
5. *Leading Up: How to Lead Your Boss So You Both Win,* Michael Useem, Crown Business, 2001, p. 292.
6. CNBC Market Dispatches, December 26, 2002 (transcript available at http://moneycentral.msn.com/content/CNBCTV/Articles/ Dispatches /P36658.asp).
7. *Forbes,* October 19, 1987, cover story, p. 122.

Pattern 4: Differentiate Using the 20/80 Principle of Performance

1. NHTSA Report no. DOT HS 806 572, "Final Regulatory Impact Analysis; Amendment to Federal Motor Vehicle Safety Standard 208; Passenger Car Front Seat Occupant Protection," pp. IV-3–IV-16 (http://www.nhtsa.dot.gov/cars/rules/regrev/evaluate/806572. html).
2. "The March of Progress," Jerry Useem, Business 2.0. August 2001 (http://www.business2.com/articles/mag/print/0,1643,16689,00. html).
3. *Paul Revere's Ride,* David Hackett Fischer, Oxford University Press, 1995.
4. Ibid., pp. 56–59.
5. Michael Reene, vice president/general manager, ChoicePoint, Inc.

6. *How to Win Friends and Influence People,* Dale Carnegie, Dorothy Carnegie, Arthur R. Pell, Pocket Books, 1998.
7. http://www.fortune.com/fortune/bestcompanies.
8. "Right Away and All at Once: How We Saved Continental," Greg Brenneman, *Harvard Business Review,* September–October 1998; *From Worst to First: Behind the Scenes of Continental's Remarkable Comeback,* Gordon Bethune, John Wiley and Sons, 1998.

Pattern 5: Find the Right Fit (Strengths, Passions, and People)

1. "How to Stay Stuck in the Wrong Career," Herminia Ibarra, *Harvard Business Review,* December 1, 2002.
2. *Investment Under Uncertainty,* Avinash K. Dixit, Robert S. Pindyck, Princeton University Press, 1994.
3. *First, Break All the Rules: What the World's Greatest Managers Do Differently,* Marcus Buckingham, Curt Coffman, Simon & Schuster, 1999.

The Patterns of Extraordinary Organizations

1. *The War for Talent,* Ed Michaels, Helen Handfield-Jones, Beth Axelrod, Harvard Business School Press, 2001.
2. *The Tipping Point,* Malcolm Gladwell, Little, Brown and Company, 2000.
3. Spencer Stuart Venture Capital Study survey, November 2001.
4. "The Talent Myth: Are Smart People Overrated?" *The New Yorker,* July 22, 2002 (http://www.gladwell.com/2002/2002_07_22_a_talent.htm).
5. *Creative Destruction: Why Companies That Are Built to Last Underperform the Market—and How to Succesfully Transform Them,* Richard Foster, Sarah Kaplan, Doubleday, 2001.
6. *Leading the Revolution,* Gary Hamel, Harvard Business School Press, 2000.
7. *The War for Talent.*
8. *The Tipping Point.*

Conclusion: Putting the Patterns into Practice

1. *Emotional Intelligence,* Daniel Goleman, Bantam Books, 1997, pp. 81–83.

SUPPLEMENTAL READING

Bolles, Richard N. *What Color Is Your Parachute 2002: A Practical Manual for Job-Hunters and Career-Changers.* Ten Speed Press, 2001.

Britton Whitcomb, Susan. *Resume Magic: Trade Secrets of a Professional Resume Writer.* Jist Works, 1998.

Buckingham, Marcus, and Donald O. Clifton. *Now, Discover Your Strengths.* Free Press, 2001.

DeLuca, Matthew. *Best Answers to the 201 Most Frequently Asked Interview Questions.* McGraw Hill Professional Publishing, 1996.

Fischer, Roger, Bruce Patton, and William Ury. *Getting to Yes.* 2nd ed. Penguin USA, 1991.

Fox, Jeffrey J. *Don't Send a Resume: And Other Contrarian Rules to Help Land a Great Job.* Hyperion, 2001.

Hough, Lee, and Neil Yeager. *Power Interviews.* New York: John Wiley & Sons, 1990.

Kennedy, James H. *Kennedy's Pocket Guide to Working with Executive Recruiters.* Kennedy Publications, 1996.

Krannick, Caryl, and Ron Krannick. *Dynamite Salary Negotiations.* 4th ed. Impact Publications, 2001.

ACKNOWLEDGMENTS

I t is one of life's great gifts to be able to follow your passions. For us, our work at Spencer Stuart, partnering with our clients to build their top management teams, is one of our loves. But another is having the opportunity to use our work as a laboratory for ideas and then transforming our experience into a book. *The Five Patterns of Extraordinary Careers* has been a three-year exercise in passion.

We are deeply appreciative to everyone who helped make this book a reality. They are our clients, with whom we work each and every day, our colleagues, who together form the most professional and enjoyable firm in our industry, the hundreds of individuals who we interviewed, who shared their career stories, thought patterns, successes, and setbacks, and the thousands of individuals who participated in our in-depth surveys that laid the analytical underpinning for the book.

Let us single out a few from among these groups who made exceptional contributions.

We would first like to thank Michael Reene, Executive Vice President and General Manager of Services at Choicepoint. Michael has been an inspiration to us from the moment we conceived of this project and selflessly offered many creative and important thoughts and suggestions along the way. He is one of the most insightful thinkers related to career success, and many of his ideas on career management challenged and motivated us to create the frameworks included in this book. Several of his thoughts were directly incorporated into this work. For his wisdom, guidance, encouragement, and direct contribution, we are tremendously grateful.

None of the data-driven insights revealed in this book would have been possible without the underlying two-year research effort, led and coordinated by Yu-Chieh Wang in Spencer Stuart's Atlanta office. Yu-Chieh worked tirelessly to help us structure the research, manage the efforts of our dispersed research team, and ensure that everything was completed efficiently and on schedule. Additional contributing members of our research team included Choka, Justin, and Isabella, all of whom are MBA graduates from Emory's Goizetta Business School, who helped structure and facilitate the broad statistical analysis, working with more than one million different points of data in our search for the most compelling patterns of career success. Rob Stavert, a Harvard University student who interned with us, contributed his intellect and effort in the research and development of the Spencer Stuart Human Capital Index. Maria Popovic, with support from Brian McGreevey, was critical to our basic research and the design, facilitation, and analysis of our groundbreaking survey of executive success. Without their efforts, we would have never come close to our ultimate incredible 25 percent response rate.

Throughout our exploration of career success over the years, our thoughts have been shaped by literally thousands of people in many countries. While we are thankful for the perspective and contribution that each of these people have afforded us, we would like to specifically recognize several individuals who had a particularly powerful impact on our thinking: Roderick Gilkie, Andrew Ward, Sean Seitzinger, Allen Chan, Mark Mykitician, Beth Polish, Roger Fransecky, John Haworth, Lee Esler, Scott Gordon, and Sam Pettway.

We are grateful to be able to include the Spencer Stuart Job Survival Guide in this book, a practical and valuable tool for professionals in transition. This section is the direct result of actual Spencer Stuart client work, led by Cathy Anterasian, Claudia Kelly, and John Keller. Claudia, who specializes in recruiting chief human resources officers, is one of the most insightful and strategic thinkers related to human capital issues in our firm, and in addition to co-authoring this critical piece of the book, Claudia has provided us with invaluable guidance and imagination during this process. Her wisdom and imagination are an inspiration.

We would also like to thank our firm, Spencer Stuart, for its belief in and support of this project from its initial conception. Specifically, we would like to recognize David Daniel, Dayton Ogden, Kevin Connelly, Manolo Marquez, Sharon Hall, William Reeves, Bill Clemens, and Rich Kurkowski, who provided critical management support. In addition, we benefited greatly from the wisdom and efforts of our global marketing team, led by Kim Brisley and supported by Tracy Jackson and Alastair Rolfe, and our legal counsel, led by Dave Rasmussen. We also thank Patty Block, whose ideas and energy managing "e-outreach" and other channels have greatly aided the book's marketing, communications, and promotional effects. Finally, Jim's administrative assistant, Karen Steinegger, served as a tireless sounding board, advisor, and logistical captain for this entire effort.

Turning such an ambitious project into an entertaining and readable book is rarely the result of the authors alone, and such was the case with *The Five Patterns of Extraordinary Careers*. We would like to thank Joshua Macht, who supported us with his editorial expertise and who worked with us in the development of the manuscript from the very beginning, offering ideas, direction, and incredible editorial content. It is because of him that a book written by two authors with distinct styles and thought processes comes across with one clear voice. In addition, we thank Mickey Butts, another incredible writer, who helped us conceive of our earliest outline and draft of the manuscript. His contribution to distilling and organizing our thinking was crucial to getting our arms around the hundreds of potentially disparate ideas and hypotheses we were originally considering.

We would also like to thank John Mahaney, our editor from Crown Business. Throughout the development of the manuscript, John challenged us to always dig deeper, push farther in our thinking, and always take the perspective of "every reader" into consideration. When we may have been content to stop, feeling satisfied with our work, John would push us that much farther, inevitably leading each time to breakthrough new thoughts, frameworks, and presentation. We also appreciate the work of John's extended Crown team, including Tara Gilbride and Shana Wingert Drehs, who have been outstanding supporters and partners in this process.

We would also like to thank Rafe Sagalyn, of the Sagalyn Literary Agency, who has been our agent for nearly five years and is simply the best in the business. His candor, open and honest feedback, incredible depth of experience, and true partnership has served as an invaluable resource throughout this project. We are proud to call him a friend.

Finally, we would like to thank our families: Gail, Lily, Oliver, and Teddy Citrin, and Lori, Arden, Adam, and Laine Smith, for their unwavering support of our work. With robust executive search practices, the vast majority of the creation of this book has been completed at nights, on weekends, and during holidays. Many a book's creation is the result of personal family sacrifice, and we are indebted to the contribution, love, and support that our families have provided us these three years.

INDEX

ABOUT THE AUTHORS

JAMES M. CITRIN leads Spencer Stuart's Global Technology, Communications, and Media practice and is a member of the firm's worldwide board of directors. He is also a member of the firm's Board Services practice. Citrin has recruited some of the top CEOs, presidents, and board directors, including the CEOs and/or presidents of Yahoo!, America Online, Motorola, Vodafone, Eastman Kodak, Discovery Communications, Gartner, The Reader's Digest Association, Gruner + Jahr Publishing USA, Penguin Publishing, The Financial Times North America, L.L. Bean, *TV Guide*, HotJobs, Ziff-Davis, Kinko's, Six Continents Hotels & Resorts, Westin Hotels & Resorts, The John & Mary Markle Foundation, and Outward Bound USA. He has also advised the governments of Mexico and the European Union on achieving success in today's technology-driven economy.

Citrin is author of *Zoom: How 12 Exceptional Companies Are Navigating the Road to the Next Economy*, as well as the co-author of *You're in Charge—Now What?: The 8 Point Plan* and *Lessons from the Top: The 50 Most Successful Business Leaders in America—and What You Can Learn from Them*. His articles have been published in the *New York Times*, *Directors & Boards*, and *Strategy and Business* and for nearly three years his column "Talent Monger" appeared in *Business 2.0*. He serves as a member of the *Business 2.0* editorial advisory board.

Prior to joining Spencer Stuart in 1994, Citrin was director of corporate planning at The Reader's Digest Association, served as senior engagement manager with McKinsey & Company in the United States and France, an associate with Goldman, Sachs & Company, and a financial analyst with Morgan, Stanley & Co.

A 1981 graduate of Vassar College, Phi Beta Kappa, with a B.A. in economics, Citrin serves as a member of the Vassar board of trustees. He earned an M.B.A. from the Harvard Business School, graduating with distinction in 1986. He is on the board of the Harvard Business School Club of New York.

Citrin lives in Connecticut with his wife, Gail, and their three children: Teddy, Oliver, and Lily.

RICHARD A. SMITH is a respected author, thought leader, and commercial and social entrepreneur. He is currently the CEO of World 50, Inc., which brings together the world's most influential executives for strategic collaboration. Previously, Smith was a consultant with Spencer Stuart, one of the youngest directors ever hired to the firm. There, he gained extensive experience recruiting CEOs, COOs, and board directors for public and private companies around the world.

Smith is the author of the widely cited CEO study and white paper *Top Tier Talent: Investment Strategies for Human Capital*. He contributes a biannual feature article for the *Venture Capital Review* and is the co-creator of Spencer Stuart's Human Capital Market Index (HCMI). He has published numerous articles on leadership, organizational performance, competitive strategy, management assessment/recruitment, and professional career development.

Prior to joining Spencer Stuart, Smith held senior positions with Diamond Cluster International, and strategy and business development positions with EDS in the United States and in Central and Eastern Europe.

Smith is the founder of 21st Century Atlanta, is a founding board member of TechBridge, and has previously served on the regional board of the American Cancer Society and the Children's Museum of Atlanta.

Smith obtained an M.B.A. in marketing and strategy from the J.L. Kellogg Graduate School of Management at Northwestern University and a B.S. in finance from the University of Florida. He is also a Certified Management Accountant. Smith moonlights as a semiprofessional singer/songwriter and has written and recorded more than 100 songs.

Smith lives in Atlanta, Georgia, with his wife, Dr. Lori Smith, and their three children: Arden, Adam, and Laine.

Also by James M. Citrin

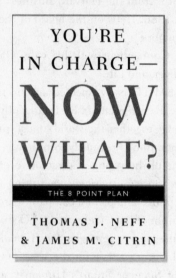

YOU'RE
IN CHARGE—
NOW
WHAT?

THE 8 POINT PLAN

THOMAS J. NEFF
& JAMES M. CITRIN

The eight-point how-to-succeed guide for anyone
about to start a new job, based on lessons learned
from 100 recent leadership transitions, both successful and not.

1-4000-4865-6
$25.00 hardcover (Canada: $35.00)

Available from Crown Business wherever books are sold

CROWN
BUSINESS
NEW YORK

CrownPublishing.com